Time Discounting
and Future Generations

Time Discounting and Future Generations

THE HARMFUL EFFECTS
OF AN UNTRUE ECONOMIC THEORY

Erhun Kula

QUORUM BOOKS
Westport, Connecticut • London

338.9
K96t

Library of Congress Cataloging-in-Publication Data

Kula, Erhun.
    Time discounting and future generations : the harmful effects of
an untrue economic theory / Erhun Kula.
        p.   cm.
    Includes bibliographical references and index.
    ISBN 1–56720–090–7 (alk. paper)
        1. Economic policy.   2. Environmental policy.   3. Errors.
    4. Decision-making.   5. Social choice.   6. Time and economic
    reactions.   I. Title.
    HD87.K838   1997
 338.9—dc21   96–46714

British Library Cataloguing in Publication Data is available.

Library of Congress Catalog Card Number: 96–46714
ISBN: 1–56720–090–7

First published in 1997

Quorum Books, 88 Post Road West, Westport, CT 06881
An imprint of Greenwood Publishing Group, Inc.

Printed in the United States of America

The paper used in this book complies with the
Permanent Paper Standard issued by the National
Information Standards Organization (Z39.48–1984).

10   9   8   7   6   5   4   3   2   1

For Karen

Contents

viii					Contents

Preface

> To me it is far more pleasant to agree than to differ; but it is impossible that one who has any regard for truth can long avoid protesting against doctrines which seem to him to be erroneous. There is even a tendency of the most hurtful kind to allow opinions to crystallize into creeds. . . . A despotic calm is usually the triumph of error. In the republic of the sciences sedition and even anarchy are beneficial in the long run to the greatest happiness of the greatest number.
>
> William Stanley Jevons

This book is the fruit of 20 years of effort to correct an untrue and unjust theory, and practical methods that stem from this theory. I started on this journey as a research student when I discovered the underlying assumption of the conventional social discounting theory that individuals live forever. My early efforts made me realize that I was not going to be treated kindly by some "establishment academics," a process which intensified in later years exceeding all my expectations, especially when I became an academic with determination to publish my views.

According to M. Reder (1982), scientific progress is a process of creative destruction. What is destroyed is the intellectual capital of other scientists whose resistance to accepting new and genuine contributions is understandable. It is only by overcoming this resistance that genuine new contributions are made and more numerate invalid proposals are avoided. However, I doubt there is a fallacious theory such as the conventional discounting either in economics or other branches of social science which has survived for more than 70 years, mainly due to the efforts of a handful of mathematical economists who regard themselves as the "establishment." As Wiseman (1991) puts it, "there consequently exists a classic situation in which the dominant paradigm can sustain its position through such means as (e.g.) control of established outlets (the 'recognised journals'); encouragement of conformity through control of power structures; mutual citation; and so on.''

The Association of University Teachers, the largest representative body of professional academics in the United Kingdom, defines academic freedom as ''without fear of penalty to teach, research and put forward views in areas which may not find favour with the establishment, with colleagues or within prevailing orthodoxies'' AUT (1992). Most of us enter into an academic profession because we are interested in ideas and discoveries. In democratic countries we are provided with security, such as academic tenure, so that we can conduct free inquiry into our chosen branch of science without fear and favor. Unfortunately, the academic tenure which helped me to put forward my views has now been substantially undermined by the government in the United Kingdom, and will no doubt have far-reaching consequences for academic freedom in the country.

About one-quarter of this book stems from more than two dozen articles in books as well as in journals such as *Environment and Planning A, Journal of Agricultural Economics, Environmental Management* and *Project Appraisal*. Although they are all refereed international journals of good reputation (the first three are included in the Social Science Citation Index), none would be described by the ''economic establishment'' as the top mainstream outlets in the subject. Initially, I submitted most of my articles to the most coveted economic journals, but on many occasions, in spite of favorable reports by independent referees, editors declined to publish them. A few years ago I sent one of my articles on alternative discounting to a leading journal. The paper was refereed independently by two expert referees, both of whom made recommendations for publication. The editor overruled these recommendations, trying to justify his position with incorrect arguments. I wrote back to the editor to reconsider his decision; failing that I appealed to the serving members of the learned Society which publishes the journal. A few individuals wrote back offering support, a couple suggested that I should try to publish elsewhere and one person, the president, contended that there was no justice in my complaint.

For a number of years the British government, by commissioning some individuals (mainly establishment academics), has been carrying out a research assessment exercise to identify the research strength of the United Kingdom universities. On the basis of grading given to each subject area studied at universities, billions of pounds of public money have already been reallocated in the system in favor of departments with high ratings. The fourth research assessment exercise was well underway at the time of finalizing this book in 1996. One of the most important criteria in identifying the research strength of each subject area is publication in ''coveted'' mainstream international journals. The case which is mentioned here makes it very clear to me that decisions to publish research papers in some leading establishment journals are sometimes, or perhaps even often, arbitrary and biased. This raises serious doubts about the validity of the research assessment exercise and the reallocation of large sums of taxpayers' money for research purposes in the United Kingdom.

As for the current state of economics, as an economist who has spent all of his adult life studying the subject, I feel saddened. Many invalid or even strange theories and practices that stem from such theories are still maintained. Those who challenge them are sidelined and not given, sometimes by way of dubious practices, a platform in mainstream journals, and in this way the nonsense has been perpetuated.

It was not all Byzantine-inspired operations, as many fair-minded individuals (there are a lot in the profession) made positive contributions; modified discounting would not have come this far, nor would this book have been written, without their help. First, I would like to thank the many anonymous referees, whoever they are, who thought that the established line should be changed and ideas on alternative discounting must be put in place. I am also grateful to book as well as journal editors who paid attention in a professional manner to referees' recommendations and published many pieces on the subject. To me, they are the top journals.

As for comments on this book, my thanks extend to Dr. William K. Bellinger of Dickinson College, Pennsylvania, who made valuable remarks on the first four chapters. Dr. Kristin Shradder-Frechette of the University of South Florida read sections on the philosophical foundation of the modified as well as ordinary discounting methods. Dr. Stanley Logan of S.E. Logan and Associates, Santa Fe, New Mexico, commented on sections regarding nuclear waste disposal, and prevented me from committing a number of errors. Mr. Malcolm Beaty of Forest Service, Belfast, read sections on afforestation and made a number of recommendations. Dr. Andrea Wrobel and Dr. Tony Horsley of the London School of Economics helped out on the application of modified discounting to optimum forest rotation problems. Ray Hickey helped to simplify some of my formulas, and Erkut Sezgin provided material for the debate between Russell and Wittgenstein.

My deepest gratitude goes to my wife for her forbearance and support during long years of adversity and hardship which came about as a result of my ideas on social discounting and my determination to put the case across. I dedicate this work to her.

General Introduction

GUIDE TO THE ORGANIZATION OF THE BOOK

In the heart of this book there is a notion of intergenerational justice by way of time discounting, a cornerstone in economic science. The main contention is that in a just society public sector policy-makers ought to treat all individuals, present and future, in an equitable manner. Although the roots of this idea are very old, as they go as far back as Aristotle, or even beyond, the basic principles established here are put into a modern philosophical framework, namely, the Rawlsian theory of justice.

Nowadays, in the appraisal of many communal projects throughout the world, especially in democratic countries, economic criteria are widely used to ensure that they are of value to society, beneficial to future as well as present generations. Proposed projects in infrastructure, industry, health, education, energy, environmental improvement and so on, are normally assessed by a team of economists as part of a general fact-finding mission to aid the decision-making process. To what extent public policy-makers act on the basis of information provided by economic analysts is an interesting issue, but it is beyond the scope of this book.

Large-scale communal projects involve a considerable transfer of natural as well as man-made resources between generations and in this way raise moral questions. Some projects, such as nuclear waste management, are most unusual in the sense that they could undermine, seriously, health, safety and civil liberties of generations yet to be born. For example, by building an underground nuclear waste repository we would be imposing small, but not negligible, health risks on future generations for millions of years to come. Of course, there are risks, possibly of a greater magnitude, in not constructing a permanent repository, as large volumes of highly dangerous nuclear residues are being kept in temporary storage in many locations throughout the world. How do economists assess projects that have undeniable intergenerational moral dimensions? This book will try to throw some light on this issue by way of time discounting.

Projects like nuclear waste storage lasting millions of years, involving numerous generations, are not science-fiction material; they are real and urgent. It will be demonstrated in this book that what has become science-fiction material is a body of economics that has been developed, especially during the last few decades, by mathematical economists who now dominate the scene. In the face of real-life projects such as construction of a nuclear waste repository, the main body of discounting theory, which is pivotal in economic appraisal of such projects, becomes ridiculous. Even when harmful long-term effects are identified and quantified, they do not become an economically significant factor in the decision-making process, as conventional discounting wipes them out.

However, it must be said that it is very difficult to quantify the long-term effects of large-scale communal projects in the first place, although this cannot be an excuse for ignoring them. It is even more frustrating to identify the long-term effects and then hand them over to the practitioners of conventional methods to be killed off. As it will be demonstrated in this book, some economists have taken a lot of trouble in identifying the long-term health costs of nuclear projects only to see them reduced to minute net present value figures.

There is a growing body of economists, including this author, who have become increasingly vocal in criticizing the conventional economic theories not only on moral grounds, but on conceptual aspects as well. For example, Nove (1992) contends that most legitimate and relevant points of view suggested by the so-called dissenting economists seem to be water off the duck's back. Even at the time when we are in need of new and relevant economics to solve increasingly urgent human problems, the conventional bandwagon is racing ahead, oblivious to all the legitimate criticisms.

This book is split into two parts: theory, which contains four chapters, and practice, which includes five case studies in areas of nuclear waste storage, forestry, agriculture and urban transport in three countries—the United States of America, Ireland and Great Britain.

Chapter 1, after emphasizing the importance of time in economics, looks at its treatment in various economic models. The main focus is on the rationale for time discounting in which three concepts are emphasized: pure myopia, risk and uncertainty regarding future prospects, and the diminishing marginal utility of increasing consumption over time. All these factors play an important part in the psychology of individuals when they are faced with intertemporal choices. Fisherian synthesis, which puts together marginal productivity of capital and the psychological time preferences in a perfectly competitive world, turns out to be obsolete in real-life situations, due to a number of factors such as market imperfections, institutional and natural barriers and the so-called isolation paradox. The last concept tries to incorporate, without much success, the claims of future generations into the body of a communal discount rate. The chapter concludes that all these distortions create a gap between social productivity of capital and the communal psychological discount rate, raising many theoretical problems.

Chapter 2 focuses on the practical importance of identifying a social rate of discount. In this respect the efforts of public sector policy-makers in the United States and the United Kingdom are reviewed in a historical context. Governments of the United States and Britain were the first to study the issue of identifying the elusive social discount rate for various resource allocation policies. However, as the chapter concludes, the British government in particular ended up in a situation in which various rates of discount are now prescribed for various public projects, which is bound to create inefficiencies.

Chapter 3 explains that the mainstream welfare economics treats society as if it were a single individual with an eternal life, or individuals live forever. The roots of this assumption go back to Ramsey's 1928 paper, "A Mathematical Theory of Saving," in which the question of "how much should a nation save?" was explored. After that, especially in the 1960s and 1970s a single-person society assumption became a standard practice in many theoretical analyses, mainly for the purpose of mathematical model building. It will be demonstrated, with the help of a simple societal model where every member is mortal, that the conventional discounting theory, and practices that stem from it, lead public sector policy-makers to a morally indefensible discrimination against future generations.

Chapter 4 explains the foundation of the modified discounting method in which public sector policy-makers first accept that individuals are mortal, then treat all generations, present and future, equitably. Although the philosophical foundation of the new method is grounded in the Rawlsian theory of justice, it is emphasized that economics as a social science has an old tradition of just conduct in almost all areas of its jurisdiction. This chapter also reports on a number of debates which have taken place in a number of journals on modified discounting in recent years. It ends with the derivation of communal psychological discount rates (the social time preference rate which is the appropriate interest rate in the new method) for the United States and the United Kingdom.

Part II (chapters 5 to 9) contains specific case studies in which ordinary as well as modified discounting methods are used in their economic appraisal. The reader will discover that the new method yields results dramatically different from those obtained by way of conventional criteria. However, I should mention at the outset that some of these case studies are extraordinarily complex, technically, environmentally, socially as well as economically. Although discounting is pivotal in their economic evaluation, there is much more to these projects than simple micro-economics. For example, when we consider a country like Finland where trees cover over 70 percent of the land surface and forestry is one of the nation's most important environmental and business assets, finding the optimum cutting age becomes highly complex. The nuclear waste disposal issue is even more demanding, as the United States Senator, Howard Baker, a member of the Joint Committee on Atomic Energy, contended, that "the containment and storage of radioactive wastes is the greatest single responsibility ever consciously undertaken by man" (ERDA 1976). Some feel that this is not an exaggerated statement, especially when we consider the existence of large volumes of highly toxic and long-living wastes in many countries, waiting to be disposed of.

Chapter 5, after a brief introduction to the history of the nuclear industry and the proposed methods of waste disposal, focuses on the health and monitoring costs of nuclear waste storage. The specific case study is the Waste Isolation Pilot Plant, WIPP, in New Mexico, which is likely to become the United States' first permanent nuclear-waste dumping site.

Chapter 6 is about a cost-benefit analysis of afforestation in Northern Ireland. The project is a 100-hectare plot located in a severely disadvantaged region in the province, with a 45-year gestation period.

Chapter 7 looks at a sizeable land drainage project in the Republic of Ireland constructed for the purpose of improving agricultural yields. In this analysis the traditional benefit-cost ratio is used as the economic appraisal method.

Chapter 8 deals with the issue of finding the optimum cutting age for trees, which is one of the oldest technical problems known to economists as well as forestry scientists. The model used stems from the works of Faustman, Samuelson and Ohlin. One of the most interesting aspects in this chapter is that the modified discounting method brings about a solution which is very close to foresters' maximum sustainable yield.

Chapter 9 is about the economic appraisal of a large-scale live urban transport project, the Victoria Underground Railway in London, with an estimated life of 56 years.

Part I

Theoretical Foundation of Ordinary and Modified Discounting

Chapter 1

Foundation of Discounting

TIME IN ECONOMICS

Discount rate is the price, or cost, of time. Discounting is a method in which this cost is calculated over a specific time horizon. All economic activities are time dependent, as there can be no instantaneous achievement in consumption or production as both must be planned beforehand, often meticulously, in a modern economy. Therefore, time discounting is, or must be, a main pillar of economic science.

If market participants were completely indifferent about time, that is, if they had no time preferences, the discount rate would be zero. But the reality is that individuals are not indifferent about time considerations; they do have time preferences. Most economists and philosophers who have contributed to the time discounting debate contend that there is a systematic preference for sooner rather than later, which gives rise to a positive discount rate with which the future is systematically undervalued. Mises (1966) and Rothbard (1970) make the case that a positive discount rate is a logical imperative in which individuals prefer a given amount of consumption now to the same amount at a future date. Lindstone (1973) puts it even more strongly by suggesting that there may be a genetic basis for man's focus on the present which is necessary for survival in frequently hostile circumstances. After all, present survival is a precondition for acquisition of future utilities.

If the present value of a future event, consumption, production, pain, pleasure, or whatever was to be valued at more than its actual worth when it occurs, then this would imply a negative discount rate. In other words, if individuals had a negative discount rate this would mean that they value future more than present. This is thought to be highly unlikely and may occur only in exceptional circumstances.

Time is a cornerstone in production where entrepreneurs try to convert resources into final goods such as wheat, corn, shoes, and so on. In Jevons's scheme of things, capital goods consist of those proportions of the produce of industry existing in it which may be directly employed either to support human beings, or to facilitate production. Capital is not confined to the food that feeds the labor force but includes machinery, tools, buildings, and so on, which can be applied to assist and enhance production; and that takes time. "The single and all important function of capital is to enable the labourer to *await* the result of any long-lasting work—to put an interval between the beginning and the end of an enterprise" (Jevons 1871). Many other classical economists, such as Mill (1826) and Hern (1864), emphasized the importance of time in production. In the simplest agricultural operations there is the seed, time and the harvest. In mining operations there is a long delay before the deposit is reached. A mine could not be worked out by an entrepreneur unless the person either dips into his/her own assets or is given sufficient credit, or, in other words, capital, for the venture. A similar situation prevails in industrial and service sectors. When an entrepreneur uses up his/her readily available assets for operations he/she gives up interest that would have been earned had he/she made funds available to others. When the person borrows money for his/her enterprise then he/she must pay the lender a similar income.

Capital goods are related to consumption goods and vice versa. Future supply and demand considerations for consumption commodities, say wheat and corn, have implications for production decisions with respect to capital goods, a part of which is seed. Likewise, consumption activities which spread over time have implications for capital goods that exist at a particular point in time.

An economic theory which omits time is not only incomplete but it must be unreal as well. Take the neoclassical equilibrium theories, for instance, which have relevance when analyses are confined to the allocation of resources at a particular point in time (Hahn 1980; Graham and Walsh 1980). It has been argued by Garrison (1984) that attempts to make timeless and unreal neoclassical theories real by occasionally allowing time through the back door have been largely unsuccessful. When time is allowed in neoclassical models, market conditions are assumed to remain constant, which makes time only a facade, and thus essentially timeless neoclassical theories, say, general equilibrium models, fail to explain reality (also see Shackle 1972; Mainwaring 1990). Furthermore, when no time preference is assumed in economic models this would mean that the equilibrium value of the inputs of each production process would completely exhaust the value of the output. In other words, ignoring time considerations would make factors of production unproductive in the classical sense that they would produce no surplus value (Garrison 1984).

Therefore, time considerations are imperative in consumption as well as in production. In the former, time is related to individuals' psychology in valuing future net consumption benefits, as seen from the present when future utilities, or disutilities as the case may be, are systematically undervalued. The more distant in time these utilities are, the smaller the values that are attached to them. In other words, time here acts as an undermining agent. In production, however, time acts as a fructifying agent where a given stock of capital, properly invested, physically grows over time (Hicks 1965). According to Menger (1871), a resource has a value because of individuals' expectations of its productive potential. Man has a tendency to attach the value of ends to the means needed for their achievement. In the Fisherian scheme of things, capital has a value because it is a source of income; when invested it could enhance the owner's consumption capacity in the future. Capital just like other factors of production is productive in time.

The psychological time preference of individuals and the time productivity of capital was first brought into equilibrium via loanable funds of consumers and of producers by Fisher (1907, 1930). Before him, analyses of these two sources of assets, that is, funds for consumption and funds for production, were generally conducted separately. In Fisherian analysis, market forces bring households' decisions to save into equilibrium with investors' plans to invest which, under certain conditions, results in a single rate of interest. By borrowing and lending at that rate market participants arrange their expenditures in such a way that total satisfaction during the entire period for which their plan extends is at a maximum, as judged by their present preferences. Firms invest up to a point where the rate of return on capital projects, at the margin, is equal to the interest rate. Consumers' plans to save are brought to equality with producers' plans to invest and the ruling interest rate reflects both the time preference of consumers and returns which can be earned on capital projects.

NEWTONIAN AND REAL TIME

What are the underlying factors that affect individuals' psychology when they express a preference for present satisfaction over future satisfaction of the same magnitude? Later on in this section I shall review a number of concepts which many contributors to this debate have thought to be parts of the jigsaw. But before that, let me discuss some views on the treatment of time in economic analysis.

In Adam Smith's early and rude stage of society which precedes both the accumulation of stock and appropriation of land, nature, left to its own devices, will produce, naturally, a certain quality and quantity of consumption goods. With the exchange mechanism in operation these natural consumption goods will have a market value based upon individuals' subjective value assessment. At that stage consumption goods are the main objects of economic analysis, as production operations are confined to hunting and gathering. In the next stage we allow intervention in the natural process where labor and capital are used in the process of production and consequently, greater and better quality of output is realized. At the more advanced state of the economy more capital is used in production because, due to accumulation, it is now available in a greater volume.

O'Driscoll et al. (1985) contend that in an extensively capital-using economy, although interrelationships between various stages of production and consumption grow in complexity, the essential feature of the analysis remains the same. The Austrian school views this relationship as a pattern of productive acts that move through time from one stage to the next until the final destination, consumption, is arrived at (Böhm-Bawerk 1884; Hayek 1935a). The objective in the Austrian tradition is to ascertain how the market can transform the desired pattern of consumption in the future into a pattern of production in the present. Elsewhere, Keynes (1936), thinking along a similar line, stated that one important question in economics was how the investors defeated the dark forces of time and ignorance which envelop their future.

Although the Austrian school places strong emphasis on variations in the time structure of production, the neoclassical treatment of capital theory is fundamentally different. For example, in Knight's theory of capital, under equilibrium conditions production and consumption are simultaneous (Knight 1946). As O'Driscoll et al. (1985) put it, "there is no structure in Knight's theory because he fully adopted the Newtonian conception of time." This collapses the time structure of production into a cross-section of the economy's stages in which future is spread out over instantaneous space.

The Newtonian concept of time resembles space as its passage is represented by movements along a line where different dates are portrayed as a succession of line segments, either in discrete or continuous forms. In Newtonian tradition, just as an individual allocates portions of his/her space to specific purposes, say, a house is divided up into functional units, he/she allocates portions of his/her time to specific activities. The fact is that what can be true for space cannot be true for time, as the latter is not divisible nor is it homogeneous. Just as a line can be divided and subdivided continuously, time in the Newtonian tradition receives the same treatment where these divisions can be made arbitrarily small. No matter how small the units of division, there will always be some space left between them; that is, each segment of time becomes independent of the others. Furthermore, each segment becomes identical to all others. Specialized time is a temporal position; it is an empty point ready to be filled with imposed changes.

One implication of Newtonian time is that it can pass without economic agents learning. As mentioned above, in neoclassical theory and in general equilibrium models, adjustments take place instantaneously which give rise to the Newtonian paradox; if adjustment is instantaneous, why is change ever necessary? Things could be right at the beginning (Myrdal 1939).

In Bergsonian tradition (Bergson 1910), real time is defined as a flow of subjective and novel experiences. "This flow is not in time, as would be the case from a Newtonian perspective; rather, it is or constitutes time. We cannot experience the passage of time except as a flow; something must happen or real time will cease to be" (O'Driscoll et al. 1985). In real terms, individuals' perspectives involve past experiences (memory) and anticipation of future to come; the present links the two. As an analogy, hearing a single note of a melody is not enough to capture the experience of music. The experience at any point includes memory of elapsed notes and anticipation of the ones to come. It is not possible to divide and subdivide a melody without fundamentally altering the experience. As the real time flows the individual's memory is constantly enriched and his/her anticipation of the future is changing. That is, unlike Newtonian time, real time is heterogeneous.

According to its critiques, one implication of the Newtonian approach to economic analysis is that the learning process, in a way, remains outside of time. The entire learning function of economic agents is assumed to exist as if it is compressed into a single, conscious present. In other words, the present, somehow, captures everything. Although this results in a greater mathematical tractability, it also reduces economic theory to a set of comparative static prepositions. An economic model based upon differential equations is actually concerned with current rates of change where past and future are not involved. In Newtonian neoclassical models the future always looks the same, irrespective of from where it is viewed. But when we allow a change in perspective with real time, the future would look different from where it is seen; the swelling of memory alone changes the view of the world.

The use of the Newtonian time concept in neoclassical economic modeling greatly undermines the forecasting ability. In such models there is no continuous refinement of future plans and knowledge is not gained in the process of projecting. Strotz (1955) contends that if economic agents commit themselves to their original plan, regardless of the change in perspective, they are likely to underachieve or, on occasions, fail in their objectives. A truly dynamic plan involves revisions and alterations in the course of time.

One of the most important aspects of the debate on Newtonian versus real time (which is relevant here) is the emphasis placed upon the individual, which is inherent in both traditions. Indeed, time with or without a learning process is a subjective matter and thus discounting in any economic analysis must be connected specifically with individuals who are undergoing an experience over time. As the reader will discover later on in Chapter 4, modified discounting, being a strictly individualistic approach, captures the subjectivity of time discounting. Ordinary discounting, on the other hand, in communal projects, disregards individuals by assuming that society is a single unit with eternal life. In discounting literature, views such as parents regarding their lives as continuing after death in their children (Fisher 1930: 86); stock of capital handed on from one single period to its successor links time periods (Hicks 1965: 36); and present is linked to the past through the inherited value of wealth (Hey 1981: 52) are confusing, to say the least. Fisher's view, in which only individuals without children appear to be mortal and each person with children passes his/her entire life experience to a child, or a number of children, is nonsensical. In the remaining two, at least one question must be asked: whose capital and wealth are linking whose time?

REASONS FOR TIME DISCOUNTING

Pure Time Discount Rate. What are the factors that encourage individuals to value present more than future? This question has been puzzling economists and others for a long time. One group contends that time discounting is partly due to irrational human behavior. As early as 1871, Jevons argued that when it comes to the distribution of income over time individuals do not act with good sense and perfect foresight, as they tend to undervalue their future needs. In effect, to secure a maximum benefit in life, after allowances being made for their uncertainty, all future incidents should have the same impact on us as present, regardless of their remoteness in time. But no human mind is constituted in this way and therefore a future utility is always less compelling than a present one (Jevons 1871).

Böhm-Bawerk (1884) puts it even more strongly: that our tendency to prefer small but earlier consumption to a much larger one in the future is due to backwardness, which is most noticeable amongst primitive tribes and uninstructed groups in our society. This human weakness is well-known to the business community, as many schemes of hire purchase require no down payment now and nothing due for several months.

Strotz (1955) argues that the more primitive the tribe or underclass in our society the greater their preference for early consumption. Backwardness and extreme selfishness may be two sides of the same coin. As Rae (1905) put it, "when I die, let the world burn." This was a guiding principle for many wild and selfish communities in the past, which eventually vanished.

Pigou (1929) is perhaps the best-known economist in the time discounting debate, since he coined the phrase "defective telescopic faculty." According to him, when market participants have a choice between two satisfactions they will not necessarily choose the greater of the two, but will often devote themselves to acquiring a small benefit now in preference to a much larger one some years hence. The main reason for this is that our telescopic faculty is defective and thus we see future gains as well as pleasures on a diminishing scale. As the years to which satisfactions are allocated become more remote, they will be represented by a scale of magnitudes continuously diminishing. Therefore, individuals tend to distribute their resources between the present, the near future and the remote one on the basis of wholly myopic and irrational preferences.

Fisher (1930), writing on the theory of interest at the same time as Pigou, seemed to be in agreement with all these views on discounting. According to him, discounting the future involves a variety of factors, some of which are shortsightedness, selfishness, lack of self-control and habit of extravagance. These tendencies are particularly high amongst some sections of society such as bachelor sailors and soldiers, whose motto seems to be "a short life and a merry one,'' as they frequently indulge in extravagant living at the expense of future well-being.

Obviously, many distinguished economists in the past believed that there is an irrational, backward, selfish and myopic aspect to human nature which affects intertemporal decisions. These tendencies, however, are not equally distributed amongst all individuals, as some groups are more vulnerable than others. This part of time discounting was sometimes called the pure time preference rate, and was branded as morally indefensible by Ramsey (1928), mainly because it tends to reduce the rate of saving and creation of capital which would be beneficial to future individuals.

It has been pointed out by Hirschleifer et al. (1960) that myopic and selfish tendencies of individuals will be mitigated by their love for others, especially children and other close relatives or even friends. Love and affection for others may prevent individuals, to a certain extent, from depleting their incomes in hasty consumption. Even if individuals did not care for their families, dependents or friends, they would still save for their own retirement and against misfortune. Whatever the saving motivation is, when an individual dies somebody else reaps the reward in his absence. This takes us to the second component parameter of time discounting—risk.

Risk. There are two risk components in time discounting: risk of death and risk of savings being lost—a stronger preference for present consumption can be justified on these two grounds. The fact of mortality is a perfectly rational factor to make individuals prefer beneficial things today to things of equal value tomorrow. Fisher (1930) is careful not to condemn the pure time preference rate as irrational; since all individuals are mortal it is reasonable for them to exhibit a preference for consumption today, because they may not survive to enjoy it tomorrow. After all, present survival is the precondition to acquiring all benefits because termination of life now brings the termination of a person's enjoyment of present as well as future income (Lindstone 1973).

Eckstein (1961) sees the possibility of calculating a pure time discount rate based upon survival probabilities in which the utility to be enjoyed at each future moment ought to be multiplied by the probability of being alive at that time. Since this probability falls with the remoteness of the period, a rational time discount rate will emerge. Numerical values for a time discount rate based upon survival probabilities can be computed from mortality statistics. ''For consumption one year after the present moment, the factor is equal to the probability of not surviving the next year; for longer intervals, it is a geometric average of annual rates'' (Eckstein 1961).

At a societal level the mortality-based time discounting rate can be estimated by taking into account the life expectancies and age/sex structure of the population. Eckstein (1961) and Henderson (1965) felt that such a rate for countries like the United Kingdom and the United States is likely to be in the order of one percent. Later on, by using the method suggested by Eckstein (1961) and Lutz (1940), I shall obtain much higher rates for these countries. If one accepts that the societal time preference rate ought to be derived on the basis of individuals' preferences, then the figure would contain time preferences of mortal individuals.

The second part of the risk in time discounting is that although an individual may survive from one particular time point to the next, his/her deferred consumption, that is, saving, may diminish or disappear completely because of adversities of the market. Savings put into a bank deposit may vanish if the bank goes out of business. Indeed, the recent collapse of the Bank of Credit and Commerce International (BCCI) left its savers high and dry throughout the world. Commercial banks, having received deposits, make the money available to others in the form of business or consumption loans at higher rates than depositors receive. The interest charged on each loan is different, depending on the duration of the loan and also the reason for the transaction and creditworthiness of the borrower (Hicks 1946). Every loan is essentially a gamble and thus the interest charged must reflect not only the base rate, but compensation for risk-taking in every transaction. Therefore, nobody, including banks, can be, or should be, 100 percent certain that loans will turn into greater sums at a future date.

Diminishing Marginal Utility of Consumption. A positive time preference rate is also justified on the grounds that in most societies the standards of living enjoyed by individuals are improving. As the income of a person increases steadily the satisfaction gained also increases, but at a slower rate because each absolute addition to his/her income yields a successively smaller increase in economic welfare. Figure 1.1 shows the situation. Vertical axis measures total as well as marginal utilities in relation to Good X. As the consumption level increases by one unit, $X_1X_2 = {}_2X_3X = \ldots$, the utility gained is also increasing but at a diminishing rate, $U_1U_2 > U_2U_3$, shown along the total utility function.

The diminishing marginal utility of income is an older concept than pure time discount rate, as its source can be traced to the works of Dupuit (1844), Gossen (1854) and Jennings (1855). In spite of its great potential in economic analysis, this concept went largely unnoticed for a long period of time. Stigler (1972) attributes this to lack of professionalism in economic science. More than 80 years after its first appearance, Fisher (1927) used it in justification of progressive income tax. Now, diminishing marginal utility of income appears to be the backbone of time discount rate.

However, Lipsey (1960) contends that the diminishing marginal utility is a debatable concept because as the income of a person increases, he/she is assumed to consume more of the same goods. That is, the diminishing marginal utility of income implies that consumers have clearly specified tastes in the neighborhood of their current consumption position. It is quite conceivable that as a person's income increases he/she moves to a different consumption pattern than was available when the income level was low. In other words, the consumer learns what his/her tastes really are and develops them into new dimensions as consumption possibilities advance. Likewise, Sen (1967) believes that as in-

Figure 1.1
Diminishing Marginal Utility of Consumption in Relation to Commodity X

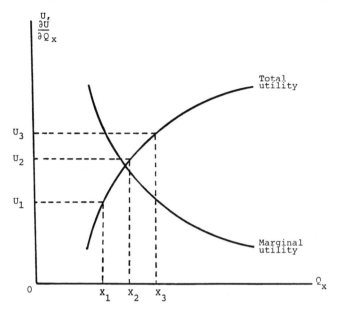

comes grow the tastes and preferences may change, weakening the applicability of the diminishing marginal utility of income hypothesis. But he also sees that there is a commonsense case for not ignoring this concept, especially when we are considering individuals in developing countries, where they improve their condition from bare subsistence to a more tolerable level of economic existence.

FISHERIAN SYNTHESIS

In view of what has been said above, it should be clear that there are two sides to the discount rate coin: consumption and production. Fisher (1907) was the first economist who put the two together. In the revision of his book, *The Rate of Interest*, he emphasized the two aspects of discounting by a long but clear subtitle, "The Theory of Interest: As Determined by Impatience to Spend Income and Opportunity to Invest." An extra unit of saving by individuals has two consequences: a reduction in present consumption by that amount and an increase in future production leading to a greater consumption opportunity. In economic literature the interest rate which relates to the latter is referred to as the marginal productivity of capital or the opportunity cost rate.

In a simple, two-period analysis where an investor allocates his/her endowment to be consumed in two successive periods, say years, the psychological rate of discount will be found in his/her indifference map. The marginal pro-

Figure 1.2
Two-Period Equilibrium

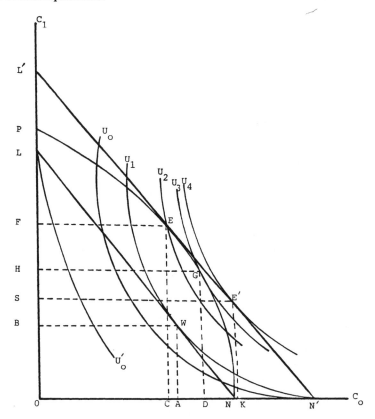

ductivity of capital will be along the physical investment opportunity schedule. By using Feldstein (1964a) and Samuelson (1967), it is possible to confine the analysis to a single individual first, then move on to all individuals who make up society at any two successive time points. In the Fisherian analysis this is not a superficial description of supply and demand of consumable/investable funds but rather a formulation that analyzes these to their ultimate source in psychology and technology.

In Figure 1.2 consumption in year zero, C_0, is measured along the horizontal axis and consumption in year one C_1 along the vertical. If the economic agent decides to have zero consumption in year one, we may represent his/her situation by point N on the horizontal axis, indicating that he/she will use up the entire endowment in year zero. Conversely, if he/she decides to consume all his/her endowment in year 1, he/she will be at L and on indifference curve U'_0. The line NL represents the borrowing-lending possibility frontier equivalent to the budget line in static consumer analysis, which can be found in any textbook on micro-economics. The slope of this line indicates the interest rate; when the interest rate is positive the slope of LN will be greater than one, which is the case here.

The person can redistribute his/her consumption between the two time points by moving to any point along LN by lending and borrowing. At this stage the economic agent has no direct investment opportunity. At point W the agent reaches the highest available indifference curve (with no direct investment opportunity) where present consumption becomes OA and future consumption OB. Next we introduce real, or physical, investment opportunity curve, NP (envisage an individual setting up a small business, constrained by his/her limited resources). The slope of this curve at any point measures the marginal productivity of capital or the opportunity cost rate for the agent. The rate decreases as the quantity of capital invested increases, which is in line with the law of diminishing returns.

If the economic agent follows the usual internal rate of return or present value criteria, he/she will invest CN putting him/her on indifference curve U_2 which is higher than U'_0 or U_1. At that point, E, the marginal productivity of capital equals the market rate of interest. The agent's present consumption will be OC and future consumption OF. It has been contended by Hirschleifer (1958) and Wright (1963) that in a two-period analysis both internal rate of return and net present value criteria will yield the same result.

It is now possible for the agent to reach an even higher indifference curve. If DN is invested the agent will be at point G on the transformation schedule and on U_3 indifference curve consuming OD at present and OH in the next period. But by using a combination of market interest rate and his/her physical investment opportunity curve, NP, he/she can move on to an even higher indifference contour U_4 by investing and borrowing. Then present consumption will be OK and future consumption OS.

From the case of a single individual we now move to all individuals who make up society at a given point in time. In traditional capital theory a single discount rate equates the marginal time preference of savers with the marginal rate of return on capital. Preference patterns for consumers include desired distribution of expenditures over time; by borrowing and lending at the market rate of interest they arrange their expenditures in such a way that the total satisfaction during the entire period for which their plan extends is at a maximum, as judged by their present preferences. Firms invest up to a point where the rate of return on marginal projects is equal to the interest rate. Consumers' plans to save are brought to equality with producers' plans to invest and the ruling interest rate reflects both the time preference of consumers and the rate of return on capital. In equilibrium the optimum rate of saving/investment is achieved for the community at a given point in time.

The unfettered market equilibrium can be seen in Figure 1.3. PP¹ shows the aggregate production possibility frontier which is in conventional shape. That is, a movement from P to P¹ implies that, *cateris paribus*, the marginal productivity of capital diminishes as more of it is used. The slope at any point along

Figure 1.3
Communal Time Preference Rate and Equilibrium/Disequilibrium

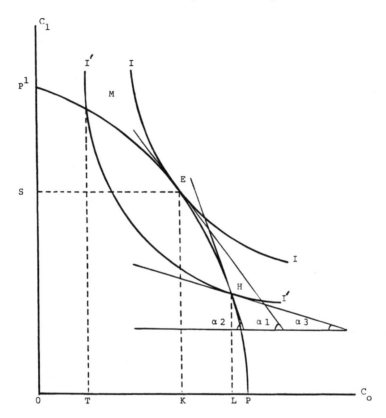

the transformation schedule measures the marginal social productivity of capital. Feldstein (1964a) draws attention to the fact that a closed economy can redistribute consumption through time only along the PP^1, not by monetary borrowing/lending line.

The communal indifference map is aggregated by registering the preferences of all individuals who exist at any given point in time. When we superimpose the communal indifference map on the communal transformation frontier, one contour will be tangent to it. This happens at point E where the slope of the transformation schedule is equal to the slope of the social indifference curve, shown by angle α_1.

At this point I should mention that there are some aggregation problems associated with both transformation curve and indifference schedules and these are argued to be especially acute in the latter. Arrow (1963) looks at the possibility of a meaningful aggregation of individual preferences into a social preference function by arguing that any aggregation process must simultaneously satisfy a number of conditions—the so-called impossibility theorem. These are, briefly: the aggregation rule must apply to all logically possible sets of individual orderings and not just a selected few, to make sure that the social welfare function is wide enough in scope. The association between individual orderings and social ordering must move in the same direction. For example, if one alternative social condition rose in the ordering of individuals we would expect a rise, or at least not a fall, in the social ordering; the social welfare function must be independent from irrelevant issues including taboos; the social welfare function must not be dictatorial or be imposed on society by a particular group of individuals.

Then Arrow demonstrates that no construction process can satisfy these conditions simultaneously. Tullock (1967), in his article "The General Irrelevancy of Impossibility Theorem," argues that although no decision process will meet Arrow's criteria perfectly, the majority voting process normally leads to a determinate outcome which is apt to be reasonably satisfactory. This common decision process meets Arrow's conditions to a very high degree of approximation and this permits us to reconcile the theoretical impossibility with the practical success of democracy. Marglin (1963b) contends that the entire social preference map is needlessly ambitious; all we want to find is the marginal social preference rate in the neighborhood of the optimal rate of interest.

It is evident that in Figure 1.3 there is a direct link with the amount of saving and the communal psychological discount rate and marginal productivity of capital. In an optimum situation where the saving ratio is KP/OP both discount rates are the same. If, on the other hand, the level of saving was, say, LP, this would not only wedge a gap between social time discount rate and social opportunity cost of capital, but would place the community on a lower level of welfare, indifference curve I'I'. At this low state of welfare where saving is suboptimal and the social indifference curve cuts into the transformation schedule, point H, the slope of the former is less than the slope of the latter: angle $\alpha2>$ angle $\alpha3$. Here society is effectively expressing a preference for a higher level of saving and investment. If no restrictions were imposed the community would move from H to E by increasing saving/investment level toward K where the discrepancy between the two discount rates diminishes and eventually disappears. Point M is an opposite case where the community is investing too much, TP, and as a result the communal psychological rate of discount is greater than the social opportunity cost of capital, which also places society on a below-optimal indifference curve, I'I'.

BARRIERS TO FISHERIAN EQUILIBRIUM

A number of economists such as DeGraaff (1957), Feldstein (1964a), Baumol (1968, 1969) and Mishan (1971) argue that the point of optimality in which a single interest rate equates the community's desire to save with investors' plans to invest is unlikely to be achieved due to a number of intratemporal as well as intertemporal problems. These are as follows:

Inequality in Distribution of Wealth. When individuals lend and borrow money in the market they are likely to make errors of judgement or become victims of unfortunate events. The wealthier the borrower the better placed he/she is in any problem arising from misjudgement or misfortune. Therefore, given the differences in wealth it would be irrational for lenders to lend as much to the poor as to the better-off members of society, or at least to lend the same amount on the same terms to each. Therefore, in order to have a single interest rate, the ideal market also requires that market participants are equally wealthy and wise. Such a market also requires that all traders have the common characteristic of being honest. If a person was permitted to borrow any sum from the perfectly competitive capital market at the going rate, he/she could borrow the money for any period, say five years, and could repay the loan on maturity simply by borrowing a larger sum and repeating the operation until the end of his/her life.

In the real world, the situation is very different as wisdom, wealth and honesty are unequally distributed. Every loan is a gamble and thus interest rates must reflect the risk on every transaction. This gives rise to varying rates of interest, depending on the position of the borrower.

Ignorance and Interdependence. In the perfect market, it is assumed that market participants, in their intertemporal allocations of consumption, must foresee their future incomes as well as the future prices of all goods and services. Individual saving rates depend on the expected future prices, which are influenced by the saving decisions of others. No single individual acting separately has any means of knowing what other individuals' intentions are. To put it differently, market participants cannot have the necessary information to determine optimally their saving levels. On the investment side, the revenue from one project depends on the investment decisions on other projects. The individual investor, just as the saver, cannot have the information necessary for rational intertemporal decision-making (also see Nove 1992).

Institutional Barriers. Baumol (1968, 1969) contends that there are institutional barriers such as taxation which prevent the community from attaining the optimal level of saving/investment. Let us assume that in an economy all goods and services are provided by corporate bodies who finance their investment projects by equity issues. The corporate income is subject to a uniform tax rate of, say, 50 percent. Finally, there is a unique interest rate, say 5 percent, at which government borrows money to finance public works, which requires input resources. Since corporations are the only owners of inputs they can only be transferred to public domain by taking them out of corporate hands. The opportunity cost of input resources can then be calculated by determining the returns which would have been obtained if they had been left in corporate hands.

In a riskless world investors would expect the same rate of return on money invested in either the private or public sector. This means that corporations must return at least 5 percent to their shareholders. But a 50 percent tax on corporate earnings means that corporations must provide a gross yield of 10 percent for their shareholders. In other words, resources, if left in the hands of the private sector, would have yielded 10 percent in real terms.

This model has significant consequences for public policy; with a 5 percent rate of interest on government bonds, the rate of discount on government projects is not 5 percent, but is in the region of 10 percent. Baumol adds that whether resources are transferred from private to public sector by borrowing or by taxation does not matter. Equally, it makes no difference whether the resources are drawn to the public sector from private investment or from private consumption; all that matters is that the transfer must take place through the agency of the corporations. The transferred inputs would have brought corporations 10 percent as a result of consumers' marginal valuation of those commodities.

Natural Barriers. In order to open the road to Fisherian optimality one may contend that all distortive taxes, including corporation tax, should be abolished. Unfortunately, this would not solve the problem because there is another even bigger barrier—risk. Since the national investment portfolio consists of a large number of projects, it is reasonable to expect that some will exceed their estimates while others underachieve, or even fail completely, and in this way there will be an overall compensation. Society benefits from the entire set of investment projects, whether they are public or private. The transfer of an investment project from private hands to the government does not affect its flow of benefits to society, nor does it mean that risks can be offset to a greater or lesser degree against other projects.

Unlike Samuelson (1964) and Arrow (1966), who argue that risk premium should be excluded from the discount rate, Baumol (1968, 1969) concludes otherwise. Since risk does exist from the individual investor's point of view, it plays exactly the same role as corporation tax by driving a wedge between the psychological time discount rate and marginal rate of return on capital. Firms will invest only up to a point where expected returns are higher than they would be in the absence of risk. Consequently, the economy will be stuck at the point of low investment and low state of well-being. (For further details of natural and institutional barriers, see Nicholas 1969; Ramsey 1969; James 1969.)

Isolation Paradox. This is about the interdependence of welfare between generations and the resulting social discount rate, which first appeared in the writings of Landauer (1947) and Baumol (1952). They argue that an individual may be perfectly willing to make a sacrifice on his present consumption to benefit future generations if others do so. A single person would not make the sacrifice alone since he knows that his own loss would not be compensated for by a future gain.

Sen (1961), by building on the ideas of Landauer and Baumol, argued that the present rate of saving, and hence the resulting discount rate, not only influences the division of consumption between now and later for the same group of people, but also between the consumption of different generations, some of whom are yet to be born. If democracy means that all the people affected by a decision must themselves take part in the process, directly or through represcntatives, then clearly there can be no democratic solution to the optimal level of saving. He then questions whether the rate of discount revealed by individuals in their personal choices is an indication of views of present generations of the weights to be attached to their own consumption or that of the consumption of future individuals. The isolation paradox proves a negative answer to this question. Assume a situation in which a man, in isolation, is facing the dilemma of choosing between one unit of consumption now and three units in 20 years' time. He knows, for some reason, that he will be dead in 20 years time, and may well decide to consume the unit. But now imagine that a group of men come along and tell him that if he saves the unit, they will follow suit; then it may not be irrational for the first man to change his mind and save the unit. This is because the gain to future generations would be much greater than his loss and he could bring this about by sacrificing only one unit of consumption. Therefore, without any inconsistency, he may act differently in two cases. This indicates that although individuals are not ready to make the sacrifice alone, they may well be prepared to do so if others are ready to join in. Sen concludes that the saving and investment decision, and hence the resulting social discount rate, is essentially a political decision and cannot be resolved by aggregating isolated decisions of individuals.

Later Sen (1967) pointed out that the earlier view of Baumol (1952) was not the same as his concept of the isolation paradox. In isolation individuals would like to see others invest but abstain personally unless forced to participate in a joint action. Otherwise they would choose to be free riders. In order to secure a collective investment, a compulsory enforcement is needed. In Baumol's case the problem is one of assurance; that is, individuals are willing to invest if they feel others will do the same. In other words, for each individual to invest as a separate unit, faith is enough and compulsory enforcement is not necessary.

Marglin (1962, 1963b), dealing with similar issues, argues that private investment decisions in which benefits appear only after the investor's death are undertaken because of the existence of a market which makes it possible to exchange the returns which occur after the investor's death for consumption benefits before the investor's death. But why do governments require citizens to sacrifice current consumption in order to undertake investments which will not yield benefits until those called upon to make the sacrifice are all dead, despite the fact that there is no market by which one generation can enforce compensation on the next? Is it because there is a difference between the way individuals view their saving versus consumption decisions collectively and individually?

One possible explanation is that individuals have dual and inconsistent time preference maps; one map representing the selfish side of our characters and the other the responsible citizens. For example, an individual acting as a citizen may

Figure 1.4
Saving Levels and Resulting Discount Rates with and without Isolation Paradox

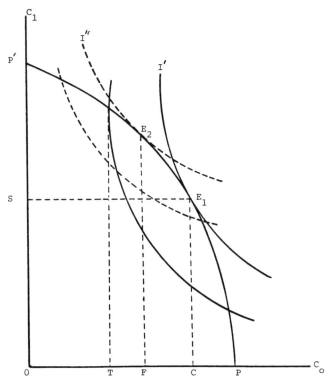

favor a strictly enforced system of traffic laws, but when caught as an offender may attempt to bribe the arresting officer. Figure 1.4 illustrates the situation. Indifference curves depicted as solid lines are derived by aggregating the unilateral decisions of individuals acting in isolation in the marketplace. The optimal point of equilibrium is established at point E_1, where I' and PP' schedules are tangent, requiring a saving level of CP. However, if individuals' preferences were aggregated with the assurance that others would participate in the collective decision, the resulting indifference curves would be less present-orientated vis-à-vis those of the curves derived by aggregating the isolated decisions. In Figure 1.4 these curves are shown as dashed lines, and the optimum equilibrium point is E_2, requiring a saving level of FP. Clearly, the equilibrium reached by one indifference map is not optimal by another one. Of course, the most important question is, which preference map is relevant? One can argue that since actions speak louder than words the preference patterns revealed in the marketplace are more genuine and should be considered by the decision-making body.

Marglin's analysis triggered off further discussion and it will be revealing to formalize it by setting up a simple model with a number of assumptions. Time is divided into two periods, present and future. All members of the present community die at the end of present, and their places are taken by individuals who come into existence fully grown at the beginning of future. The same investment opportunities are open to all individuals. Members of society are alike in the sense that they have similar time preference maps. The utility function of one individual is:

$$U_i = f(C_i, C_f, C_p - C_i) \tag{1.1}$$

where:

$$U_i = \text{utility function of the ith individual.}$$
$$C_i = \text{consumption of ith individual.}$$
$$C_f = \text{consumption of future individuals.}$$
$$C_p - C_i = \text{consumption of ith individual's contemporaries.}$$

Differentiating equation (1.1) we get:

$$dU_i = \frac{\delta U_i}{\delta C_i} dC_i + \frac{\delta U_i}{\delta C_f} dC_f + \frac{\delta U_i}{\delta (C_p - C_i)} (dC_p - dC_i) \tag{1.2}$$

where:

$$\frac{\delta U_i}{\delta C_i} = 1; \frac{\delta U_i}{\delta C_f} = \alpha; \frac{\delta U_i}{\delta (C_p - C_i)} = \beta > 0 \tag{1.3}$$

That is, the marginal utility of each item in the utility function is positive. The marginal utility of the ith individual's consumption is unity, that of future generations is α and his contemporaries is β. Assume now that the marginal rate of transformation between present and future is $\bar{r}$. That is, at the margin one pound of present sacrifice adds $\bar{r}$ pounds to the consumption level of the next generation.

The individual is willing to invest a pound as long as:

$$dU_i \geq \alpha \bar{r} - 1 \tag{1.4}$$

But instead of him investing, if somebody else invests he will still get satisfaction because the utility of future generations will increase to the same extent, but the loss in his eyes would be only β instead of unity. Therefore, the ith person will be pleased if somebody else invests so long as:

$$dU_i \geq \alpha \bar{r} - \beta \tag{1.5}$$

A third person is also guided by (1.4). This means that nobody wants to invest personally, though each would like to see others invest. Each individual would be willing to invest provided others did so, for in this case the gain from the investment of others would outweigh the loss on one's own investment. If there are n individuals in the community, investment will take place if the following holds:

$$dU_i \geq n\alpha \bar{r} - 1 - \beta(n - 1) \qquad (1.6)$$

$n\alpha \bar{r}$ = utility gain to ith person via future generations' benefit.
1 = utility loss to individual for his sacrifice.
$\beta (n - 1)$ = utility loss to individuals due to contemporaries' sacrifice.

Each is made better off so long as:

$$n \alpha \bar{r} \geq 1 + \beta(n - 1) \qquad (1.7)$$

If the numerical values for the parameters were:

$$\alpha = 0.10; \beta = 0.15; \bar{r} = 2$$

we would need at least 17 people ($n = 17$) to participate in a joint action to satisfy equation (1.7).

Tullock (1964), Usher (1964) and Lind (1964), commenting on Marglin's analysis, argue that his model is extremely sensitive to changes in the assumed values of the parameters. In Marglin's model a less altruistic value of α, say, 0.074, with other parameters being the same, leads to a completely different result. No matter how large n there would be no collective investment because equation (1.7) will not hold. Instead, the sacrifice should be made toward contemporaries rather than posterity. In effect, in making charitable contributions we normally require to know by how much the recipients are worse off than ourselves. An increase in the consumption of a person who is already consuming more than we are does not improve our state of satisfaction. It is quite reasonable to assume that even at the market-determined rate of saving, and discount rate, the next generation is going to be better off than the present one. A collective saving of the kind which is recommended by Landauer, Baumol, Sen and Marglin suggests taxing the poor in order to help the rich. Individually, some wealthy members of our generation might make charitable gifts to future generations on the grounds that the consumption levels, on average, are likely to be lower than the consumption levels of those who make the contributions. Alas, even this argument does not seem to be convincing. Since the poor have always been with us, it is more than likely that the next generation will also have some poor and needy. Therefore, some wealthy members of the present generation may choose to make a charitable contribution on the condition that the recipients should be the less fortunate members of future society. The existence of many foundations set up by the rich is the obvious indication for this choice.

Marglin's evidence for future-orientated altruism is dubious, as he asks: why do governments want citizens to undertake sacrifices, the returns from which will not come about until a long time interval has elapsed? One can also argue about the necessity of a present-orientated altruism by putting forward equally hearsay arguments, such as governments are too forceful, income tax is excessively burdensome, and so on.

Isolation paradox, if it existed, would have a bearing on the magnitude of the communal rate. However, as I shall demonstrate later on, in some cases such as nuclear waste storage it would be totally ineffective in achieving the desired objective: avoidance of injury to future generations. In many other cases such as forestry, air pollution, and so on, it is largely ineffective because it essentially recommends some reduction on the individual discount rate. For example, let us say that a social discount rate without isolation paradox was estimated to be 5 percent. With future-orientated altruism it would probably come to, say, 4.5 or at the most to 4 percent, which would not have a dramatic impact on long-term projects when used in the conventional manner (see Chapter 6, for instance). Nevertheless, the point of importance is that advocates of the isolation paradox meant well by implying that economic policy-makers should be caring and compassionate toward future generations.

Chapter 2

Search for an Appropriate Discount Rate

BACKGROUND

In addition to theoretical difficulties in identifying the elusive social discount rate, a number of economists, especially practitioners of cost-benefit analysis, have been in search of a figure for a long time. After all, whatever the theoretical problems may be, at the end of the day public sector economists need a discount rate. In effect, it is the necessity of having a social discount rate that gave rise to many theoretical developments, as economics has largely been a problem-driven discipline. Pearce (1983) contends that those who practice cost-benefit analysis have a real-world task to attend to, as they must rank proposed projects in order. The niceties of theoretical exchanges in learned journals did little to aid those who had these tasks.

In a historic context, the public works program in the United States after the First World War demonstrates how the public decision-making process has changed to take account of economic advice. During the Great Depression, expansion of public works as a means of combatting unemployment became an important policy option for the government. In 1930, acting on the recommendation of President Hoover, the U.S. Congress authorized the expenditure of nearly $1 billion (in 1930 prices) for a public works program, including the Hoover Dam on the Colorado River. Following the Employment Stabilization Act of 1931, 31 leading economists convened in New York, recommending a further $5 billion for public works programs, without delay, to be financed by a bond issue. On the state level, Governor Franklin Roosevelt of New York established a committee for planning of public works and work-sharing schemes amongst workers. Roosevelt also called a seven-state conference and urged both the federal and the state governments to initiate public works.

There were problems with expanding public projects at all levels. Due to the deepening recession, federal revenue was declining, which restricted the financing of proposed works. Apart from increased taxation, printing money and bond issues appeared to be the only means of creating funds for such projects. However, state and local governments were unable to print new money or new bank deposits by selling bonds to a controlled banking system. In effect, they were forced to cut back their spending to levels of their declining receipts. In the meantime, President Hoover himself was having second thoughts about his favorite policy of public works. Such works were ineffective to the needs in remote areas and to those who were not skilled enough to take part. Nevertheless, the Hoover administration increased state and local government spending by $1.5 billion during the recession. At the end of his term of office he pointed out that the number of public works created during his presidency was greater than in the entire previous 30 years. Amongst them, the projects of which he was most proud were the San Francisco Bay Bridge, Los Angeles Aqueduct and Boulder Dam. Public works as a major government policy in Western countries came to the fore during the Roosevelt administration.

In the meantime, economists as well as public sector policy-makers were beginning to think about establishing objective criteria as to the selection of public works. For example, should the government have given the Boulder Dam project priority over an extended highway network in Colorado? How should the costs and benefits of public works be accounted for? Should the benefits and costs be discounted; if so at what rate?

The 1936 Flood Control Act is considered by some to be a landmark on the road to establishing an objective criterion for desirability of public works. It is stated that a project be declared feasible if the benefits to the public are greater than the estimated costs. Although this Act did not spell out what benefits were to be taken into consideration, it was clear that the Act was referring to the construction costs of public works and did not include wider costs such as externalities which could impose a substantial welfare loss to the community. Similarly, inter- as well as intragenerational distributional aspects of public projects were ignored, alongside discounting. The next notable publication was the so-called Green Book (see U.S. Government 1950). In this the United States Federal Inter-Agency River Basin Committee attempted to formalize procedures to identify and compare costs and benefits associated with infrastructure projects. Two years later a budget circular made further inroads into establishing a methodology for assessing the worth of public works (Budget Circular 1952).

Following the publication of these documents a number of economists became interested in appraisal methodologies and produced volumes of work, mainly in relation to water projects (see Eckstein 1958; McKean 1958; Krutilla and Eckstein 1958; Maass 1962; Dorfman 1975). The main thrust of these publications was to link cost-benefit criteria with welfare economics so that a substantial body of welfare theory could be brought to bear on appraisal of water projects. The most popular project appraisal method turned out to be the benefit-cost ratio and almost everybody agreed to discount costs and benefits. The next question was at what rate future costs and benefits should be discounted.

PROPOSED RATES

Market Rate of Interest. Many who contributed to the discounting debate at the early stages of cost-benefit analysis believed that the ideal discount rate to be used in public sector capital projects was the one which would achieve a rate of capital formation maximizing social welfare. This involves a temporary sacrifice on present consumption. The value of sacrificed consumption then becomes the key to the selection of a discount rate, as it comes closest to representing the marginal opportunity cost of extra capital formation. The interest rate determined by the capital market provides a starting point in discount rate selection.

However, many economists were quick to realize the shortcomings of the market-orientated approach (James and Lee 1971). First, volatility had been a notable feature of all markets including capital markets. For example, immediately after the Second World War, due to increased savings, interest rates were low in the United States. In the 1960s the rates were high because of abundant investment opportunities. A public project approved by using a low market rate of interest at one period may not qualify during the era of high interest rates. Second, imperfections can exist in financial markets as well as in goods and labor markets. Financial markets in some Western economies are dominated by a few banks who tend to behave as a collective monopoly.

Modern governments have become closely entwined with capital markets as regulators as well as major participants. A large budget deficit requires heavy borrowing and increases the interest rate. The main reason for this tends to be politically attractive, excessive public spending. Furthermore, government regulates the money supply by its monetary policy which affects interest rates. Since monetary policy can be modified by political considerations at will, then in the selection of public projects politics rather than economics becomes a decisive factor. In addition, as mentioned in Chapter 1, there are many interest rates in the market reflecting the circumstances of borrowers/lenders. A lender normally charges a higher rate to those less likely to repay. Essentially, a government department is a secure borrower and thus its ability to repay is not normally in doubt. James and Lee (1971) contend that a public project should be judged on its own merit rather than the financial security of the borrower or the lender.

According to Eckstein (1961), capital markets are too imperfect; they are rife with rationing, ignorance, differential tax treatments; they are reluctant to finance investments from external funds, and have a slow adjustment process, all of which destroy the normative significance of actual rates. On the plus side, market rates, however imperfect or numerous, do exist. Their existence alone can be a considerable help to policy-makers in identifying a figure.

Government Borrowing Rate. The use of the long-term government borrowing rate as appropriate social discount rate was thought to be a much better alternative than the market rate of interest, for a number of reasons. First, since public sector capital projects are essentially risk-free in their economic evaluation, what we need is a risk-free interest rate. The public sector investment portfolio in any given financial year contains a large number of start-up projects. It is true that some of these projects will underachieve; a few may even fail entirely. Some other projects, on the other hand, will exceed their estimates and in this way there will be an overall compensation. In addition to a large portfolio situation, governments, in order to avoid political embarrassment, tend to initiate rescue packages for struggling projects. Just like communal projects, interest rates on government bonds were thought to be one of the most risk-free discount rates in the early literature of cost-benefit analysis. The second rationale for this rate was thought to be that it represented the cost of capital used in the construction of public projects.

Taking the second alleged merit of the government borrowing rate first, it is not correct that it represents the cost of capital used to finance projects. In reality governments raise only a small proportion of their revenue by borrowing; the bulk of their money comes from taxation. As for the riskless nature of bonds, their market value as well as the interest rate promised is subject to risks. The market value of bonds is affected by fluctuations in the base rate of interest. For example, take a long-term bond of £1,000 issued at a fixed interest rate of 5 percent at the time when the base rate was also 5 percent. If the base market rate goes up to 10 percent, then nobody will pay £1,000 for this bond as one could earn twice as much by putting the money into a bank account. Therefore, a doubling of the base rate of interest, *cateris paribus*, would halve the market value of the bond. This problem would be moderated in the long run, as falls and rises in the market value of bonds tend to cancel each other out. Fixed interest rate on bonds will also be affected by variations in the purchasing power of money. Let us say that at the time when the above-mentioned bond was issued the rate of inflation was zero. After a few years the inflation rate becomes, say, over 5 percent, which will make the real rate negative. Because of all these problems, nowadays most economists do not advocate the use of interest rate on government borrowing in public sector projects.

In the past the U.S. government agencies used bond rates in economic evaluation of capital projects. Until 1968, the official policy in the United States was:

The interest rate to be used in plan formulation and evaluation for discounting future benefits and compounding costs, or otherwise converting benefits and costs to a common time basis shall be based upon the average rate of interest payable by the Treasury on interest-bearing marketable securities of the United States outstanding at the end of the fiscal year preceding such computation which, upon original issue, had terms to maturity of 15 years or more. Where the average rate so calculated is not a multiple of one-eighth of 1 percent, the rate of interest shall be the multiple of one-eighth of 1 percent, next lower than such average rate. (The President's Water Resources Council 1962)

From 1960 onward the bond rate rose slightly, reaching 3.25 percent in 1965 and remaining at that rate for 3 years. In 1968 the Federal Water Resources Council recommended a rise in discount rate which was followed, and the figure was increased to 4.6 percent. Federal agencies were using higher rates for discounting benefits and private costs than they were for public costs with the rationale that private groups pay higher interest rates on their borrowing. But this practice was eventually dropped because of the planning distortions created by multiple discount rates (Douglas and Lee 1971).

The Social Opportunity Cost Rate of Capital. A large number of economists contend that since capital funds are limited, a public sector project will displace other projects in the economy. Therefore, in economic appraisal of commercial projects the appropriate rate of interest must be the one that reflects opportunity cost of capital. Generally, the next best alternatives are thought to be in the private sector and the objective behind this approach is to avoid displacing good capital projects in the private sector (Krutilla and Eckstein 1958; Hirshleifer et al. 1960; Kuhn 1962; Joint Economic Committee 1968).

However, it is commonly agreed that the rate of return in the private sector cannot be used to measure social profitability. First, in private rate of return calculations external costs such as noise, pollution and congestion are not normally taken into consideration. Second, profits and hence rate of return to capital may be quite high in the private sector, not as a result of efficient operation, but as a result of restrictive practices such as monopoly, cartel or oligopoly, all of which work against the public interest. Most economists believe that the private profits and resulting rates of return on capital require a substantial social adjustment before they can be used in public sector project evaluation.

In addition, it was questioned why it should be assumed that public projects always displace private investment rather than private consumption (Eckstein 1961; Marglin 1963a, 1963b; Feldstein 1964, 1972; Henderson 1965). It may well be the case that funds used to construct public projects partly displace private investment and partly private consumption.

As explained in Chapter 1, at a theoretical level social opportunity cost rate corresponds to the gradient of the social transformation schedule. At a practical level, how can such a rate be calculated? There seem to be two methods available: rate of return on a comparable project in the private sector, or the reciprocal of the capital output ratio, both of which yield widely diverging rates. In considering the gap between private and social rates of return some economists believe that the latter is a much more reliable method. For example, Feldstein (1964a, 1964b) argues that in a fully employed economy investment projects increase the productivity of labor and hence the wage rate improves. This increment is a cost to private investors who calculate the rate of return net of factors other than capital. From the communal viewpoint the increased income of the wage earners is a gain and thus the social rate is likely to be much greater than private efficiency of capital. In developing countries the situation is also similar. Harberger (1972) contends that in such countries where structural unemployment prevails, the shadow price of labor will be zero, especially for the unskilled. In other words, wages are not cost, in real terms, to public projects that draw labor from the unemployment pool. In such cases the output must be attributed to capital, broadly defined so as to include land and the like. Then the social rate of return on capital becomes the ratio of net product to the stock of capital, which is a much more sensible way of measuring social productivity of capital.

Timbergen (1956) points out that, for long periods, values for the capital output ratio of about three have been observed in some countries. A capital output ratio of three would imply a yield of about 33 percent, whereas ordinary investors get a few percent on their liquid capital. Obviously, the two methods, that is, the output-capital ratio and earnings on private capital, yield very different figures. On this point Henderson (1965) comments that ''it is a rather sad commentary on the state of economics that different sets of authors should be advocating such widely divergent criteria for measuring benefits, with little apparent meeting of minds simply because they happen to have approached the question from different directions.''

The Social Time Preference Rate. Another school of welfare economists believe that the correct rate of discount for commercial projects is the social time preference rate (STPR), which is also called the consumption rate of interest (CRI) or communal psychological discount rate (CPDR). The rationale for their argument is simple but compelling. The purpose behind all investment decisions, private or public, is to increase future consumption, which involves a sacrifice on present consumption. In other words, the relevant discount rate is the consumption rate of interest. This rate is a measure for changes in the marginal consumption levels of members of the community at different time points. Technically, in a two-period analysis it is the marginal rate of substitution of consumption between two time points less unity. Assuming a two-period social utility function:

$$U = f C_0, C_1)$$ (2.1)

where C_0 is present and C_1 is future consumption. Differentiation results:

$$dU = \frac{\delta U}{\delta C_0} dC_0 + \frac{\delta U}{\delta C_1} dC_1$$ (2.2)

Communal indifference curves were explained in Chapter 1. If dU equals zero, as it must when utility remains constant, as we move along the social indifference curve then (2.2) will be zero. From there the marginal rate of substitution of consumption will be:

$$MRSC_{0,1} = \frac{\delta U/\delta C_0}{\delta U/\delta C_1}$$

Then by definition the social time preference rate, S, will be:

$$S = MRSC_{0,1} - 1 \tag{2.3}$$

If the members of the community were indifferent between an extra unit of consumption now and the next period, then we have:

$$\frac{\delta U}{\delta C_0} = \frac{\delta U}{\delta C_1}$$

which will make the social time preference zero.

As explained in Chapter 1, we anticipate that $\delta U/\delta C_0 > \delta U/\delta C_1$ which means that judged from today, the marginal utility of a unit of present consumption is greater than the marginal utility of the same unit in the next period. Then the social time preference rate must be a figure greater than zero. The component parameters of this rate are: mortality-based pure time discount rate, myopia or irrationality, and diminishing marginal utility of consumption.

Weighted Average Rate. In welfare economics the theoretical consistency requires that in the choice of social rate of discount both the social opportunity cost rate and the social time preference rate must play a part. In an unfettered market which rests upon a set of heroic assumptions these two rates are thought to be equal (Chapter 1). In the real world, however, due to many factors such as distortive taxes, risks, intergenerational interdependence, ignorance, and so on, the rates of social opportunity cost and social time preference could not be equal; on the whole, probably the latter will be less than the former. What rate should we use in such a world?

One proposed solution is a synthetic rate weighted on the basis of proportion of displaced consumption and investment. That is:

$$w = (p)r + (1 - p)s \tag{2.4}$$

where:

w = weighted average rate
r = social opportunity cost rate
s = social time preference rate
p = proportion of funds related to displaced investment
$1 - p$ = proportion of displaced consumption

Arrow (1966), Diamond (1968) and Harberger (1968, 1969) tend to favor this type of approach to public sector discounting. For example, Harberger, by considering debt finance, contends that borrowing for commercial projects increases the market rate of interest which implies less investment elsewhere. Then new government revenue can be divided into a proportion that would have been consumed and a proportion that would have been invested.

An Algorithm. Feldstein (1972), by arguing against weighted average rates, suggests that in a second-best world there is a need for two types of price in public sector investment evaluation. One is the relative price of consumption and the other is the relative price of investment. On the other hand, the weighted average provides only one price. As an alternative to synthetic weighted average, Feldstein proposes the shadow price algorithm. In this, first all costs and benefits of communal projects are expressed in terms of equivalent consumption and then discounted back to the point of decision-making at the consumption rate of interest (the social time preference rate).

The logic behind the shadow price algorithm is that every investment decision is put into motion in order to increase the future consumption capacity. Every pound invested now results in a future stream of consumption. The social opportunity cost of £1 displaced private investment is its expected future stream of consumption discounted at the social time preference rate. In the world of second best, where the social rate of return on private investment exceeds the social time preference rate, the opportunity cost of £1 displaced private investment exceeds 1, that is, £1 private investment has a greater value than £1 private consumption.

THE BRITISH GOVERNMENT'S POLICY—DISCOUNT RATE GALORE

Having realized the importance of discounting in economic policy-making, the British government since the early 1960s has been studying practical as well as theoretical developments in this field with a view to having a national policy. Although the intention and efforts of the government must be highly appreciated, as it will become obvious at the end of this chapter that the end result can only be described as "the discount rate galore" in which different rates are prescribed for different projects and regions which must create resource misallocation.

The nationalized industries were the first focus of attention in public sector portfolio, due to a 1961 White Paper (Cmnd 1337) which made a number of recommendations on the aims and objectives of publicly owned industries. The main emphasis was on the fact that industries should "pay their way." In order to achieve this they must operate in such a fashion as to earn a sufficient rate of return on their capital and build adequate resources to deal with contingencies which might occur from time to time. With a low rate of return on capital the operation of these industries will, sooner or later, damage the economy. As their activities expand this will result in either high taxes or greater borrowing by the Exchequer in order to provide for their developments. In this way too much of the nation's savings will be channelled into an area where nationalized industries show poor results.

It was also mentioned in the White Paper that there was a public expectation that the products of nationalized industries should be provided cheaply. In fact, the boards of these industries had been subjected to pressure from public opinion to keep their own prices down even when costs and prices were rising elsewhere. In this way they contributed substantially to efforts to stabilize prices, but on the other hand their own positions suffered. It was recommended that the pressure on public enterprises should be minimized, enabling them to manage their own affairs without outside interference.

The Test Rate of Discount. How do we ascertain that public corporations are earning adequate returns and paying their way? This was made clear in the 1967 Subcommittee Report on nationalized industries and the following White Paper, "Nationalised Industries: A Review of Economic and Financial Objectives" (Cmnd 3437). The White paper recommended that nationalized industries must use the best possible appraisal technique in their investment appraisal. The discounted cash flows method, which had already been widely used by many institutes, was recommended for all important projects, with an 8 percent test rate of discount. This figure was broadly consistent, having regard to differing circumstances, in relation to tax, investment, grants, and so on, with the average rate of return, in real terms, earned as a low-risk project in the private sector. In August 1969, this rate was increased to 10 percent; in 1972 it was reviewed but not changed. In a way the test rate of discount was a test of marginal performance in the public sector as compared with the private sector.

Many appeared to be satisfied with the choice of net present value criterion and the test rate of discount. For example, Alfred (1968) calculated a typical rate of return of 6.2 percent for the United Kingdom economy as a whole; then after considering the income tax on profits he increased his figure to 7.1 percent which was close to the government's first proposal of 8 percent. In view of the government's replacement of income and profit tax by a 42.5 percent corporation tax in April 1965, Alfred modified his figure to 10.1, a figure remarkably close to the test rate of discount.

Some others pointed out a number of problems with the choice as well as the magnitude of the test rate of discount. First, the test rate of discount was based entirely upon the opportunity cost concept. As explained above, the theory suggests that both social opportunity cost and social time preference rates must play a part in the choice of a social discount rate. Nowhere in the above-mentioned White Papers was there a mention of the social time preference rate.

Second, in estimating the social opportunity cost rate as a basis for the test rate of discount, the government used extremely crude measures. The treasury specified, in a memorandum submitted to the select committee on nationalized industries in 1969, how the figure was chosen (HCP 371-III, appendices and index, appendix 7). It was the minimum return which would be regarded as acceptable on a new investment by a large private firm. Obviously, the commercial rate of return on private capital was adjusted neither for market imperfections nor for externalities. Moreover, a crude average rate of return, rather than the marginal one, was taken in the choice of a figure for the test rate of discount.

Third, the funds that were used to finance the capital investments of nationalized industries were assumed to displace private investment rather than private consumption. In order to finance public projects, if the government borrowed the entire funds from the capital market, then the social opportunity cost rate could have been relevant, provided that the private rate of return was adjusted for market imperfections and externalities. However, in most cases in the United Kingdom, projects are financed by tax revenue, a large proportion of which comes from the reduction in private consumption. The appropriate course of action in this case would be the use of consumption rate of interest rather than the social opportunity cost.

Required Rate of Return. All these criticisms of the test rate of discount turned out to be fruitful. In 1975 an interdepartmental committee of administrators and economists was set up to review the test rate of discount and to consider its relevance to a wide range of public sector ventures. These included the investments of public sector trading bodies and the nationalized industries' new capital projects which take place in an environment of changing technology and market conditions. The committee recognized the fact that in public sector investment appraisal, the chosen rate of discount should reflect ideas on the social time preference rate as well as the social opportunity cost rate. The committee also stated that a justifiable figure for the social time preference rate would almost certainly be below 10 percent.

In addition, there was no point in imitating the private sector unless the rate of return there correctly reflected society's view of profitability. Also, it was hardly convincing to regard a public investment as diverting resources entirely from private investment rather than private consumption. In view of all these considerations, the committee recommended a rate of 7 percent in real terms as striking a balance between the social profitability of capital and the social time preference rate.

After the committee finished its study in late 1976 there was a great deal of discussion during the run-up to the White Paper, "Nationalised Industries" (Cmnd 7131) in 1978. The appropriate rate of discount was considered in more detail with the departments directly concerned. The main change from the original recommendation was a reduction in the figure. The original 7 percent was the average of the 6–8 percent range. The later data showed that the appropriate profitability in the private sector was between 5 and 7 percent, and in the end 5 percent was chosen. This figure was called the required rate of return.

In the spring of 1989 the British government revealed its new policy on discounting in a parliamentary exchange, when Mr. Boswell rose to ask Mr. John Major, then the Chancellor of the Exchequer and later the Prime Minister, whether the government would make a statement on new investment in nationalized industries and the discount rate used for appraising investment in other parts of the public sector.

In response, Mr. Major stated that

the government have reviewed the level and use of discount rates in the public sector. These were last reviewed in 1978. Since then the rate of return in the private sector has risen to around 11 percent. In the light of this, the government have decided to raise the required rate of return for nationalised industries and public sector trading organisations from 5 percent to 8 percent in real terms before tax. The new required rate of return of 8 percent will be an important factor in setting new financial targets, but there will be no impact on pricing during the life of the existing financial targets. (Hansard 1989)

At present, the choice of discount rate is a matter for individual nationalized industries or trading bodies to decide in consultation with sponsor departments and HM Treasury. The government's main concern is that the industries' approach should be compatible with achieving the required rate of return on the program *as a whole*. In appraisal of new capital projects risk should be given proper attention. The effect of full allowance for risk will often be implicitly equivalent to requiring a higher internal rate of return on riskier projects.

The British government also decided that the discount rate to be used in the nontrading sector should be based on the cost of capital for low-risk projects. In the conditions that prevailed in 1989 this indicated a rate of not less than 6 percent in real terms. Risks were to be analyzed separately and projects that were more risky were required to demonstrate correspondingly lower costs or higher benefits. This would ensure that projects in the nontrading sector would be as demanding as in the trading sector. In particular, they would provide a comparable basis for the consideration of private participation in public sector activities by taking account of the full economic cost of the public sector option. Table 2.1 gives the details of rates of return in various sectors of the British economy which formed the basis of the government's calculation.

Forestry Rates. The review process of the social discount rate was keenly watched by the forestry lobby in the United Kingdom. This is because as a long-term project, afforestation is extremely sensitive to the chosen magnitude of the discount rate (see Chapter 6). When the test rate of discount was first established the strongest objection to it came from foresters, as they argued that the 10 percent rate had ended the hopes of an economic rationale for forestry invest-

Table 2.1
Rates of Return in Various Sectors of the British Economy, 1960–1986

	Rates of Return		
Years	All Sectors	Manufacturing Non-North-Sea	Manufacturing Companies
1960	13.1	13.1	14.5
1961	11.3	11.3	12.0
1962	10.3	10.3	10.8
1963	11.4	11.4	11.5
1964	12.0	12.0	11.8
1965	11.4	11.4	11.5
1966	10.0	10.1	9.5
1967	10.1	10.2	9.6
1968	10.2	10.3	9.3
1969	10.1	10.2	9.6
1970	8.9	8.9	8.0
1971	9.1	9.1	6.8
1972	9.5	9.5	8.1
1973	8.9	9.0	7.9
1974	5.2	5.4	4.0
1975	4.0	4.3	2.6
1976	4.4	4.4	2.9
1977	7.5	6.8	5.7
1978	7.9	7.1	5.9
1979	7.4	5.7	4.2
1980	6.4	3.9	3.1
1981	6.2	3.0	2.0
1982	7.5	3.8	3.6
1983	9.1	4.8	4.1
1984	10.7	5.6	4.8
1985	11.4	7.2	6.1
1986	10.0	8.9	7.2

Source: British Business, 9 October 1987.

ment in the United Kingdom. Indeed, some earlier studies on forestry in Britain revealed that a very low discount rate was needed, on the order of 2 percent, so that a positive discounted cash flows figure could be obtained (Walker 1958; Land Use Study Group 1966; Hampson 1972). Some economists such as Thompson (1971) contend that in most cases it is not possible to earn more than 3 percent compound from forestry in Britain without subsidies, even with the most optimistic assumptions about future timber prices.

By using the discounted cash flows method with an interest rate as high as 10 percent the power of discounting practically wipes out the distant benefits that arise from felling in forestry. In order to salvage afforestation projects, some forestry economists such as Price (1972, 1976) have persistently argued for the use of lower rates of interest than the test rate of discount. Their defense is that unlike fabricated goods, the risk of land-based projects such as forestry becoming worthless in the distant future is extremely low. Since forestry is more or less a risk-free investment, then it should be discounted at a specially low rate.

When the test rate of discount was replaced by 5 percent required rate of return in 1978 there was a sigh of relief by some foresters. However, not everybody was relieved to the same extent, as many maintained that even a 5 percent discount rate was too high to justify the United Kingdom's forestry program on commercial grounds. Indeed, figures revealed by the Forestry Commission in 1977 showed an expected rate of return of about 2–2.5 percent on 60 percent of the Forestry Commission's acquisitions in Britain without subsidies (Forestry Commission 1977a).

After the publication of the 1967 White Paper (Cmnd 3437), some forest economists suggested that forestry rates of return should be enhanced by taking into account a number of factors. First, returns from forestry fail to take into account the increasing value of land acquired by afforestation. This was indeed a factor in the 1960s and 1970s in the European Community countries, but the situation has now been changed as land prices have been falling during the last decade. Second, a cost-benefit analysis should not be based on current prices, which fail to take into account the historic fact that the price of timber rises. The future as opposed to current price of timber should be used in any meaningful analysis. Potter and Christy (1962) and Barnett and Morse (1963) confirm that the long-term price of lumber shows an annual increase of over 1.5 percent in real terms in the United States, between 1870 and 1957. In the United Kingdom a similar trend has been observed in this century to 1963 (Hiley 1967). Third, forestry provides recreational and environmental benefits which must be incorporated into cost-benefit analysis.

In 1971 an interdepartmental government team was set up to carry out a cost-benefit analysis of British forestry. In this study a wide definition of profitability was taken as the criterion. The team considered the environmental, landscape and recreational benefits of forestry along with the value of timber produced. Also, the team tried to impute shadow prices for the inputs as opposed to distorted market prices. Various sensitivity analyses were also carried out; in one, a 20 percent premium for import saving was levied on the home-grown timber. After all these painful and time-consuming calculations to improve the profitability, the maximum rate of return from forestry was increased to 4 percent, well short of previous as well as new required rates of return (HMSO 1972a).

In the meantime, some simply refused to accept the view that the United Kingdom's forestry program should be judged on the basis of profitability, even if it was widely defined. For example, the chairman of the Forestry Commission in 1971, Lord Taylor of Gryfe, in a speech to the Scottish Woodland Owner's Association on 4 May 1971, said,

the Forestry Commision should not be regarded as a large commercial state enterprise but should be recognised for what it is—as the forestry authority concerned not only about the state enterprise, but concerned about the propagation and development of forestry as a whole in Britain. Therefore, I consider it my mandate and responsibility to speak as effectively as I can for forestry as distinct from any particular section. (*The Times*, 5 May 1971)

Following the 1971 cost-benefit study of British forestry the government revealed its forestry policy in a document which stated that afforestation would continue in Britain as before (HMSO 1972b). It was spelled out that this policy was guided by but not based on the conclusion of the cost-benefit study. With regard to the discount rate, the Forestry Commission in Britain was given a target rate of return of 3 percent, in real terms.

In another part of the United Kingdom, Northern Ireland, the Forest Service has been using the Treasury rate in land acquisition and in valuing growing timber in their own trading and other accounts. This rate has traditionally been 5 percent.

Discount Rate for Decommissioning of Nuclear Power Plants. The development of nuclear power for commercial purposes in the United Kingdom shows a similar pattern to that of the United States which started in the early 1950s (see Chapter 5). In 1955 the Conservative government announced its nuclear power plan which was based upon Magnox reactor technology. At the time the government did not expect the Magnox program to be economical; nevertheless nine stations were announced.

In 1964 the Labour government announced Britain's second power program based upon the advanced gas-cooled reactor technology. This involved a 20-fold scaling up from a small prototype with the order of three different designs. The Energy Committee (1990) contends that this was a disastrous decision, especially when there was scarcely sufficient engineering expertise for one. Consequently, by the early 1970s difficulties over construction of these reactors were mounting. In 1978 two more advanced gas-cooled reactors were ordered and the Central Electricity Generating Board (CEGB) and the United Kingdom Atomic Energy Authority (UKAEA) were authorized to undertake safety and design work.

In 1979 the newly elected Conservative government announced a third reactor program, pressurized water reactor, costing £15 billion in terms of 1979 prices. However, there were doubts about the size and the capacity of this program as well as the energy forecasts for the future. After a long public inquiry in 1987 the government announced the construction of the first pressurized water reactor, Sizewell B, which is the most favored design, a modification of the United States' Standardized Nuclear Unit Power Plant system. By 1989 nuclear power reached an important position, providing 20 percent of Britain's energy requirement.

The decades of expansion of nuclear power in Britain came to an abrupt end with the government statement of 9 November 1989 in which plans to build new pressurized water reactors were shelved in line with the curtailment of public support for the nuclear industry in general. The real reason for the policy reversal was the failure to sell the nuclear industry to the private sector. Indeed, the privatization process of the electricity industry served the useful purpose of revealing not only how much nuclear electricity costs, but also its future liabilities. After a long inquiry the Energy Committee (1990) put it that "after years of official assurances that nuclear power was (or could be) the cheapest form of electricity generation, parliament and the public are entitled to know why it was only faced with the commercial discipline of life in the private sector that nuclear power (from both existing and proposed reactors) suddenly became an expansive form of generation."

The reasons for the private sector to shy away from nuclear power were many. First, the cost of generating power in nuclear reactors was much higher than in fossil fuel plants and this cost has been going up over the years, partly because of the rising cost of capital (nuclear power is highly capital-intensive) and partly because of the tightening of regulatory standards. In November 1989 the Secretary of State revealed to Parliament that "the costs of nuclear power remained hidden throughout nationalisation, and it was only the preparations for privatisation that brought them to light" (House of Commons 1989). The Energy Committee (1990) confirms that on the basis of the evidence it received there has been a systematic bias in the Central Energy Generating Board's costing in favor of nuclear power by ignoring risks, failing to provide for contingencies, and in putting forward best expectations rather than more cautious estimates.

Second, the private sector has seen nuclear power as an open-ended liability both for reprocessing as well as for final disposal of wastes. Third, a nuclear power plant may turn out to be a bad performer and for a variety of technical reasons may fail to produce its expected output. In effect, the nuclear industry throughout the world is littered with such plants. Fourth, delays in construction and accidents not only would increase the cost of operation, but would reduce greatly the output. Furthermore, third party damages such as deaths, injuries, illnesses, property damage and clean-up would also affect profitability. Although the Nuclear Installations Act of 1965 and the Energy Act of 1983 limit the liabilities of generating bodies, this could still amount to £200 million. Fifth, a fall in the prices of competing fuels, especially fossil fuels, during a reactor's lifetime could make it uneconomic. Finally, there is the uncertainty regarding the dismantling of nuclear power generating units. No commercial reactor anywhere in the world has yet been fully decommissioned and there is no experience with the difficult stage of taking apart and disposing of the most contaminated parts of the reactor.

Apart from the "front-end" stage which involves uranium extraction and delivery, a nuclear reactor's life goes through three phases: construction, operating and decommissioning. Also there is the permanent disposal of highly contaminated parts and wastes which is probably the most complicated part. The Department of Energy and Kleinwort Benson (advisors to the department) regard 40 years as a reasonable operating life for a pressurized water reactor. But the Energy Committee (1990) points out that no pressurized water reactor has yet operated for more than 23 years. As for the decommissioning (i.e., the final return of sites to green-field status), this will not take place until 100 years after the reactors close.

Following the British government's policy to increase the required rate of return for tradeables from 5 percent to 8 percent in April 1989, the Central Electricity Generating Board used this rate as the standard for appraising its projects. However, some believe that in view of its high-risk nature the nuclear industry should use a much higher rate in its appraisal of new projects (Dimson 1988; Energy Committee 1990). The former recommends a discount rate of 11 or even 16 percent for the industry. As for the decommissioning cost the Central Electricity Generating Board has been using a 2 percent discount rate, which is much lower than the required rate of return or forestry target rate.

In 1996 the British government was planning to privatize the country's nuclear industry. In May 1995 the government decided to opt for swift privatization of the industry's most modern reactors. The Trade Secretary, Mr. Michael Heseltine, had been working on a major restructuring of the industry to make privatization a success. Earmarked for sale were the modern reactors of the Nuclear Electric and Scottish Nuclear who would operate them as subsidiaries of a new holding company to be called British Energy, in which shares would be offered to investors. The country's aged Magnox reactors would remain state owned. The Labour Party has criticized the government for compromising safety and for rushing the sale in order to raise cash for preelection tax cuts.

Discount Rate for British Rail. The British government has a commitment to privatize British Rail's railtrack division and the rolling stock. In 1996 the British government intensified its efforts to go ahead with sales. A couple of years ago the Treasury had calculated that on a replacement cost basis railtrack was worth about £7 billion. On the basis of 8 percent required rate of return for the tradeable sector and £7 billion asset base, railtrack must earn £560 million per annum. In order to achieve this operators must charge sufficiently high prices which are likely to make the rail service uncompetitive and reduce the interest amongst potential private operators.

In order to make the privatization initiative attractive, the Treasury agreed to set railtrack's initial rate of return not at 8 percent but at 5 percent, in 1994–1995, raising it by 1 percentage point a year until it reaches 8 percent. This, government believes, would encourage more private operators to bid for franchises under the government's privatization scheme. In other words, in order to make British Railways attractive to the private sector the government yet again bent the rules of discounting by creating one more special case.

Although the efforts of the British government to identify an appropriate social rate of discount must be appreciated, what has happened until now is far from encouraging: sharp fluctuations in the prescribed rate, and a current policy of discount rate galore, which is highly damaging from both resource allocation and equity viewpoints. The summary of the situation is as follows:

Test Rate, first proposal	8%
Test Rate, second proposal	10%
Required Rate of Return	5%

Current Required Rate, tradeables	8%
Current Required Rate, nontradeables	6%
Treasury Rate for Forestry Trading	
Account in Ulster	5%
Forestry Target Rate, Great Britain	3%
Decommissioning Rate for Nuclear Industry	2%

British Railtrack Target Rate, 1994-95	5%
" " " " 1995-96	6%
" " " " 1996-97	7%
" " " " 1997-98	8%

No matter what the government tries to do with its discounting policy it does not work. No matter what rates are used, ordinary discounting fails to yield a coherent policy because it rests upon a premise that is untrue as well as unjust. In the next chapter I take up this case.

Chapter 3

The Tyranny of an Untrue
and Unjust Theory:
Ordinary Discounting

INTRODUCTION

Conventional or ordinary discounting has been the backbone of all time-dependent social theories in economics during the last 60 years or so. It has been widely used all over the world in theoretical exploration of economic issues and on practical case studies, that is, evaluation of real-life projects. Despite its immense popularity in theory and practice, conventional discounting is wrong, as its rests upon an assumption that individuals live forever. Furthermore, this assumption leads public sector policy-makers to a morally indefensible discrimination against future generations; that is, the established welfare economics based upon conventional discounting theory is not only unreal but it is unjust as well.

Apart from myself, a number of economists have also expressed concern about the conventional theory. For example, Mishan (1988) argues that there is a convenient but absurd assumption in the established theory of cost-benefit analysis that all persons affected by a communal project are expected to remain alive until the end of its life, no matter how long this may be. In other words, nobody is permitted to die during the lifetime of a communal project evaluated by economists. A few years before that, Collard (1979), as part of his writings on the economics of ethics, was exploring the consequences of ordinary discounting in an article entitled "Faustian Projects and Social Rate of Discount." His analysis had some similarity to mine, but for some reason Collard did not develop his argument.

The results of ordinary discounting will also be valid if we substitute the assumption of immortal individuals with the one that society is like a single individual who has an eternal or very long life. This, of course, would detach communal identity from individuals who in fact make up a society. In effect, this idea is very much in line with the communal view of the Marxist school, which at the height of its power viewed society as a collective entity destined to live forever, evolving into perfection. In its scheme of things individuals, or individualism, in theory, received no attention. As I shall demonstrate later on, a good many economic models explicitly assume a unitary and nonindividualistic structure for society, similar to the one in Marxist ideology whereas others state that individuals live forever. Ironically, as far as I know, economists who were instrumental in laying down the foundation of conventional discounting in social economics would not remotely associate themselves with Marxism.

ORDINARY DISCOUNTING IN VARIOUS FORMS

Some economists, such as Dasgupta and Pearce (1972), Sassone and Schaffer (1978) and Pearce and Nash (1981), highlight the 1936 U.S. Flood Control Act as being instrumental in paving the way for the development of cost-benefit analysis as a tool to analyze the economic worth of communal projects. The stated principle that flood control projects should be deemed desirable if the benefit to whomsoever they may accrue are in excess of the estimated costs, introduced, to all intents and purposes, the discipline of welfare economics into the practical world of decision-making. After the passage of the Flood Control Act the development of the theory of cost-benefit analysis gathered momentum on both sides of the Atlantic in relation to two different sets of projects. In the United States water resource projects were the catalyst in laying down guidance on the use of cost-benefit techniques (see Chapter 7). In the United Kingdom, however, the transport projects took the lead (Chapter 9).

Two main pillars of cost-benefit analysis—identification and pricing of net benefits and discounting—came to the fore in the 1960s and 1970s. In valuation of net benefits of public projects in developed countries, it was assumed, rightly or wrongly, that markets were reasonably competitive and prices there, with some minor adjustments, could be used in assessing the value of proposed projects. But in developing countries the situation was different, as actual market prices decisively failed to reflect the scarcity value of inputs as well as outputs associated with communal projects. Different writers chose different numeraries for evaluation. For example, Sen (1972b) and Marglin et al. (1972) chose aggregate consumption at domestic prices. Little and Mirrlees (1969, 1974) and Squire and Van der Tak (1975) adopted the use of world prices. With regard to discounting, various principles, all based upon ordinary discounting method, were constructed to find "improved" ways of deflating future costs and benefits.

Almost all the textbooks written on cost-benefit analysis advance the discounting debate on the basis of an argument explained below, or similar to that one. For example, see Frost (1971), Kendall (1971), Mishan (1971, 1972), Dasgupta and Pearce (1972), Layard (1972), Squire and Van der Tak (1975), Zerbe and Dively (1994) and Layard and Glaister (1994). If an individual has a marginal time preference of, say, 5 percent per period (year), then he/she is indifferent between the alternatives of one extra unit of current consumption, year zero, and $(1 + 0.05)$ units of consumption in year one $(1 + 0.05)^2$ in year 2. Although each individual's time preference rate is subjective, it is through the operation of capital markets that they are revealed. Assuming perfect competition, which relies upon a set of heroic assumptions and the absence of risk, all intertemporal traders will be able to borrow and lend at the market rate of interest. If an individual's time preference rate is greater than the market rate, he/she will choose to borrow; if it is lower, the money will be lent. The ordinary discounting formula is:

$$1/(1 + r)^t; \ e^{-rt} \tag{3.1}$$

where r is the market rate of interest and t is time $(0,1,2, \ldots)$, normally expressed in terms of years. If we assume a long-term market project which throws off £1 net benefit every year, the discounted values for each year can be obtained by using (3.1). Appendix 1 gives the ordinary discount factors for years 1–50 for interest rates 4–12 percent and 15 percent. Of course, the discount factor for year zero is one. These numbers give the net present value of £1 net benefit expected at any one year in the future. For instance, the current market value of £1 which is expected in year 50 is £0.0085 at 10 percent interest rate.

Conversely, ordinary compounding, that is, the opposite of ordinary discounting, is given by:

$$(1 + r)^t; \ e^{rt} \tag{3.2}$$

That is, £1 invested at 10 percent interest rate will amount to £117.39 in 50 years' time.

The use of ordinary discounting in economic analysis of social projects has been a very widespread practice. (3.1) immediately grabs the attention of the reader in every book on cost-benefit analysis and indeed in many other texts. It is in numerous journal articles which deal with various aspects of intertemporal welfare economics. It is so deeply embedded as to be very rarely examined. It is eye-catching, intimidating, to some establishment figures it is beyond question. According to Price (1993), this small expression has been a career maker as well as a wrecker for quite a few academics. It is ominous.

In the business of cost-benefit analysis ordinary discounting appears in various forms. Here are some of these forms.

Net Present Value. This is the most popular method by which net benefits generated by communal projects over time are discounted year by year and then summed to obtain an overall figure. If this figure is greater than zero, then the project in question becomes feasible; otherwise it fails, indicating that it does not generate discounted benefits large enough to offset discounted costs. That is:

$$NPV = \sum_{t=0}^{n} \frac{1}{(1 + r)^t} NB_t,$$ (3.3)

or

$$NPV = \int_{0}^{n} NB_t e^{-rt} dt$$

where t is time $(0,1,\ldots n)$ normally expressed in years; n is the project's life; NB_t is net benefits (benefits minus cost) at year t; r is appropriate social discount rate; and $1/(1 + r)^t$ and e^{-rt} are ordinary discount factors.

Internal Rate of Return. This is the twin sister of the net present value criterion. The internal rate of return yields a zero net present value figure for the project under consideration, that is:

$$\sum_{t=0}^{n} \frac{1}{(1 + x)^t} NB_t = 0;$$ (3.4)

$$\int_{0}^{n} NB_t e^{-xt} dt = 0$$

where x is the internal rate of return (unknown) which satisfies (3.4). Having calculated the internal rate, the policy-maker compares it with a predetermined rate. If the internal rate proves to be greater than the predetermined rate then the investment project becomes acceptable.

Benefit-Cost Ratio. It is the ratio of the project's discounted benefits to discounted costs which must be greater than one, that is:

$$BCR = \frac{\displaystyle\sum_{t=0}^{n} \frac{1}{(1 + r)^t} B_t}{\displaystyle\sum_{t=0}^{n} \frac{1}{(1 + r)^t} C_t} > 1;$$ (3.5)

or

$$BCR = \frac{\int\limits_{0}^{n} B_t e^{-rt} dt}{\int\limits_{0}^{n} C_t e^{-rt} dt} > 1$$

where B_t is benefit at time and C_t is the cost.

Shadow Price Algorithm. As explained in the previous chapter, this investment evaluation method was created by Feldstein (1972) who believes that in a world of second best, where the social opportunity cost and social time preference rates are different, we need two types of price in the appraisal of communal projects: the relative price of future consumption in terms of current consumption and the relative price of private investment in terms of present consumption. The shadow price algorithm contains these two prices. In Feldstein's method the costs and benefits of public sector projects are transferred into the consumption and then discounted to the present at the consumption rate of interest.

The method uses ordinary discounting to deflate the future consumption stream of communal projects, that is:

$$NPV = \sum_{t=0}^{n} \frac{1}{(1 + s)^t} \{B_t - [(p)S + (1 - p)]C_t\} \tag{3.6}$$

where s is the social time preference rate, S is the shadow price of £1 private investment, p is the proportion of funds displacing private investment, $1 - p$ is displaced private consumption, and n is the project's life.

Normalized Internal Rate of Return. This method was devised by Mishan (1967, 1971, 1975) in order to eliminate the problem of multiple roots that exist in the ordinary internal rate of return criterion. The method involves compounding (3.2) as well as discounting (3.1). First, benefits generated by a public project should be compounded forward to a terminal date, usually the end of the project's life, to obtain a terminal date. The encashable benefits should be compounded by the social rate of return on capital, because the money used in public projects has an opportunity cost. The nonencashable benefits conferred on the community, on the other hand, should be compounded at the consumption rate of interest. Then we try to find what rate equates the total terminal benefits of the project to the initial capital cost. Since the total terminal value and the initial capital cost are both positive, the normalized internal rate of return would be a positive single figure.

AN INSIGHT INTO ORDINARY DISCOUNTING

In social economics the underlying assumption of ordinary discounting (i.e., individuals live forever or society is like a single individual who has an eternal or very long life) leads the societal policy-makers to a morally indefensible discrimination against future generations, as they give less and less weight to the welfare of more and more distant generations. For all intents and purposes, beyond a certain point, depending upon the magnitude of social discount rate, future folk just do not matter at all. In effect, ordinary discounting becomes a handy tool in the hands of current policy-makers to deprive future generations in a most appalling way. For example, it permits present generations to undertake lopsided projects such as nuclear power, the heavy cost of which will fall upon future members of society (see Chapter 5). It encourages present individuals to deplete the world's forests and prevents them from undertaking afforestation (Kula 1986a, 1986b, 1988a). It forces the community to reduce the size of fish stocks and deplete fossil fuel deposits in a hasty manner (Kula 1994). It allows present generations to leave a more polluted environment to future folk than the one they inherited. Overall, it guides those who are alive now and in a position of advantage to behave in a reckless manner toward future generations. In other words, it brings the worst out in present generations. As Samuelson (1976) puts it, "let us make no mistake about it, the positive interest rate is the enemy of long-lived investment projects." In actual fact ordinary discounting, with a low or high interest rate, is the enemy of future generations.

Below, I shall demonstrate precisely, with reference to the net present value criterion, how future generations are discriminated against. I have chosen the net present value for this demonstration because it is the most widely used criterion in economic analysis. Some economists have noticed that despite its general popularity this method has serious limitations when it comes to evaluating projects in which the costs and benefits are separated by a long time interval, a feature of many public sector projects. The discount factor used to deflate future benefits or costs is a decreasing function of time approaching zero over time. Multiplying distant costs and benefits by the relevant factor reduces them to insignificant figures. That is, with ordinary discounting the distant consequences of communal projects become immaterial and thus do not play a decisive role in the decision-making process. By following the path of ordinary discounting, present generations could pass great costs on to future generations by undertaking investments, the heavy costs of which will appear in the distant future, or failing to undertake projects which may have a low establishment cost now, but yield large benefits in years to come (Nash 1973).

Having said all this, now let me outline, by making a number of simplifying assumptions, a basic model which will demonstrate what the net present value does to future generations.

Assumption 1. Let us say that our society in its current form consists of only three individuals: person A, person B and person C.

Assumption 2. The life expectancy of individuals is three years, but they are of different ages. Person A is the most senior member of the community being two years old, having one more year to live; person B is one year old and has two full years to live; person C is the new arrival with three years of life expectancy.

Assumption 3. The size of the population and life expectancy of its members are constant. That is, there are always three members at any time point and life expectancy of each person is three years at birth. Individuals are mortal, but the society lives on. Currently, period one, we have persons A, B and C. At the beginning of the second period person A dies and is replaced by person D. At the beginning of the third period, person B dies at the age of three and person E joins, and so on.

Assumption 4. Currently, period one, three existing individuals, persons A, B and C, decide jointly to undertake an investment project which will outlive them. The project has an economic life of, say, five years, and as a consequence, in addition to the decision-making population, future members of society who are yet to be born will be affected.

Assumption 5. The initial construction cost of the project, say £1, is shared equally by the existing members at the time, A, B and C. These costs are regarded as negative benefits accruing to them, that is, $\bar{C}_A = -£0.333$, $\bar{C}_B = -£0.333$ and $\bar{C}_C = -£0.333$. Also assume that the money comes from a source displacing each person's private consumption by that amount.

Assumption 6. From the second year onward, the project yields net consumption benefits over its lifetime. The certainty equivalent of these benefits is £1 every year. When these net benefits become available at the end of each year they are distributed equally between the existing members of society who are alive at the time, that is, £0.333 each. Each person consumes his/her share of the benefit immediately when it becomes available. At the end of the fifth year the project is written off with no cost.

Assumption 7. Since it is assumed that the project is financed through a reduction in individuals' private consumption, and the resulting benefits are also consumed by the individuals when they become available, the analyst needs to know the social time preference rate, or the consumption rate of interest, to deflate the net consumption stream. It is convenient to assume that all members of society, at any point in time, have the same time preference rate of, say, 10 percent. Then the communal time preference rate would be 10 percent at all times, a figure reflecting all individual rates at any point in time.

By using the net present value criterion on this project we get:

$$NPV = \frac{-1}{(1.1)} + \frac{1}{(1.1)^2} + \frac{1}{(1.1)^3} + \frac{1}{(1.1)^4} + \frac{1}{(1.1)^5} \qquad (3.7)$$

$NPV = £1.97$

The overall figure is positive so the project qualifies as a viable investment at a 10 percent discount rate. Note that in this, society is treated as a single individual, as no attention was paid to individuals who come and go during the lifetime of the project.

Now, in view of the assumptions of our model, let us rewrite (3.7) in detail by taking into consideration who receives what and when. That is:

$$
\begin{aligned}
NPV = & \left[\frac{-0.333}{(1 + s_A)} - \frac{0.333}{(1 + s_B)} - \frac{0.333}{(1 + s_C)} \right] + \\
& \left[\frac{0.333}{(1 + s_B)^2} + \frac{0.333}{(1 + s_C)^2} + \frac{0.333}{(1 + s_D)^2} \right] + \\
& \left[\frac{0.333}{(1 + s_C)^3} + \frac{0.333}{(1 + s_D)^3} + \frac{0.333}{(1 + s_E)^3} \right] + \\
& \left[\frac{0.333}{(1 + s_D)^4} + \frac{0.333}{(1 + s_E)^4} + \frac{0.333}{(1 + s_F)^4} \right] + \\
& \left[\frac{0.333}{(1 + s_E)^5} + \frac{0.333}{(1 + s_F)^5} + \frac{0.333}{(1 + s_G)^5} \right]
\end{aligned}
\tag{3.8}
$$

This takes into account births and deaths, and who receives how much and when: s_i is the time preference of the ith person alive at that time, which is 10 percent throughout. Then the NPV becomes:

$$
NPK(£) = -0.909 + 0.826 + 0.751 + 0.683 + 0.621
\tag{3.9}
$$

$NPV = £1.97$.

Equation (3.8) allows us to deal with the core of society (i.e., individuals) by taking into account births and deaths. In other words, we are somehow relaxing the assumption of a single-person society by allowing individuals to take part. As soon as we do this, discrimination against future generations becomes obvious. Each number in (3.9) is in fact the ordinary discount factor, that is, 0.909, 0.826, 0.751, 0.683, 0.621, which can be compared directly with the factors in Appendix 1, column 8, page 175.

At the beginning of the first year, the members of society who initiate the project and pay for its construction cost wait one year for their share of consumption loss. Their subjective valuation of these costs, seen from the project's initiation point, the present, is expressed in the first square bracket of equation (3.8). The discounted value of the construction cost to each person is −0.333.

In the second year, however, person A is no longer in the society. He/she died at the end of the first year, immediately after incurring his/her share of the cost, and is replaced by a newcomer, person D. The discounted value of the second round of net benefits to the society seen from the beginning of the first year is expressed in the second square bracket. Persons B and C, indeed, wait

Table 3.1
Time Association between the Project and Population

Yrs (1)	Total Net Benefits Arising (£) (2)	Persons Born at Beginning of Each Period (3)	Persons Alive at Each Period (4)	Individuals' Net Share of Benefits (£) (5)	No. of Yrs. Each Person Waits to Acquire His/Her Share (6)	Power of (1+s) in NPV (7)	Weights Given to the Share of Each Beneficiary (8)
1	-1	C	A	-0.33	1	1	$1/(1.1)$
			B	-0.33	1	1	$1/(1.1)$
			C	-0.33	1	1	$1/(1.1)$
2	1	D	B	0.33	2	2	$1/(1.1)^2$
			C	0.33	2	2	$1/(1.1)^2$
			D	0.33	1	2	$1/(1.1)^2$
3	1	E	C	0.33	3	3	$1/(1.1)^3$
			D	0.33	2	3	$1/(1.1)^3$
			E	0.33	1	3	$1/(1.1)^3$
4	1	F	D	0.33	3	4	$1/(1.1)^4$
			E	0.33	2	4	$1/(1.1)^4$
			F	0.33	1	4	$1/(1.1)^4$
5	1	G	E	0.33	3	5	$1/(1.1)^5$
			F	0.33	2	5	$1/(1.1)^5$
			G	0.33	1	5	$1/(1.1)^5$

two years for these benefits which they acquire at the end of year two. For person D, however, equation (3.8) assumes that he/she also waits two years to get his/her share. In fact he/she does not; person D waits one year for this.

In the third year the situation is the same. The decision-maker looks at the third round of benefits from the vantage point of the beginning of the first year and assumes that each recipient waits three years for his/her share of net benefit. Person C's share of £0.333 is deflated by the discount factor $1/(1 + s_C)^3$ assuming that he/she waits three years, which is so. On the other hand, persons D and E wait two years and one year respectively to acquire their shares which arise at the end of the third year, and this fact is not recognized in (3.8).

The same treatment is given to the individuals who receive their shares of net benefits at the end of the fourth and fifth years, that is, they all wait four and five years, respectively, which is not true.

Table 3.1 summarizes the relationship between the project and the members of society over time. Column 6 illustrates the number of years each beneficiary waits in order to acquire his/her share of net benefits. Column 7, on the other hand, shows the power to which $(1 + s)$ rises in the net present value equation.

Column 8 shows the actual weights attached to each individual's share of net benefit as seen from the beginning of year 1, which is the time point that the project is initiated.

Once we take into account the composition of society with regard to individual members who actually make up a society, the discrimination against future generations becomes clear, as the model illustrates. The more distant future individuals are from current generations, the less weight is attached to their shares. For the benefits arising in the fourth year, person F waits only one year for his/her share and is given a weight of $1/(1.1)^4$. For the benefits arising in the fifth year, person G, who is a more distant member of society to the project's decision-maker than person F, also waits one year to acquire his/her share but this is given a weight of $1/(1.1)^5$.

It is worth noting that if this project was the only one of its kind initiated by the community for a long time there would be a lot of winners and some losers. Person A would clearly be a loser as he/she does not live long enough to benefit from the project but pays one-third of its establishment cost. Person B pays £0.333 as part of his/her share of the cost but gets it back at the end of the second year. However, in terms of net present value, person B would also be a loser because the discounted value of his/her share of cost is greater than the discounted value of benefit accruing in the second year. Persons C, D, E, F and G are all net gainers. But when we assume other projects of similar nature started in earlier years persons A and B would be compensated. I shall come back to this issue later on as it was raised in some debate papers.

Within the confines of our model how can we justify the practice that the communal decision-maker can systematically discriminate against future members of society by giving less and less weights to their share of benefits? The more distant a future person is from the policy-maker the less importance is given to his/her welfare. Although I shall discuss this issue in some detail later on, let me mention at this point that discrimination against future generations is in conflict with the views of some economists who made passing statements on the subject. For example, Pigou (1929) argues that "it is the clear duty of government, which is the trustee for unborn generations as well as for its present citizens." Marglin (1963b) argues likewise, "since the generations yet to be born are every bit as important as the present generations." These economists indicate that, in their view, the welfare of each generation, present and future, is equally important and thus the public sector policy-maker should give equal weight to each generation's share of benefits or losses. Clearly, this does not happen in methods based upon ordinary discounting.

Mishan (1988), in the fourth edition of his popular book *Cost-Benefit Analysis*, argues that conventional welfare models in economics implicitly assume that all persons affected by a public sector project are expected to remain alive over the investment period even if this turns out to be a very long time horizon

(Mishan 1988: 294). Only in this way will the usual Pareto criterion be met. But when gainers and losers come into being at some point in time later than the beginning of the project, as in the case of my illustrative model the conventional analysis will fall flat on its face.

Mishan emphasizes that the Pareto criterion is based upon the premise that the value to be attributed to a good or bad at any point in time is the value which is placed upon it by the persons themselves at that point in time, and economists take this as given, just as a medical doctor accepts his/her patient's complaint about, say, a back pain or a headache. Assume an individual expected to receive £1,000 from a project in 100 years time. If the market value of this benefit was £1 now, given the assumption about the magnitude of discount rate which will yield this result, he/she can hardly be indifferent between receiving £1 in year zero and £1,000 in year 100 if he/she is going to be born in year 60. Mishan concludes that once a time gap between any generation or individual exists, their comparison by way of discounting has to be ruled out as an invalid procedure.

By focusing mainly on the Kaldor-Hicks compensation criterion in intergenerational gains and losses, Mishan contends that difficulties will be circumvented by assuming that each person affected by the project remains alive during the entire investment period, whatever that may turn out to be—thousands or even millions of years. At this stage let us explore what will happen to the conventional discount factors once we assume that persons associated with communal projects are assumed to live on alongside the communal project. Let us modify our hypothetical societal model by assuming that when there is a birth in the community the newcomer remains alive during the lifetime of the project, which is five years. The decision-making individuals also live on. That is, nobody dies and because of births the size of the community is growing. This satisfies Mishan's requirement but our interest here is to find out what happens to the conventional discount factors. So the previous assumptions that constant life expectancy and unchanging size of population are altered along with mortality. Individuals are not expected to live forever in our model because the communal project is only five years of life expectancy. All that is required is that every communal member remain alive during the entire investment period.

Persons A, B and C, the decision-makers who start the project, are alive in year 1. In year 2 person D, in year 3 person E joins in, and so on. Nobody dies. When net benefits become available they are distributed equally among the existing members of society. In year 2, £1 net benefit is shared by persons A, B, C and D (i.e., £0.25 each). In year 3 we have five individuals in existence, A, B, C, D and E, so each gets £0.20. Last, but not least, we assume that all individuals have 10 percent psychological discount rate at all times. The conventional discount factors, by using the model outlined above, can now be obtained in the following way:

$$NPV = \begin{matrix} (A) & (B) & (C) \\ \left[\dfrac{-0.333}{(1.1)} - \dfrac{0.333}{(1.1)} - \dfrac{0.333}{(1.1)} \right] \end{matrix} \qquad (3.10)$$

$$+ \begin{matrix} (A) & (B) & (C) & (D) \\ \left[\dfrac{0.25}{(1.1)^2} + \dfrac{0.25}{(1.1)^2} + \dfrac{0.25}{(1.1)^2} + \dfrac{0.25}{(1.1)^1} \right] \end{matrix}$$

$$+ \begin{matrix} (A) & (B) & (C) & (D) & (E) \\ \left[\dfrac{0.2}{(1.1)^3} + \dfrac{0.2}{(1.1)^3} + \dfrac{0.2}{(1.1)^3} + \dfrac{0.2}{(1.1)^2} + \dfrac{0.2}{(1.1)^1} \right] \end{matrix}$$

$$+ \begin{matrix} (A) & (B) & (C) & (D) & (E) & (F) \\ \left[\dfrac{0.167}{(1.1)^4} + \dfrac{0.167}{(1.1)^4} + \dfrac{0.167}{(1.1)^4} + \dfrac{0.167}{(1.1)^3} + \dfrac{0.167}{(1.1)^2} + \dfrac{0.167}{(1.1)^1} \right] \end{matrix}$$

$$+ \begin{matrix} (A) & (B) & (C) & (D) & (E) & (F) & (G) \\ \left[\dfrac{0.14}{(1.1)^5} + \dfrac{0.14}{(1.1)^5} + \dfrac{0.14}{(1.1)^5} + \dfrac{0.14}{(1.1)^4} + \dfrac{0.14}{(1.1)^3} + \dfrac{0.14}{(1.1)^2} + \dfrac{0.14}{(1.1)^1} \right] \end{matrix}$$

$$NPV = \begin{matrix} (A) & (B) & (C) \\ [- 0.333 - 0.333 - 0.333] \end{matrix}$$

$$+ \begin{matrix} (A) & (B) & (C) & (D) \\ [0.207 + 0.207 + 0.207 + 0.227] \end{matrix}$$

$$+ \begin{matrix} (A) & (B) & (C) & (D) & (E) \\ [0.150 + 0.150 + 0.150 + 0.165 + 0.182] \end{matrix}$$

$$+ \begin{matrix} (A) & (B) & (C) & (D) & (E) & (F) \\ [0.114 + 0.114 + 0.114 + 0.125 + 0.138 + 0.152] \end{matrix}$$

$$+ \begin{matrix} (A) & (B) & (C) & (D) & (E) & (F) & (G) \\ [0.093 + 0.093 + 0.093 + 0.098 + 0.107 + 0.118 + 0.131] \end{matrix}$$

$$NPV = (-0.909) + (0.848) + (0.797) + (0.757) + (0.732)$$

Each term on the right hand side of equation (3.10) is the communal discount factor for each single year and they differ from factors in (3.9). The reason for this is that the calculation for each newcomer is conducted from the year of his/her entry. Each number in square brackets belongs to an individual. In effect, each number is a discount factor for a single individual in a particular year. The bracketed letter above each number indicates the "owner" of the factor. Equation (3.10) gives the collective factors for each year.

Conventional factors will be obtained when we bring each newcomer, no matter what time point he/she enters, to the commencement of the project. In other words, everybody who is associated with the project is imagined to be present not in body but perhaps in spirit at the time of decision-making. That is:

$$NPV = \left[-\frac{\overset{(A)}{0.333}}{(1.1)} - \frac{\overset{(B)}{0.333}}{(1.1)} - \frac{\overset{(C)}{0.333}}{(1.1)} \right]$$

$$+ \left[\frac{\overset{(A)}{0.25}}{(1.1)^2} + \frac{\overset{(B)}{0.25}}{(1.1)^2} + \frac{\overset{(C)}{0.25}}{(1.1)^2} + \frac{\overset{(D)}{0.25}}{(1.1)^2} \right]$$

$$+ \left[\frac{\overset{(A)}{0.2}}{(1.1)^3} + \frac{\overset{(B)}{0.2}}{(1.1)^3} + \frac{\overset{(C)}{0.2}}{(1.1)^3} + \frac{\overset{(D)}{0.2}}{(1.1)^3} + \frac{\overset{(E)}{0.2}}{(1.1)^3} \right]$$

$$+ \left[\frac{\overset{(A)}{0.167}}{(1.1)^4} + \frac{\overset{(B)}{0.167}}{(1.1)^4} + \frac{\overset{(C)}{0.167}}{(1.1)^4} + \frac{\overset{(D)}{0.167}}{(1.1)^4} + \frac{\overset{(E)}{0.167}}{(1.1)^4} + \frac{\overset{(F)}{0.167}}{(1.1)^4} \right]$$

$$+ \left[\frac{\overset{(A)}{0.143}}{(1.1)^5} + \frac{\overset{(B)}{0.143}}{(1.1)^5} + \frac{\overset{(C)}{0.143}}{(1.1)^5} + \frac{\overset{(D)}{0.143}}{(1.1)^5} + \frac{\overset{(E)}{0.143}}{(1.1)^5} + \frac{\overset{(F)}{0.143}}{(1.1)^5} + \frac{\overset{(G)}{0.143}}{(1.1)^5} \right]$$

The last term in the second square bracket belongs to the newcomer in the second year, person D. Although this person enters the world in the second year, the discount factor for him/her is $1/(1.1)^2$, that is, person D is assumed to wait two years for £0.25. In the third, fourth and fifth square brackets similar treatment is given to all newcomers, that is, they are imagined to be present at the commencement of the project. The resulting communal factors are:

$$NPV = 0.909 + 0.826 + 0.751 + 0.683 + 0.621,$$

which are ordinary factors that are the same as those in (3.9) or in column 8, Appendix 1. That is, in order to verify the conventional discount factors we should assume that each person who will be affected by a real life project is present, perhaps in spirit form, right at the start of the project. This applies to individuals who will be born hundreds of years from now! This is science fiction economics.

An unequal distribution of benefits between members of the community would make no difference to ordinary factors. Now let us assume that the original decision-makers, A, B and C, are getting more than the latecomers and the early entrants are also getting more than later ones. We give each newcomer a treatment as if he/she was present at the commencement of the project, that is:

$$NPV = \left[-\underset{1.1}{\overset{\underset{(A)}{0.333}}{}} - \underset{1.1}{\overset{\underset{(B)}{0.333}}{}} - \underset{1.1}{\overset{\underset{(C)}{0.333}}{}} \right]$$

$$+ \left[\underset{1.1^2}{\overset{\underset{(A)}{0.3}}{}} + \underset{1.1^2}{\overset{\underset{(B)}{0.3}}{}} + \underset{1.1^2}{\overset{\underset{(C)}{0.3}}{}} + \underset{1.1^2}{\overset{\underset{(D)}{0.1}}{}} \right]$$

$$+ \left[\underset{1.1^3}{\overset{\underset{(A)}{0.25}}{}} + \underset{1.1^3}{\overset{\underset{(B)}{0.25}}{}} + \underset{1.1^3}{\overset{\underset{(C)}{0.25}}{}} + \underset{1.1^3}{\overset{\underset{(D)}{0.15}}{}} + \underset{1.1^3}{\overset{\underset{(E)}{0.10}}{}} \right] + \cdots$$

$$(3.11)$$

$$NPV = -0.909 + 0.826 + 0.751 + \cdots$$

which is nothing but ordinary factors. This must be obvious without the details because since the denominators in each square bracket are the same and since the numbers in the numerators add up to unity, then there will be no change in the communal factors no matter how unevenly £1 gets distributed over time.

But, of course, distribution would make a difference if we take each person's entry point as base year for that person, that is, the model leading up to (3.10). To show the difference:

$$NPV = \left[-\underset{1.1}{\overset{\underset{(A)}{0.333}}{}} - \underset{1.1}{\overset{\underset{(B)}{0.333}}{}} - \underset{1.1}{\overset{\underset{(C)}{0.333}}{}} \right]$$

$$+ \left[\underset{1.1^2}{\overset{\underset{(A)}{0.3}}{}} + \underset{1.1^2}{\overset{\underset{(B)}{0.3}}{}} + \underset{1.1^2}{\overset{\underset{(C)}{0.3}}{}} + \underset{1.1}{\overset{\underset{(D)}{0.1}}{}} \right]$$

$$+ \left[\frac{0.25}{1.1^3} + \frac{0.25}{1.1^3} + \frac{0.25}{1.1^3} + \frac{0.15}{1.1^2} + \frac{0.10}{1.1} \right] + \cdots$$

$$(3.12)$$

$$NPV = -0.909 + 0.835 + 0.7784 + 0.6504 + \cdots$$

These numbers are different from the ones in (3.10) except the factor for the first year.

ROOTS OF THE PROBLEM

At the early part of the twentieth century, some philosophers such as White-head and Russell (1910) were arguing that any verbal statement could be put into mathematical notations and rigorously developed without confusion to its logical conclusion. According to Russell the chief triumph of modern mathematics consists in having discovered what mathematics really is. In one of his essays, ''Mathematics and Metaphysicians,'' Russell argues that all pure mathematics is built up by combinations of the primitive ideas of logic, and its propositions are deduced from the general axioms of logic. The subject of formal logic shows itself to be identical with mathematics. He then goes on to discuss concepts of infinitesimal, infinite and continuity. Mathematicians have not only advanced these problems but have completely solved them. The solutions, for those acquainted with mathematics, are so clear as to leave not the slightest doubt of difficulties. This achievement is probably the greatest of our age.

Some earlier studies like Irving Fisher's *Mathematical Investigations into the Theory of Value and Prices* (1892) and Francis Edgeworth's *Mathematical Psychics* (1881) became the models for a reformulation of economic principles on the new foundation of analytical logic. According to Fusfelt (1966) a number of critics quickly pointed out the flaws in the mathematical approach to economic problems. The new approach was attacked as being essentially static just like Newtonian physics, and thus not well adapted to analysis of an economy in constant change. Similar criticism still exists today and I shall mention a few names later on.

The sternest critic of mathematics as logic was Wittgenstein, who argued that the formal logic had not shown itself to be identical with mathematics. It has rather completely deformed the thinking of mathematicians and philosophers. The work of modern mathematicians such as Weierstrass, Dedekind and Cantor was far from being the greatest achievement of our age. In relation to the rest of mathematics, it was a cancerous growth, seeming to have grown out of the normal body aimlessly and senselessly. According to Wittgenstein, the notions of infinitesimal, infinite and continuity had not been clarified by the definition of them given by mathematicians, but, rather distorted.

If we see mathematics as a series of techniques, the question of what it was about simply would not arise. In a series of lectures in 1939, Wittgenstein argued that Russell and his followers did infinite harm and mathematics must be rescued from the clutches of philosophical theorists. For a good review see Monk (1990).

However, a number of economists including Keynes were already attracted to the ideas of Russell. Irving Fisher, one of the leading figures in the development of capital theory, always wanted to bring scientific rigor into economics in order to understand the great complexities of the subject. One way to achieve this was the use of mathematical methods and he was one of the earlier economists to try this out in his Ph.D. thesis. According to Samuelson (1967), Fisher's project is one of the greatest Ph.D. theses ever written in economics.

When Keynes became the editor of *The Economic Journal* in 1911, a position he retained for 33 years, he gave a lot of encouragement to economists to write articles containing mathematical methods. However, at the time not many economists had impressive mathematical skills, but this began to change gradually in later years. Harold Hotelling and Frank Ramsey were some of the earliest to demonstrate competent modeling skills in economics. The latter, with the encouragement of Keynes, published an article, "A Mathematical Theory of Saving" in *The Economic Journal* for the purpose of finding an answer to the question: how much of its income should a nation save? He reasoned that the rate of saving multiplied by the marginal utility of money should always be equal to the amount by which the total net rate of enjoyment of utility falls short of the maximum possible rate of enjoyment (Ramsey 1928).

In order to develop his model, Ramsey made a surprising assumption that society is like a single unit who has an eternal life. "In order to justify this rule it is, of course, necessary to make various simplifying assumptions: we have to suppose that our community goes on forever without changing either in numbers or in its capacity for enjoyment or in its aversion to labour." In his further elaboration of the mathematical theory of saving, Ramsey emphasized further that "men, or rather, families, were to live forever" (Ramsey 1928: 558). With Keynes at the helm the age of mathematical economics was beginning to rise. Paul Ormerod, in *The Death of Economics* (1994), argues that the rise of mathematical economics suffocated and eventually killed the subject.

In spite of his extensive writings in economics, Keynes has remained a deeply controversial figure for economists and others. Andrew Roberts, author of *Eminent Churchillians* (1994), argues that Keynes is responsible for modern ills ranging from appeasement to hyperinflation, from the excessive growth in state power to the breakdown of the family.

Another dominant figure in the development of mathematical economics and the spread of conventional discounting in communal models has been Paul Samuelson. For example, in his analysis of Irving Fisher's capital theory at individual level he suddenly turns to a communal model by arguing that Fisher never faced up to an infinite-period equilibrium model. Take the consumption-saving tastes of the community:

$$U = \sum_0^\infty \frac{U(C_t)}{(1 + R)^t}$$

where U is communal utility, C_t is consumption at time t and R is the subjective communal discount rate (Samuelson 1967: 34). Clearly, like Ramsey, Samuelson is treating society as a single entity with infinite lifespan without due regard to individuals who make up the society.

Elsewhere, Samuelson (1976) develops his forestry model by assuming, after initial planting, an infinite chain of harvesting and replanting, mainly in the context of private sector forestry, but implies that his solution is applicable to communal forests. Furthermore, he puts his model in a general equilibrium setting and by making explicit reference to Ramsey's optimum control theory:

"And suppose a planner for this society acts to solve a Ramsey (1928) optimum-control problem, namely for t restricted to integral values,"

$$Max \sum_{t=0}^{\infty} U[C(t), Q(t)]e^{-pt}$$

On another occasion, in the development of an economic model he assumes a large finite span to the human race—one million generations—and uses discounting in the usual manner (Samuelson 1958).

Marglin (1963a), in his analysis of the opportunity cost of public sector investment, thinks in exactly the same way as Samuelson: "We plan public projects to maximise their net present value at the marginal social rate of discount," then specifies a communal benefit function stretching from now to eternity.

Apart from the above-mentioned economists, Ramsey's optimum control theory with ordinary discounting has been extended in many directions, such as the economic growth theories by Shell (1967), Mirrlees and Stern (1973) and Ng (1973). A few years after the publication of "A Mathematical Theory of Saving," Hotelling (1931) established a criterion for the optimum depletion of destructible resources, which is in the same spirit as Ramsey's paper. The major objective in Hotelling's work was to examine the optimal extraction rate for nonrenewable resources from the viewpoint of the government, who wanted to maximize the social welfare from exploitation of these resources. After the first oil shock of 1973 the concern about resource depletion began to grow, which encouraged mathematical economists to establish their numerous resource depletion models by using the work of Hotelling. For an introduction to this subject, see Solow (1974a) and for elaboration of many models, see the 1974 Symposium Issue of the *Review of Economic Studies*.

The mathematical attraction of a single-person society with an infinite lifespan, coupled with ordinary discounting, e^{-st}, in economic model building is obvious. It is easy to handle and also it yields neat results.

I am sure that it was not Ramsey's intention to start a fashion in economics that would yield theories and consequently practices that are discriminatory against future generations. In effect, Ramsey expressed concern about future individuals by suggesting that the pure time preference part of the social discount rate should not be used by the public sector policy-makers. He believed, within the confines of his model, that the pure time preference rate was morally indefensible.

Ramsey was one of the earliest mathematical economists who, probably, wanted to practice his mathematical skills by making an untrue but highly convenient assumption, which he clearly pointed out, to build an economic model. He probably never thought that in future years his assumption about the "nature of society" would be accepted by his colleagues without question because of its mathematical convenience. Especially during the 1970s and 1980s, the wall-to-wall equation period in economics, there was not a great deal of enthusiasm in the profession about concepts such as truth and justice. Mishan (1988) believes that ignorance was the main factor: "Economists have never explicitly proposed that a *potential* potential pareto improvement in the above sense be accepted as an economic ranking device for the obvious reason that they were not aware that their familiar present-discounted-value criteria (assuming then to be correct in other respects) implied as much whenever generational time was involved" (Mishan 1988: 300). It may be true, however, that many did not fully understand the implications of methods like the net present value in welfare economics and the foundation of conventional discounting, but this cannot be said for all economists.

In a subject as complicated and volatile as economics, the soul of an equation can easily become the body of untruth. No matter how "sophisticated," most equations in economics rely upon omissions, simplifications, oversimplifications, and, on occasions, false premises such as society being like a single individual with eternal life. The more equations there are in an economic model the more fragile it becomes. Baumol (1991) is not surprised that the use of extensive mathematical models has not solved problems in economic analysis. As one of those who actively encouraged the use of mathematics in economic analysis a few decades ago, he now concedes that things have gone too far.

Some economists state that their purpose in research is to achieve "excellence." Surely, the excellence of a research project in economics or in any branch of science must be measured by its proximity to the truth. If one takes a strictly utilitarian view of research, there, too, the importance of the truth, whatever it may turn out to be, is paramount as only true ideas will prove to be useful in the long run, to the majority.

Very recently, a few articles appearing in the "mainstream economic journals" have at last recognized human societies with overlapping generations implying that individuals need not have to live forever (Mourmouras 1991; John and Pecchenino 1994). The latter explores the issue of a potential conflict between economic growth and the maintenance of environmental quality in an overlapping generations model. In this, the authors state that

Environmental issues have been analysed extensively in the environmental and natural resource literatures, . . . but by assuming that the life span of individuals and the life span of the economy are the same (possibly infinite), researchers in environmental economics have for the most part restricted themselves formally to the analysis of intragenerational problems. (John and Pecchenino 1994: 1393)

If we take the year 1776, when Adam Smith published *An Inquiry into the Nature and Causes of the Wealth of the Nations*, as the beginning of modern economic thinking, then one can see that it has taken the mainstream outlets more than 200 years to accept that human societies do not contain immortal individuals, an oddity which has thankfully lasted less time than the dispute between Galileo and the church. Indeed, it took the Vatican many hundreds of years to accept that Galileo's theories after all were correct and what was done to him by the establishment of the day was inappropriate. However, one has to recognize that Catholicism is a faith like any other religion, and perhaps its leaders should not have been challenged by inquisitive and free-thinking scientists. But economics is supposed to be a science, not a religion.

It is doubtful whether a discipline can claim credibility if those in the driver's seat are trying and succeeding to perpetuate untrue and unjust theories, refusing to change models that are based upon strange assumptions, and dominate the subject for a long time by unsuitable mathematics to the most extreme levels for the purpose of achieving "excellence" or gaining "insight." However, I have no doubt that a good number of articles containing models based upon immortal individuals will continue to appear in the "leading journals" for a good while.

In his retirement from Cambridge, England, Professor Frank Hahn gave his fatherly advice to young economists:

It is true that age reduces intellectual agility, although that may be connected with a certain sense of deja vu. In any event I advise the young to strike while the iron is hot and do garner the great pleasures of discovery. The second most important reflection leads me to advise everyone to ignore cries of economics in crisis, to avoid discussion of mathematics in economics like the plague, and to give no thought at all to methodology. (Hahn 1992)

Backhouse (1992), in his reply to Hahn, stresses the importance of philosophy and hence methodology in economics. On the use of mathematics he concedes that there are areas of economics which require mathematics for rigorous treatment, but in many cases the course of research becomes dictated by requirements imposed by the mathematics. In other words (mine rather than Backhouse's), mathematics becomes a straightjacket. Alec Nove (1992) contends that currently the "mainstream economics" is obsessed with mathematical formalism and mathematical consistency of economic models even if they are totally unrelated to the economic situation in the real world. The mathematical model building appears to be the be-all and end-all of economic science which leads to inattention to those problems and statements which cannot be given mathematical expression. No matter how logical an argument may be, it goes straight through the "mainstream economists." He concludes his essay by stating that we all need a new and relevant economics.

The extensive use of mathematics with convenient assumptions in a subject like economics could make journal articles look rigorous, their authors clever, and earn them a good reputation and promotion amongst the likeminded, could bring more public money to them for similar research, but could it bring truth into the subject studied? If an analysis was rigorous but untrue what would we call it? Perhaps a rigorous untruth!

Economics must be a unique branch of science in the sense that it has been misused by so many special interest groups. At the top of my list there are politicians who are in the habit of using their carefully selected economic facts and figures to support their positions. Perhaps this is not an unfair game in democracies, as opposition groups have opportunities to scrutinize all economic "facts" and put their own versions in their place. This process of economic truth and countertruth may become confusing for the public, but as free individuals with common sense they can pass their judgement on the matter.

Social engineers are another interest group to be mentioned; I particularly have the Marxist school in mind. In their search for a perfect society they concocted "economic theories" and devised policies which ultimately proved to be unworkable, and in the process brought humanity to the brink of total destruction. In addition, there are various religious groups, essentially people of goodwill, who try to change some obvious facts of economic life such as the interest rate, which to them appears to be in conflict with the scriptures.

Last, but not least, there are a few career economists who have long realized that best results are obtained by way of collective actions and restrictive practices (Wiseman 1991). After all, as teachers of economics we explain to students how unfair competition such as monopoly, oligopoly, cartel, and so on, bring lucrative rewards to practitioners at the expense of consumers. Similarly, the economic career cartel brings lucrative rewards for a time to practitioners. At times it may indeed be tempting, from a purely career viewpoint, to trade in truth and justice for whatever the fashion requires—mathematical convenience, "rigor," "elegance," whatever.

At the beginning of this chapter, I mentioned Professor Collard's unpublished paper, "Faustian Projects and the Social Rate of Discount," which contains ideas similar to mine. There he draws attention to Dr. Faustus who makes a deal with the devil to obtain magical powers for a short while, in return for his body and soul. His paper begins:

I, John Faustus of Wittenberg, Doctor, by these presents do give both body and soul to Lucifer, Prince of the East, and his minister Mephistopheles, and furthermore grant unto them, that twenty-four years being expired the articles above written inviolate, full power to fetch or carry the said John Faustus body and soul, flesh, blood or goods, into their habitation wheresoever.

Chapter 4

Modified, or Just, Discounting

INTRODUCTION

In the previous chapter it was argued that the conventional welfare theory is based upon a concept either that individuals are immortal or society is like a single individual who has infinite, or very long, life. It was then demonstrated that these false and strange assumptions lead the public sector policy-maker, by way of discounting, to a morally indefensible discrimination against future generations. The roots of the problem were traced to Ramsey's 1928 paper, a mathematical theory of saving, written in Russellian spirit, where a simplifying assumption was made in order to construct a mathematical model to discover the optimum level of saving from a societal viewpoint.

In later years, Ramsey's assumption about the "nature of society" became widely used, mainly, but not exclusively, for mathematical model building, in nearly every branch of economics from growth to resource exhaustion. Such utilization was especially widespread in cost-benefit analysis. Furthermore, during the 1960s and 1970s, when the development of cost-benefit analysis gathered speed, a number of investment evaluation methods, based upon ordinary discounting (which includes discrimination against future generations), were established for theoretical as well as practical purposes.

Some economists such as Pearce (1971, 1983) argue categorically that "cost-benefit analysis makes no claim to produce morally correct decisions." A cost-benefit analyst is essentially a preference counter, not a moral judge of economic matters. He/she counts the preference of society defined as nothing more than the collection of individuals who make it up. Pearce thinks in terms of a point in time when he refers to society, that is, the sum of people at a point in time when communal decisions are made, although on occasions he mentions future generations who may be affected by such decisions. Sections on social welfare function in Dasgupta and Pearce (1972) are even more explicit as the recorded preferences of current individuals are referred to when various social welfare functions are specified. In a scheme like this, morally correct decisions can only be coincidental, especially when we make another convenient assumption that registered preferences of individuals who exist at a point in time are morally correct. When intertemporal decisions are based upon registered preferences of present individuals, it is hoped that they contain care and consideration about future generations.

We know that the registered preferences of the majority, or even in some cases the ruling minority in totalitarian regimes, can be profoundly unjust. Take, for example, the former South African economy, where for many years the white minority had made economic, social and political decisions for the nonwhite majority and where public sector policy-makers seldom regarded a nonwhite person's welfare as the same as a white person's well-being. Let us say, for argument's sake, that one nonwhite person's well-being carried a weight which was one-tenth the weight given to a person of European origin and this was captured by the market structure that existed at the time. In the final chapter of this book, a cost-benefit analysis for a transport project in London will be carried out, in which the main benefits will be shown to be the time saved by users of the facility. Benefits will be divided into two parts as work and leisure time. Suppose that a similar project was constructed in Johannesburg during the apartheid regime and the cost-benefit analyst differentiated between work and leisure times of whites and nonwhites on the grounds that earnings of the former, on average, were ten times higher. It would be unconvincing to argue that a black person's earning was ten times lower than a white person's salary because of his/her inferior economic performance, when, in fact, black people were at a disadvantage in South Africa, mainly because of the discriminatory market rules created against them by white decision-makers. Wouldn't conventional cost-benefit analysis, based upon the registered preference approach in South Africa, look morbid?

In the registered preference scheme of things the position of future generations is far worse than South Africa's nonwhites, who are here, vocal, with articulate leaders, and have formed alliances with many groups throughout the world to change their position and as it happens, things are going in their favor. Minorities exist in almost every country of the world and there may be cases of discrimination against them inflicted by the majority. In democracies, normally minority groups are represented in the political system and in this way they have an opportunity to improve their conditions. But future generations are not here, and have no representatives; therefore, they cannot speak out or protest.

Pigou (1929), by recognizing the inadequacy of the registered preference approach in public sector policy-making, argues that efforts of present generations directed toward the distant future will be much less than the efforts directed toward the relatively near future. The people involved in the latter case will probably be the immediate successors whose interests may be regarded as nearly equivalent. In the former, the persons involved will be quite remote in blood or in time, for whom current policy-makers scarcely care at all. The consequences of such selfishness will be less saving, the halting of creation of new capital, and the using up of existing gifts of nature to such a degree that future advantages are sacrificed for smaller present ones.

There are far more serious cases of self-indulgence demonstrated by some sections of present generations than those that Pigou mentioned in 1929; for example, the hasty plunge into the "nuclear age" for destructive (military) as well as "constructive" (commercial) purposes in nuclear science, military, business and politics. As a result of this venture we are going to pass very large quantities of highly toxic nuclear wastes, in various forms, to future generations, which could become a major threat to their health, safety and civil liberties for thousands of years. For a discussion on the nuclear age, see Shradder-Frechette (1991, 1993). How does discounting come into the nuclear debate? It is right in the center of it, as Schulze et al. (1981) point out, that in the economic evaluation of the nuclear package discounting is one of the most crucial parameters in the equation. No matter how high future costs may be, such as decommissioning power plants, storing and monitoring wastes, ordinary discounting with high or low discount rates tends to make a nuclear project "economically" attractive by wiping out its distant consequences (see Chapter 5 for a specific case study).

Recently, the Swedish government decided to phase out nuclear power by the year 2010, a decision in which waste disposal problems played an important role, even though nuclear energy currently provides about half of the country's electricity (Traiforos et al. 1990). Even so, after the closure of the nuclear program, the nation will be left with highly toxic wastes which will remain active for millions of years and could create serious problems for future generations. When the fruits of the Swedish nuclear program confined to a few decades benefiting a few million consumers and a handful of professionals and workers is set against long-term costs, the registered preference approach looks less than convincing, morally or otherwise. In effect, economic principles that yield results which could endanger health, safety and civil liberties of future generations for very long time periods are bound to make the likes of Pigou turn in their graves.

Pearce (1983) concedes that the traditional cost-benefit rules may create circumstances, such as nuclear-waste storage, where future generations could suffer, and this is indeed a problem in the conventional theory. However, the discrimination problem against future generations is overcome if we set up an "intergenerational compensation fund" which would apply the Kaldor-Hicks criterion through time but with actual compensation accruing. Suppose that current generations who are storing nuclear wastes now know, for some reason, that an accident will happen in year 500 and the cost of this is estimated to be £10 billion. In order to compensate future sufferers, all we need to do is invest in a bank deposit, say, at a 5 percent interest rate, only £0.25 now which will amount to £10 billion in 500 years' time. In this argument the Kaldor-Hicks compensation scheme becomes remarkably cost effective! For much longer periods even a smaller sum is required. Schulze (1978) dismisses this view as being bizarre as well as impractical because it assumes that the bank will remain in existence for hundreds, thousands or even millions of years—the time scales involved in nuclear storage. No institutional mechanism can seriously be expected to exist for time periods that are mentioned here.

Pearce, by noting these difficulties, mentions the views of those who contend that we cannot take account of costs to generations yet to be born, as it would widen the concept of democratic voting in an unacceptable way. There are also those who draw attention to the fact that the kind of intergenerational discrimination implicit in discounting is an increasing feature of our society. The greenhouse effect of atmospheric pollution, acid rain and depletion of the ozone layer are instances in point. Pearce believes that, despite all of its difficulties, the concept of an intergenerational compensation fund is worth pursuing despite objections by some that it is not needed anyway. This is because future generations are already compensated by the fact that communal projects will add to the capital stock which will be inherited by them.

In this way future capabilities to invest in solutions to the nuclear-waste problem, or to any problem, are already successfully shifted onto them by present generations. This line of thought, in my view, is appalling. Take the Swedish nuclear program, which is expected to be terminated in the year 2010 when all capital stock will be scrapped, at a very high decommissioning and storage cost. In effect, future Swedes will not inherit any capital stock but a waste problem unparalleled in human history. The argument that the Swedish government, by plunging into the "nuclear age," allowed the economy to create sufficient resources during its few decades of operation that will help future generations in thousands or millions of years is absurd. In effect, nuclear venture, aided by conventional discounting methods (if cost-benefit analysis were ever carried out), turned out to be a bankrupt business. In addition to waste management efforts the idea that the Swedish government now needs to invest a couple of kronas in a bank deposit to compensate future sufferers is a morbid argument of the extreme kind. This is a bankrupt idea created by unsound thought. Economists should not be allowed to disown responsibilities for their theories in this manner.

Let us assume, for argument's sake, that all Swedish institutions including the bank and its compensation fund will remain intact for a long period of time. Consequently, as the time passes the money invested now will grow to become huge sums in thousands of years to compensate potential losers. Also assume that at an unspecified date in the distant future, due to a leakage in the waste storage system, serious health problems in the form of cancer and genetic deformities will affect some Swedes. Their lawyers, after a long battle, become successful in linking their clients' illnesses to the leakage in the repository and the courts eventually order the bank to pay out sufficient sums in compensation. Would this then be considered to be the Kaldor-Hicks compensation in which gainers, say nuclear scientists, economists and politicians who started the short-lived nuclear age, compensate the losers (those who are trapped in defective and aching bodies for life) by way of the compensation fund that exists in the bank?

The absence of a proper compensation scheme aside, the suggestion that although the effect of conventional discounting is to discriminate against future generations, this would be circumvented by setting up, or pretending to set up, or even just dreaming perpetually about setting up a compensation fund is totally unconvincing. It is better to eliminate discrimination right now by abandoning conventional discounting in the appraisal of communal projects; then there would be no need to rely on a totally bizarre argument like a compensation scheme of a few pence now to sort things out in the distant future. Ordinary discounting methods, in fact, resemble guidelines used during the apartheid regime in South Africa when the ruling minority, by taking advantage of its power and privilege, had made many economic and other decisions for the majority. Current generations are only a small minority in the generational chain but they have a power over them.

THE TRADITION OF JUST CONDUCT IN ECONOMICS

Economics as a social science has an old and rich tradition of enquiry into the just conduct in almost all areas of its jurisdiction. Although rejected by some, concepts like just price, just wage, just profit, just taxation and now, just discounting, have been of interest to many scholars. The roots of this, according to some writers, go back to the economics of Aristotle (Roover 1970). When the ideas of Aristotle came into Christian Europe during the twelfth century the initial reaction of the church was negative. But in later years some Christian scholars such as Thomas Aquinas saw the possibility and desirability of incorporating Aristotelian ideas into Christian beliefs. In the synthesis of Christian theology and Aristotelian philosophy the society is an integrated system, like the universe, where God, nature and man have their own places. The virtuous life requires a societal structure in which there is a mutual exchange of functions within a hierarchy in which priest, farmer, worker, artisan, merchant and the government perform their tasks in accordance with the laws of God and nature, and each one is properly rewarded for its contribution.

Take the concept of just price, for instance, which has made many theologians, philosophers and economists think since the Middle Ages. The early medieval view was that the just price is the one enabling the supplier to live and to support his family on a scale suitable to his station in life (Ashley 1920; Clark 1939; Clough and Cole 1946). There is a duty on public authorities to fix prices in line with this principle. If they fail to regulate the price then the supplier may set it unilaterally only at a level enabling him/her to maintain his/her status. If overcharging takes place, he/she then commits the sin of avarice. Aquinas conceded that the just price cannot be fixed with precision at all times, but can vary within certain limits. If such variations are minor then they would not involve injustice.

Another view on the just price is that of the value of goods established by the rules of the market (i.e., supply and demand) at the time of the sale (Magnus 1894; Kraus 1930). A cost-based concept would be that price equals cost, including normal profit and compensation for risk-taking (Scotus 1894; Amalzak 1945). If the market price differs from the cost, the supplier must accept it as fair whether he/she gains or loses. Scotus specified that fair price is a uniform charge regardless of who is buying and for what purpose.

The common good view is that price is a social phenomenon and should be regulated with this purpose in mind; and this idea can be traced to Roman times (Roover 1970). The medieval doctrines believed that high prices on credit sales were unjust if they involved concealed usury which was socially and theologically objectionable.

The concept of just wage is as old and varied as just price, as its roots go back to medieval times and beyond. The early view that a laborer should be paid enough to sustain him and his dependents was widespread in the Middle Ages. This theory found its practical appreciation in the guild system, which was formed for the purpose of providing decent living and equal opportunities for the workers, protecting consumers against deceit, preventing unfair competition by way of restrictive or other practices. However, the guilds in the course of time degenerated into monopolistic organizations aimed at giving unfair advantage to their members.

The Marxist school believes that wages determined in the capitalist markets are profoundly unjust because such markets are based upon the exploitation of laborers. In their view labor is the only source of income as it is ultimately responsible for all output. When owners of capital, which is concentrated labor, extract profits, they are stealing value produced by the laborers.

The marginalist school contends that the just wage is the one that relates a worker's contribution to output at the margin. One of the most famous marginalists, John Bates Clark (1927), stated at the beginning of his publication that the main force motivating him to develop a theory of distribution was his desire to find an objective basis for justice in the distribution of income. He reasoned that if the net contribution of labor could be identified in a production process, then its market value would be the just reward.

On the morality of income tax, in 1927 Irving Fisher published an essay entitled "A Statistical Method for Measuring Marginal Utility and the Justice of a Progressive Income Tax" (Fisher 1927). In this he argued that since the marginal utility of income is declining, this alone would justify taxing the rich at a higher rate.

Adam Smith, who is regarded by many as the founder of modern economics, had a great deal of interest in morality and justice, as he wrote extensively on the subject. His first book was *The Theory of Moral Sentiments* published in

1759, 17 years before the publication of *The Wealth of Nations*. Campbell (1971) argues that *The Theory of Moral Sentiments* is important for understanding *The Wealth of Nations*, for it presents a broader picture of Smith's social theory, of which economics is only a part. In his *Lectures on Jurisprudence*, Smith builds a bridge between the two main works: "they connect with *Moral Sentiments* in that justice is part of morality, and they connect with the *Wealth of Nations* not only because this latter work is summarised in the lectures, but also because Smith considered economic matters to be included in 'the four great objects of law, which are given as justice, police, revenue and arms' " (Campbell 1971: 18). Therefore, in Smith's world, economics and justice are two sides of the social coin.

The concept of morally correct conduct is deep-rooted as well as widespread in economics. To argue that cost-benefit analysis, which is a branch of welfare economics, makes no claim to produce morally correct decisions is in fact alien to the subject. Especially when irreversible decisions are made which could affect future generations tens or even hundreds of thousands of years down the line, morality must be in the equation not as a side issue but as the core of the analysis. Of course, what is the morally correct decision? In this instance what is the morally correct communal discounting in economics?

RAWLSIAN FRAMEWORK FOR DISCOUNTING

As I mentioned earlier, different individuals are likely to express different or even conflicting views when the morality of a communal project is considered. This would be especially marked when these individuals come from different religious, cultural, racial or nationality groups, have opposing political convictions and above all have different interests. At the beginning the problem may appear to be intimidating and even insurmountable. What sort of bottom-line agreement can be reached when man is stripped of religion, race, nationality, political affiliation, social status and personal interest? This is precisely what John Rawls attempts to do in presenting his theory of justice (Rawls 1972).

The Rawlsian structure differs from the tradition of Hume, Smith and Bentham in the sense that it is nonutilitarian. In his view, those who opposed the classical utilitarian theory of justice failed in their mission mainly because they criticized utilitarianism on a narrower basis by pointing out the obscurities and incongruities that it contains. Rawls, in the tradition of Locke, Rousseau and Kant, carries the social contract doctrine to a higher order of abstraction which, according to him, is a superior alternative to utilitarianism.

In Smith's *Moral Sentiments* (1976), justice, in a utilitarian spirit, is a necessary condition of the existence of any society where emphasis is on sympathy; whereas in *Wealth of Nations* (1979), it is on selfishness. According to Smith, individuals are born with feelings of love for others as well as self-love. Each one of us is able to put ourselves in other people's shoes and judge whether a response to a particular situation is proper or not. We are also able to imagine how our actions look from the outside, partly because we desire approval of others, and think about the "impartial observer." However, Smith concedes that the desire for approval may not turn out to be sufficient to prevent us from behaving in a selfish manner, and thus in a society, rules of justice with legal sanctions may become necessary to prevent disruptive behavior.

In contrast Rawls makes his nonutilitarian position clear right at the beginning of his work, *A Theory of Justice*:

Justice is the first virtue of social institutions, as truth is of systems of thought. A theory however elegant and economical must be rejected or revised if it is untrue: likewise laws and institutions no matter how efficient and well-arranged must be reformed or abolished if they are unjust. Each person possesses an inviolability founded on justice that even the welfare of society as a whole cannot override. For this reason justice denies that the loss of freedom for some is made right by a greater good shared by others.

A Theory of Justice is also one of very few major philosophical works which deals, although rather briefly, with discounting, especially in Chapter 5, section 45. Rawls implies that attempts to elaborate and expand on any part of his theory of justice, including just discounting, are welcome.

The contrast between the utilitarian and Rawlsian doctrines is starkly illustrated by Shradder-Frechette (1991) by an example that an act utilitarian would be bound to accept as right the action of framing and consequently hanging an innocent person if his/her death would prevent social disturbance which could take the lives of a number of individuals. That is, in act utilitarian justice, dignity, liberty and life of a single person, or a number of persons, is expendable to benefit a greater number in the community. Act utilitarians reject all ethical rules and instead reason merely on the basis of the consequences of a particular act.[1] In Shradder-Frechette's terms the believers of egalitarian ethics, including Rawls, would not accept such a situation because maximizing the good for the majority is not the objective (also see Fried 1970, 1978; Donagan 1977).

Basic Principles

In justice as fairness, Rawls, instead of expanding Locke's and Rousseau's contract doctrine, which largely aims to set up a particular form of government, tries to establish the basic principles of justice. These principles are intended to help free and rational individuals to further their own interests, who would accept an initial position of equality as the fundamental principle. There are many important structural features of Rawlsian doctrine; the main ones which will be used in the discounting debate are as follows:

Original Position. This is a purely hypothetical situation in which rational individuals, attempting to advance their interests, negotiate to settle the basic terms of their association as equal beings. In this position, first it must be considered which principles it would be rational to adopt given a particular contractual situation, which links the theory of justice with the theory of rational choice. It must be agreed that one view of justice is more acceptable than alternatives if rational individuals would choose its principles. When circumstances are presented in different ways, correspondingly different principles would be accepted. The ideal outcome, according to Rawls, would be a unique set of principles, but this may not turn out to be the case, and he states that he would be satisfied if it produced a mere ranking of the main conceptions.

Veil of Ignorance. In order to establish a fair procedure it is essential to purify parties by nullifying the effects of specific circumstances that put individuals at odds and tempt them to exploit natural and social circumstances to their advantage. In this respect, parties are situated behind the veil of ignorance, where nobody knows his/her class, profession, income level and other social attributes in society. Individual talents, intelligence, strength and ambitions in life are not disclosed, nor are race, religion, color or nationality.

Nor does anybody know his/her conception of the good, special features of his/her psychology such as pessimism, optimism and aversion to risk. The persons in the original position do not know the particular circumstances of their own society, nor do they have any information as to which generation they belong to. These broader restrictions extending to generations are necessary because of discounting, saving/consumption levels, conservation/depletion of natural resources, and other environmental matters such as greenhouse effect, acid rain, nuclear wastes, and so on.

Although parties are ignorant about their personal circumstances, they know the general facts about human society, principles of economic theory, politics, sociology and laws of human psychology. It is important that a conception of justice should generate its own support. When the basic structure is established in the community, individual members tend to acquire the corresponding sense of justice and thus the Rawlsian concept of justice is stable. Differences between parties exist but unknown to them, since everybody is rational and similarly situated, each would be convinced by the same argument.

Two Principles of Justice. Rawls contends that in the original position the parties would agree on the two principles of justice. First, each individual is to have an equal right to the most extensive basic liberty compatible with similar liberty for others. Second, social and economic inequalities are to be arranged so that they are both reasonably expected to be to everybody's advantage and attached to positions open to all.

The items in the first group are: freedom of thought, expression and assembly; the right to vote and to be elected; the right to own personal property, accumulate wealth; and freedom from arbitrary arrest and capture as defined by the rule of law. The items in the second category are about the distribution of income, wealth and authority which is needed for the functioning of social institutions.

Difference Principle. The two principles of justice are to be arranged in a serial order with the first one prior to the second. That is, a divergence from the institutions of equal liberty cannot be justified by greater social or economic gain. The distribution of wealth and authority must be consistent with both the basic liberties and equality of opportunity. Of course, income and authority can be unequally distributed. The difference principle allows inequalities, or unequal treatment, only if such practices are to the advantage of the least well-off, whose better prospects act as incentives, so that the economic process is more efficient and innovation proceeds at a faster rate. Eventually, the resulting economic benefits spread through the system and to the least advantaged. Rawls points out that he will not consider how far these things are true (a task perhaps better suited to economists than philosophers), but something of this kind must be argued if these inequalities are to be fair.

DISCOUNTING WITHIN THE RAWLSIAN FRAMEWORK

Since discounting is time related, let us focus on the intertemporal aspects of the Rawlsian doctrine. The veil of ignorance prevents delegates from knowing the generation, natural, political, economic and other conditions of the time, which will affect them and their society during their lives. Alternatively, one could envisage that parties in the original position, after disputing the intratemporal issues, now move on to consider intertemporal problems. This position should not be thought to be a special gathering or a subcommittee of the original position which includes only the representatives from the generational chain. This would be stretching fantasy too far and the conception would cease to be a natural guide to intuition. It may be helpful to observe that a number of persons could pretend, at any time, to debate this hypothetical situation simply by reasoning in accordance with the appropriate restrictions. There would be a number of issues involved in the intergenerational debate, such as natural resource depletion, conservation, saving/investment levels and the resulting capital accumulation. As I explained elsewhere (Kula 1994), discounting enters into all of these equations as a fundamental parameter.

Although each delegate is barred from knowing his/her position in the generational chain, he/she is assumed to know the general principles of economic theory and laws of human psychology (Rawls 1972: 137). As explained in Chapter 1, discounting is a major pillar of economic science and a part of human psychology and therefore would constitute part and parcel of general facts that each delegate is endowed with. It is known to the delegates that individuals are not time indifferent, but discount their own utilities on the grounds of pure time preference, risk of death, other risks, and diminishing marginal utility of increasing consumption.

Rawls rules out pure time preference in the original position as being irrational. Indeed, rationality is a cornerstone in the Rawlsian doctrine and thus any human behavior which is deemed to be irrational is ruled out. Rationality implies impartial concern for all parts of life; the mere difference of location in time is not in itself rational. Rawls accepts discounting on the grounds of risk and diminishing marginal utility of consumption, but does not believe that parties will give any weight to mere position in time, that is, pure time discounting (see especially section 45, time preference). This part of the Rawlsian analysis is important in determining the *magnitude* of communal discounting which is relevant but essentially a different issue than the *method of communal discounting*, which will emerge a little later on.

Rawls, like most academics, at the time of his writings was not aware of the fact that in ordinary discounting a systematic discrimination is practiced against future generations. If he was, in my opinion, he would have written against it. Apart from the rationality issue, he condemns pure time preference rate on the grounds that it would discriminate against future generations. This is because the inclusion of a pure time preference rate into the communal discount rate would increase the haste to deplete communal resources which in turn would cause injury to future generations. "In the case of society, pure time preference is unjust: it means (in the more common instance when future is discounted) that the living take advantage of their position in time to favour their interest" (p. 295).

The above statement, which is boldly expressed, is crucial in understanding the principle of equality between generations in the Rawlsian doctrine. There are many other statements which are equally explicit: "the different temporal position of persons and generations does not in itself justify treating them differently" (p. 294). The principle of intergenerational equality is in fact the first principle of justice in the Rawlsian theory. In the first principle of justice we are not allowed to treat generations differently solely on the grounds that they are earlier or later in time. In our illustrative example in Chapter 3, it was made clear that the decision-making generations, the living, are not treating future generations as they were treating themselves. This practice is clearly in conflict with the Rawlsian doctrine. The consequences of discrimination against future generations by the living are grave. As explained previously, ordinary discounting allows present individuals to undertake lopsided projects, such as nuclear power, the heavy costs of which will fall upon future generations. Indeed, the net present value criterion, which is based upon ordinary discounting, with high or low interest rates wipes out enormous distant costs and in this way such projects become economically "viable."

Let us go back to the Swedish nuclear program which is likely to be terminated by 2010. In the original position the delegates will see that the fruits of the Swedish nuclear program, confined to a few decades, benefiting a few million consumers and a handful of professionals and workers, could create substantial health and safety problems for millions of years to come. In other words, the immediate economic and career benefits of nuclear energy involve small risks to health to start with, but the risks will increase substantially in the distant future because of the waste disposal problem. The veil of ignorance prevents delegates from knowing their place in the generational chain. They could turn out to be members of the present generation, benefiting not only as consumers from a relatively risk-free energy now, but, say, as career-conscious nuclear scientists, politicians and other professional groups who actively take part in its development. They could also turn out to be sufferers from cancer or genetic disorders as members of distant generations.

Mishan (1988) argues that in the original position delegates who are to be affected for better or worse by a public project will have a lively debate on the matter. In Mishan's opinion, assuming most are risk averters, they are unlikely to give their approval to lopsided projects. In accepting principles such as ordinary discounting that justify their "viability," the delegates would not be risk averters, but risk takers. Rawls contends that justice does not allow that the sacrifices imposed on a few are outweighed by the larger sum of advantage enjoyed by many. Ordinary discounting seems to be doing exactly the opposite. By making nuclear projects good, it allows a few to justify their privilege, say, as nuclear scientists, at the expense of risk imposed on numerous future generations.

I must emphasize once more that it is not required that parties in the original position are altruists; complete altruism is not in line with the Rawlsian doctrine, which only permits limited altruism or mutual disinterest:

> while parties have roughly similar needs and interests, or needs and interests in various ways complimentary so that mutually advantageous co-operation amongst them is possible, they nevertheless have their own plans of life. These plans, or conceptions of the good, lead them to have different ends and purposes and make conflicting claims on the natural and social resources available. Moreover, although the interests advanced by these plans are not assumed to be interests in the self, they are interests of a self that regards its conception of the good as worthy of recognition and that advances claims on its behalf as deserving satisfaction. I shall emphasise this aspect of the circumstances of justice by assuming that parties take no interest in one another's interests. (Rawls 1972: 127)

Recently, some economists have begun to emphasize the altruistic dimension of market participants. For example, Casson (1990) detects a gradual weakening in the concept of economic person over the years in favor of ethical person and hopes that such focus will intensify in future years, allowing economists to recapture the lost ground to other disciplines such as sociology, politics and philosophy. The ethical person envisaged by Casson operates in a world of imperfect information, dealing with vaguely specified problems. That person is constrained by the moral values of a particular time and venue and, most important, he/she, unlike the economic person, is not rational. Clearly, ethical person, as described by Casson, is at odds with the Rawlsian delegate. In the latter, rationality is a crucial attribute. Furthermore, although subject to the veil of ignorance regarding personal circumstances, the Rawlsian delegate is endowed with all the basic facts of life. Above all, his/her problem is clearly specified: to enter into an agreement with others to achieve just society with all its political, legal and economic structures.

According to Rawls, acceptance of a defective method or theory can only be permissible in the absence of an alternative. As I tried to illustrate above, ordinary discounting by practicing a systematic discrimination against future generations by present individuals, as well as by its untrue assumptions, is at odds with the first principles of justice. Furthermore, it creates situations in which lopsided projects, such as nuclear power, are justified by the living for short-term gains at the expense of long-term costs, and delegates do not have to be strict risk averters to disallow them. The alternative to ordinary discounting is modified discounting, in which public sector policy-makers treat all generations equitably, regardless of their positions in the generational chain. Also, it assumes mortal individuals.

Going back to our illustrative example in Chapter 3, I would have no quarrel with the net present value criterion as far as treatment given to persons A, B and C (Kula 1981, 1984c, 1986b, 1987a, 1988a). The actual time that those individuals wait for their share of costs/benefits is properly taken into account in equation (3.8). If the same procedure is repeated for other individuals involved (i.e., persons D, E, F and G), we would obtain different communal factors, the modified factors. This would satisfy the first principle of Rawlsian justice in which the decision-maker treats all individuals alike, regardless of their position in time. The resulting overall sum, the sum of discounted consumption flows, SDCF, measures the total worth of this project to the community which contains present as well as future generations. This figure may also be called net discounted value, NDV.

The illustrative example regarding the NPV (given in Chapter 3) assumed a 10 percent time preference rate for each individual. Using this as the price of waiting for one year, we can now obtain results for each person for his/her entire association with the hypothetical project. That is:

$$NDV = \left[\frac{-0.333}{(1 + S_A)} - \frac{0.333}{(1 + S_A)} - \frac{0.333}{(1 + S_C)} \right] \tag{4.1}$$

$$+ \left[\frac{0.333}{(1 + s_B)^2} + \frac{0.333}{(1 + s_C)^2} + \frac{0.333}{(1 + s_D)^1} \right]$$

$$+ \left[\frac{0.333}{(1 + s_C)^3} + \frac{0.333}{(1 + s_D)^2} + \frac{0.333}{(1 + s_E)^1} \right]$$

$$+ \left[\frac{0.333}{(1 + s_D)^3} + \frac{0.333}{(1 + s_E)^2} + \frac{0.333}{(1 + s_F)^1} \right]$$

$$+ \left[\frac{0.333}{(1 + s_E)^3} + \frac{0.333}{(1 + s_F)^2} + \frac{0.333}{(1 + s_G)^1} \right]$$

$$NDV = -0.909 + 0.853 + 0.828 + 0.828 + 0.828 \tag{4.2}$$

$$NDV = 2.428$$

Each of the terms on the right-hand side of equation (4.2) is a communal modified factor; these are different from the ordinary factors in (3.9), Chapter 3. The resulting net discounted value shows an overall sum of £2.428 as opposed to £1.97 in (3.9). In other words, the new discounting method makes the project more desirable. The modified discount factors from year 3 onward become the same, 0.828, given the assumptions of our socioeconomic model. At the beginning of year 3 the last member of the decision-making generation, person C, drops out of the model and the relationship between the project and future generations who are associated with it becomes stabilized. That is, modified discount factors, unlike ordinary factors, do not decline continuously; in this way the distant consequences of communal projects become important in a decision-making process. In the case of short-run projects, the results obtained by either method will not differ significantly. As for long-living projects, the modified discounting method will yield results which are considerably different from those obtained by the ordinary criteria.

Table 4.1 shows the appropriate length of time for discounting purposes to each individual member of society who is associated with the project. It also gives undiscounted and discounted net benefits for each person. Columns 2–6 show the division of net consumption benefits between individuals on an annual basis. Column 7 gives the net undiscounted share for each individual who is associated with the project. On this basis only person A is a loser. Columns 8–12 show the discounted net benefit accruing to each individual by taking into account the correct length of time for every person. In effect the second half of the last row are the modified communal discount factors (numbers under columns 8–12) and £2.43 is the sum of annual factors, that is, discounted communal worth of the project.

MODIFIED FACTORS FOR PRACTICAL PURPOSES

Our single illustrative example enables the reader to understand the nature of the modified discounting method. In this the communal decision-maker, just like estimating future costs and benefits of investment projects, estimates the number of generations who will be associated with a particular project and time frames involved. Below I shall compute modified discount factors for practical purposes for the United Kingdom, which requires a number of simplifying assumptions without seriously impairing the reality. But first we have to define generations.

A generation can be defined in a number of ways. At one end of the spectrum each individual who is associated, or will be associated or affected, with a communal project is a generation in his/her own right. That is, if a project is expected to affect 200 million U.K. citizens over its lifetime, each person will be regarded as a generation. In fact, this is done in our example but only for illustrative purposes. At the other end, we can split the living into, say, four generations as grandfather/grandmother, father/mother, son/daughter, grandson/granddaughter with, say, 20 years' age gap between each, on average.

I prefer to define a generation as individuals born in each year; that is, those who were born in 1948 are 1948 generation, those who were born in 1949 are 1949 generation, and so on. The same applies to future generations, that is, those who will be born in 2020 will be 2020 generation, and so on. For dis-

Table 4.1
Undiscounted and Discounted Net Benefits on the Basis of MDM

Person (1)	Undiscounted Benefits					Personal Total (7)	Discounted Benefits					Total (13)
	t_1 (2)	t_2 (3)	t_3 (4)	t_5 (5)	t_6 (6)		t_1 (8)	t_2 (9)	t_3 (10)	t_4 (11)	t_5 (12)	
A	-0.33	-	-	-	-	-0.33	$\frac{-0.33}{1.1}$	-	-	-	-	-0.30
B	-0.33	0.33	-	-	-	0	$\frac{-0.33}{1.1}$	$\frac{0.33}{1.21}$	-	-	-	-0.03
C	-0.33	0.33	0.33	-	-	0.33	$\frac{-0.33}{1.1}$	$\frac{0.33}{1.21}$	$\frac{0.33}{1.33}$	-	-	0.22
D	-	0.33	0.33	0.33	-	1.0	-	$\frac{0.33}{1.1}$	$\frac{0.33}{1.21}$	$\frac{0.33}{1.33}$	-	0.83
E	-	-	0.33	0.33	0.33	1.0	-	-	$\frac{0.33}{1.1}$	$\frac{0.33}{1.21}$	$\frac{0.33}{1.33}$	0.83
F	-	-	-	0.33	0.33	0.66	-	-	-	$\frac{0.33}{1.1}$	$\frac{0.33}{1.21}$	0.58
G	-	-	-	-	0.33	0.33	-	-	-	-	$\frac{0.33}{1.1}$	0.30
Total Project	-1	1	1	1	1	3	-0.91	0.85	0.83	0.83	0.83	2.43

counting purposes the convenience as well as the relevance of defining generations in this way is obvious because we normally use years as time segments.
This process is also proper as the Oxford Dictionary defines generation as "all
persons born about the same time and therefore of the same age." In this respect
I put the population into 73 age groups, which is about the average life expectancy in the United Kingdom.

Other assumptions: the size of population is constant, and the life expectancy at
birth is not changing. In the United Kingdom, over the last couple of decades the
population has remained around the 57 million mark and there is no reason to believe that it will change substantially one way or the other in the foreseeable future. Therefore, it would be realistic to assume near zero growth rate for
population. With regard to the expected lifetime of individuals, it should be noted
that the life expectancy of U.K. citizens has drifted upward over the years. The figure for the life expectancy of females at birth has gone up from 75 years in 1966
to 76 years in 1981. For males it has gone up from 69 to 70 years during the same
period (see *Annual Abstracts of Statistics*). Although it is conceivable that these
figures may continue to increase over the years, the statistics indicate that this is
likely to happen very slowly. For the time being a constant life-expectancy figure
of 73 years as an average for both sexes is assumed in the United Kingdom. Later
on a sensitivity test will be carried out to find out to what extent increasing life expectancies over time may alter our results. One further structural assumption is
that population consists of equal cohorts, and that recruitment into it, necessary
with the assumption of constant population, equals deaths.

Going back to Table 4.1, the modified discount factors for each year are
shown in the second half of the last row, excluding the last term, £2.43, which
is the overall discounted value. That is:

Years	MD Factors
t_1	−0.91
t_2	0.85
t_3	0.83
t_4	0.83
t_5	0.83

These numbers are obtained by summing numbers in columns 8 to 12.

Now instead of three individuals we have 56 million citizens who are divided
into 73 age groups, or generations. A public sector project throws off £1 every
year over its lifetime which gets divided equally between the existing generations at the time. There are always 73 generations in existence at any point in

time. I also retain the assumption that all net benefits are consumed immediately by the recipients and futhermore when costs are paid, the money is diverted from consumption. The formula for the modified discount factors are:

$$MDF = \frac{1}{n}\left[\frac{1}{(1+s)^t}(n+1-t) + \sum_{1}^{t-1}\frac{1}{(1+s)^t}\right], \text{ when } t \leq n \qquad (4.3a)$$

$$= \frac{1}{n}\sum_{1}^{n}\frac{1}{(1+s)^t}, \text{ when } t \geq 0 \qquad (4.3b)$$

where:

MDF = modified discount factors
n = life expectancy of the United Kingdom citizens, which is 73 years; it also rep-
             resents number of generations at any point in time
t = age of public sector project yielding £1 every single year
s = social time preference rate

Equation (4.3a) corresponds to the first two years of the hypothetical project and (4.3b) to the years 3, 4 and 5.

A computer model written in BASIC can be used to estimate discount factors for various discount rates. The program which is used here gives results for interest rates between one and 15 percent. That is:

```
10   SIM A (200,15)
20   INPUT "INPUT THE NUMBER OF ROWS YOU REQUIRE (N< = 200)"; N
30   T = 1
40   FOR I = 1 TO 15
50   A (T, I) = 1/(1 + (I/100))
60   NEXT I
70   REM "ROW 1 NOW FORMED"
80   REM "T IS ROW, I IS COLUMN"
90   FOR T = 2 TO N − 1
100  FOR I = 1 TO 15
110  S = 0
120  FOR K = 2 TO T
130  REM "K IS THE COUNTER FOR SUMMATION"
140  S = S + (1/N/ (1 + (1/100)) ^ (K − 1)
150  NEXT K
160  A (T, I) = S + (N + 1 − T) * (1/N) / ((1 + (I/100)) ^ T)
170  NEXT I
```

```
180   REM "ROWS T FORMED"
190   NEXT T
200   REM "ROWS 2 TO N − 1 NOW FORMED"
210   FOR I = 1 TO 15
220   S = 0
230   FOR K = 1 TO N
240   S = S + (1/N) / (1(I/100)) ^ K
250   NEXT K
260   A (N, I) = S
270   NEXT I
280   REM "ROW N NOW FORMED"
290   REM "NOW PRINT OUT MATRIX"
302   PRINT TAB (30); "DISCOUNT FACTOR"
304   PRINT\PRINT TAB (31); "PERCENTAGE (I)"
306   PRINT "YEAR (T)";
307   FOR I = 1 TO 15
308   PRINT USING "£"; I;
309   NEXT I\PRINT
310   FOR T = 1 TO N
315   PRINT USING "££"; T;
320   FOR I = 1 TO 15
330   PRINT USING "£££"; A (T, I);
340   NEXT I
350   PRINT
360   NEXT T
370   END
```

Appendix 2 gives the modified discount factors calculated for discount rates 1–15 percent over a 73-year period; factors beyond that period will be equal to the figure for year 73, given the assumptions about the structure of population. It must be obvious that the MDM contains numerous net present value calculations, one for every individual who is associated with the communal project. The association continues as long as the individual and the project survive. In other words, the modified discounting method traces the consequences of the project to its ultimate source, the individual.

Figure 4.1 illustrates the difference between ordinary and modified discount factors at a 10 percent discount rate. The gap between the two curves is narrow in the early years but widens as time passes. If a communal project was a short-lived one, the overall result by way of ordinary or modified discounting methods would not be very different. For investments with long lives, a feature of most

Figure 4.1
Ordinary and Modified Discount Factors at a 10 Percent Rate

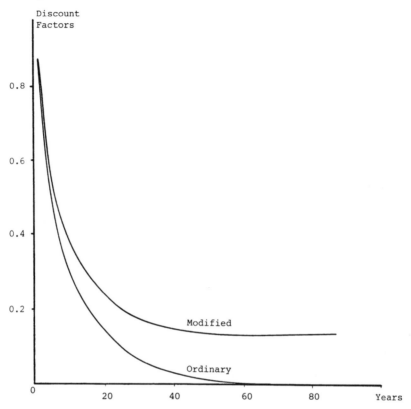

public sector projects, an appraisal based upon the modified discounting method will give very different results than the one by way of conventional methods. Chapters 5–9, in fact, are devoted to practical case studies to illustrate the difference. Unfortunately, in practice, when conventional appraisal methods are used, it is quite normal to take a cut-off point of 25–30 years because of the effect of ordinary discounting (UNIDO 1972; Ministry of Overseas Development 1977; HM Treasury 1984; Rigby 1989). In effect, the estimated lifetime of many public sector projects stretches well beyond this cut-off period.

Equations (4.3a) and (4.3b), which are based upon discrete time, can be converted, by a high degree of approximation, into a single continuous time formula as (4.3a) is converging into (4.3b). Rewriting (4.3a) in continuous time would yield:

$$MDF = \frac{1}{n}\,[e^{-st}(n - t) + \int\limits_{1}^{t} e^{-st}\,dt]$$

which becomes

$$MDF = \frac{1}{n} [e^{-st}(n - t) + \frac{1}{s} (1 - e^{-st})]$$

or

$$MDF = e^{-st}(1 - \frac{t}{n} - \frac{1}{sn}) + \frac{1}{sn} \qquad (4.4)$$

RELATED ISSUES

Broussalian (1971) contends that the first question to ask when evaluating a communal project is: for what benefit is it, and at whose expense, at intratemporal as well as intertemporal levels? But most economists believe that there is general agreement on discounting, which answers intertemporal questions and any disagreement amongst them relates only to the magnitude of the rate of discount. Then why is it that essentially an empirical question should have remained unsettled for so long, and the discounting debate seems to be dragging on indefinitely? His view is that at the heart of the problem there lies the meaning of society, which is not made up of identical individuals who either live forever or die together to be instantly replaced by other generations. "Such assumptions are, to be sure, often made in economic discussions" (Broussalian 1971).

Even within a given generation there are differences such as poor, rich, middle income, sick, invalid, those with prospects and those without, and so on. According to Broussalian, the who and the when are very important. It is in the nature of many public sector projects that they provide an unalterable profile of consumption benefits that cannot be stored, exchanged or assigned away by communal members.

Given that society is composed of heterogeneous individuals with finite and different lifespans the flow of benefits and costs would affect each one differently and this problem is not dealt with in discounting debates in public sector economics. There may be a good case for leaving conventional discounting entirely to the private sector, provided that the individual investor is the maximizer of his/her own wealth. In other words, public and private sector investments are different ball games. Let us now look at those and some other issues which are relevant.

Privately Owned Projects. Thus far I related the modified discounting method to publicly owned projects. Recently, Bellinger (1991) developed the modified discounting method to a more general stage in which privately owned as well as quasi–public sector projects[2] can be evaluated. Furthermore, his model, multigenerational value, accommodates a wide range of intergenerational weights that public sector policy-makers may wish to use.

I welcome his attempt to expand the scope of the modified discounting to encompass projects created by the private sector that generate intergenerational externalities. What is the societal value of such projects which could seriously affect future generations? This, indeed, is a fair and topical question. For example, a nuclear power station operated by private individuals creates serious intertemporal externalities in the form of highly toxic and long-living radioactive wastes which could affect the health and safety of numerous generations yet to be born. As I explained before, in the economic evaluation of a project of this kind, discounting is the most crucial parameter (Schulze et al. 1981). What should be the discounted value of a privately owned nuclear power generation unit from the viewpoint of all generations affected? This question widens the scope of modified discounting and Bellinger, by taking it one step further, makes an appreciable contribution.

To my surprise, over the years some of the supporters of modified discounting turned out to be in the private sector (i.e., businessmen/women), and this, at first, surprised me. Common sense and fairness aside, why should private companies demonstrate enthusiasm for the new method which, essentially, is a communal model? For example, after I read papers at a number of international conferences on agriculture, land use, infrastructure and the environment there were many discussions in support of modified discounting initiated by the private sector participants who normally take part in such gatherings. Their view was that in addition to intergenerational discrimination, ordinary discounting is reducing business opportunities for the private sector. This is because private companies take part in the construction and management of almost all communal projects in developed market economies. They were fully aware of the role of ordinary discounting in undermining the viability of long-term projects. Less infrastructure projects by the government, less business for the contractors. Some economists such as Galbraith (1974) argue relentlessly that in the United States the growing gap between private wealth and public squalor is largely due to the lack of communal projects.

The problem is even more acute in the developing countries. For example, the British government, over the years, advised developing countries to use evaluation methods and discount rates similar to those of the United Kingdom.

It is difficult to give practical guidance to appraisers of projects in countries where there is no centrally determined test discount rate or to governments seeking to establish this. Although current experience suggests that a discount rate of 10 percent applied to costs and benefits in constant prices is a useful operational guide over a wide range of countries, each country's accounting rate of interest is unique. (Ministry of Overseas Development 1977)

For example, in the cost-benefit analysis of the Third Bosphorous Crossing, Istanbul, Turkey, the required discount rate was at least 15 percent, with a 35-year cut-off period. This rate has widely been used in the economic appraisal of transport and other public projects in Turkey sponsored by the World Bank

(Karatas 1989). It has become obvious to private contractors that the ordinary discounting is a kiss of death for many communal infrastructure projects throughout the world.

Intragenerational Distribution. Thus far, in my illustrative and real-world models, I assumed that £1 net benefit, the throw-off, which materializes at the end of each year, is equally distributed between existing members of the community. The main reason for this is to be able to compute general modified discount factors. Of course, the net benefits of some public sector projects may not get distributed equally within the community. Furthermore, as Broussalian points out, the purpose behind a particular communal project may be to target specific groups such as the old, deprived infants, average or underprivileged college students, and so on. In cases like that the lion's share of the net benefit flow in the future would be captured by the target population, with some trickle-down to other members of the community.

It has been argued by Rigby (1989) that the modified discounting, rather than implicitly ignoring distributional effects, explicitly assumes that distributional effects are equal to all members of society within a given time period, whether in present or future generations. This may restrict the use of the new method across a wide range of projects. As I pointed out, the first step in establishing a just discounting method must be to construct a general framework. It is possible to obtain modified discount factors aimed to favor specific population cohorts, say infants, on the grounds that the project in question focuses on this group in society. Rather than tampering with the general modified factors one may wish to deal with this issue in a different and much simpler manner, say, by giving a special weight to that target group. This can be taken into account in numerators in (4.1) and consequently (4.2).

It would be extremely demanding on the cost-benefit analyst that he/she should create different modified factors for different projects. I do not think that a typical analyst would either have the time or the skill to calculate discount factors for each project.

Changing Population Structure. The structural assumptions about the United Kingdom's population may appear to be rather rigid when long-term projects are appraised. One could argue that the size of population as well as its age structure may change in future years. The crucial question, in my opinion, is not whether this change will take place, but rather will it be substantial enough to have an impact on the communal factors that are calculated here?

Take the assumption regarding a constant 73-year average life expectancy. A sensitivity test has been carried out by envisaging a situation in which the average life expectancy drifts upward from 73 years toward 79 years over, say, the next 70 years. Then by taking 76 as the middle figure, the computer program was run for n = 76 to estimate the communal factors. Comparing the results with earlier ones revealed that the numbers are not sensitive to such a change. For example, for n = 73 the discount factor at a 10 percent discount rate is 0.137 for the years between 54 and 73; for n = 76 it is 0.132 between the years 54 and 71; and 0.131 between the years 72 and 76. This change did not make any visible difference at all to the shape of the modified factor, even at a scale three times the size, shown in Figure 4.1. Of course, for countries with rapidly expanding population and changing age structure such as Mexico, Brazil, and so on, one needs to calculate different factors.

Reinvestment. So far it has been assumed that the money used to finance the communal project comes from a source displacing each individual's private consumption by that amount. Furthermore, when benefits are distributed to existing individuals each one is assumed to consume his/her share entirely. In other words, our assumptions put us into a consumption game throughout the life of the public sector project where net consumption benefits are discounted at the consumption rate of interest. What if a part of the benefit is reinvested? How would this affect the communal modified factors?

The purpose behind reinvestment is the same as the original investment decision, that is, to enhance future consumption capacity. As I discussed in Chapter 1, the Austrian school views investment/reinvestment as a pattern of productive acts to move through time from one stage to the next until the ultimate objective, the consumption, is reached. In a communal project reinvested net benefits will eventually be consumed at a future date by members of the community; then we may have to identify first what proportion of net benefits are reinvested. The analyst needs to identify when reinvested benefits eventually turn into consumption benefits.

Mishan (1988), in probing into the welfare foundation of cost-benefit analysis in relation to communal projects involving many generations, raises a similar question about reinvestment. His point is that a communal project involving many mortal generations with and without overlapping lifespans will not satisfy the Pareto criterion. But this problem will be circumvented when we assume that each beneficiary from the project was to invest the entire value of his/her benefit, leaving it subsequently reinvested at an opportunity cost rate until the end of the project's life. He notes that this is a nonsensical assumption, as economic agents do not behave in this manner. Empirical evidence reveals that only a very small proportion of net benefits are reinvested and the rest is consumed.

I have to concede that reinvestment, if it takes place, would have some impact, possibly a small one, on the modified factors because it is essentially a transfer of net consumption benefits between generations, but it would not change the nature of the method. When reinvestment is small, as Mishan points out, the effect on the general modified factors as calculated here would be negligible. In many cases public sector investments involve nonmarketable benefits where reinvestment is not an issue (Broussalian 1971).

DEBATES

Various aspects of modified discounting, including its philosophical foundation, are being debated in various journals. Price (1984, 1987, 1989a), mostly in relation to afforestation projects involving many generations, raises a number of issues. First, when afforestation projects are viewed by different generations at different time points, the decision-maker on the ground, who is in charge of felling and replanting, may be tempted to realize the investment at an earlier age than the one agreed on originally, which could even undermine the original decision. Second, even when the initially agreed-on plan is honored by all generations this could put the original decision-makers, say, present generations, who initiate the project but do not reap the benefits during their lifetimes, into a disadvantaged position, similar to person A in our illustrative example. According to Price, these problems will be overcome and intergenerational justice and efficiency will be achieved by using the ordinary discounting method with an appropriately low discount rate based solely on the diminishing marginal utility of consumption. His proposed low rate of discount excludes all other factors such as the myopic desire for early consumption, and risk of death.

Thomson (1988) contends that the well-being of all generations is not in fact of equal importance to decision-makers and therefore it is quite understandable when they favor the present folk. Even dictators or disengaged experts have to consider how society gets from this generation to the next and cannot ignore the importance of the near future. Furthermore, it is not clear to him why at birth the expectations of individuals who are associated with the project should be relevant.

Rigby (1989) asserts that, indeed, in ordinary discounting the distributional effects between individuals over time as well as at a given point in time are not captured. The welfare foundations for ignoring the distributional inequalities generally rest on the Kaldor-Hicks principle that gainers need only to be able to compensate losers. The argument is that, in applying a hypothetical compensation principle, cost-benefit analysis assumes away any effects on social welfare that result from the change in income distribution consequent upon a project. Kula is therefore correct to assert that ordinary discounting treats society as a single individual. The modified discounting method assumes the opposite in that, rather than implicitly ignoring distributional effects, it explicitly assumes that distributional effects are equal to all members of society within a given period, whether in present or future generations.

In practice, since ordinary discounting wipes out the distant consequences of public sector projects in most cases, a 25-year cut-off period is assumed which ignores costs and benefits thereafter, although residual values are often used as a proxy. The new method would make the cost-benefit analyst take serious account of costs and benefits over the life of the project. Rigby also points out that environmental and health projects with long-term benefits may gain prominence in the public sector investment portfolio when the modified discounting method is used as an appraisal criterion.

Hutchinson (1989) argues that the modified discounting method would result in a greater number of individual projects being undertaken in the public sector than would be the case under conventional public sector investment appraisal. This has obvious implications for the allocation of an economy's limited resources between the private and public sectors. Modified discounting introduces a dichotomy, the general equilibrium implication of which must be thought out carefully. Apart from changing the pattern of project mix in the public sector, the modified discounting method may also affect the profitability in the private sector. It would indeed be revealing if the new method was placed in a much broader context of general equilibrium.

Bateman (1989) points out that the modified discounting method should not be seen as complete rejection of ordinary discounting, as both methods have similarities, the most important of which is that the theoretical underpinning of the two methods is the same, that is, both techniques employ a positive time preference to discount future net benefits of an investment project. In effect, both methods obtain a net value for the investing population. Second, like the net present value criterion, the modified discounting method does not consider problems of benefit distribution within a given population by viewing this as a political rather than an economic problem.

Bellinger (1991), points out that the Rawlsian "covenant" which underpins the new method may be too restrictive to prevent future generations from exercising free choice at times when they are technologically able to do so.

Price's argument that an ongoing investment decision such as afforestation should be viewed at different time points by different decision-makers (i.e., foresters in charge of felling and replanting) is misleading. There will be times when each decision-maker will have an unfair advantage in relation to future generations. If each person misuses that time advantage then all generations will be deprived in the end. The assertion "look at the decision on when to terminate the rotation from the perspective of the forester eventually charged with either felling the crop or postponing the decision (say) ten years" fails to grasp the nature and philosophy of the modified discounting. Unlike the conventional methods such as the net present value or the internal rate of return, the ground rules for this method are laid down in the original position by the representatives from all generations, not by the present foresters who are here now and at a point of advantage in relation to future generations.

However, there seems to be a valid point that is latent in Price's analysis regarding the early generations who make a sacrifice by undertaking an investment project on a rotation basis which will bear fruit beyond their lifetime, similar to the position of person A in our illustrative example. I should like to point out that although person A is losing out in our simple investment example, overall he/she is likely to become a net gainer if we assume a number of communal projects, some of which were initiated before person A was born. In other words, person A's loss must be seen against what he/she receives from previous generations. Eventually, this line of thought will take us to the very first generation who made a sacrifice by starting off the process of capital accumulation. Indeed, this problem is recognized by Rawls as he argues that the first generation, having no predecessors, would not receive anything in return for its sacrifice and would be worse off. On the other hand, the last generation would not be required to put any capital aside to pass on.[3]

Rawls does not recommend against capital accumulation by encouraging each generation to leave no surplus behind. This would only perpetuate poverty. But he also notes that justice does not require that any generation should save so that later ones are simply more wealthy. As I demonstrated in Chapter 1, in a two-period analysis, the higher the saving ratio, the lower the social discount rate in Paretian equilibrium. An increase in saving ratio across generations, *ca-teris paribus*, would benefit even more the wealthier individuals yet to be born. The difference principle would point in the opposite direction. At the extreme, saving rate will be zero when the social time discount rate is infinitely large. Note that there is no difference between ordinary and modified factors in extreme cases. When the social rate of discount is infinitely large, both conventional and new criteria yield the same result—zero discount factor and no capital accumulation. Conversely, when the social rate of discount is zero, modified and ordinary factors become unity.

Once the difference principle is accepted, then one needs to establish a social minimum level of saving, which cannot be easily determined. In economics the precision between saving level and discount rate is often emphasized, but in the Rawlsian doctrine the concept of just saving is less precise. Each generation must not only maintain the gains of culture and civilization, but it must also put aside in each period of time a suitable sum for capital accumulation. This sum may take various forms, from net investment in tools and machinery to investment in education, and maintenance or even improving the environmental quality. It is, therefore, not possible to define precise limits on each generation's obligation regarding saving levels, but this does not mean that significant ethical constraints cannot be formulated.

Assuming a high marginal productivity of capital and distant time horizon utility maximization may lead to an excessive rate of accumulation, especially during the early years. Since there is no moral reason to discount future on the grounds that it is the future, then utilitarian doctrine may guide us to demand heavy sacrifices on the poorer generations to benefit later ones that are far better off. Even if we cannot define a precise just saving level, we should be able to avoid this kind of extreme. In the original position delegates must ask themselves how much they would be willing to save. Presumably, this rate varies depending on the state of society. The just saving principle can be regarded as an understanding between generations to carry their fair share of the burden to realize and preserve a just society.

Although Rawls rejects discounting on the grounds of irrationality, pure myopia or mere location of generations in time, he permits, or even requires, that discounting should account for changing circumstances (i.e., diminishing marginal utility of increasing income or consumption). Bellinger, by drawing attention to Brown (1987), suggests that, given per capita income growth over time, it would be justified to count future utilities less than present ones. "Therefore, Rawlsian logic may be more consistent with the discounting of future benefits than with Kula's conclusion" (Bellinger 1991: 103).

The fact is that the modified discounting method does differentiate between income levels and discounts future on grounds of diminishing marginal utility of income. Before taking up this point I should like to point out that a powerful school of thought argues that real incomes cannot grow indefinitely (Mill 1862; President's Material Commission 1952; U.S. Bureau of Mines 1970; Meadows et al. 1972; Mesarovic and Pestel 1974; Meadows et al. 1991; Goldsmith 1991; Nisbet 1991). For an equally compelling counterargument, see especially Kahn (1976) and Simon (1984, 1989).

Let us postulate that income levels are growing and will continue to grow in the future on a per capita basis, and consequently, future generations will be better off than present ones. Should the decision-maker then treat rich and poor generations alike? There is a long-established tradition in economics, the ability to pay approach, that policy-makers should be justified in taking more from the rich on the grounds of diminishing marginal utility of income (Fisher 1927); Frisch 1932). The modified discounting method is not at odds with this school nor is it in contravention of the Rawlsian doctrine, as it differentiates between income levels in the process of discounting. In order to see that clearly, consider the following argument.

The modified discounting method uses the social time preference rate (STPR) as the appropriate rate of discount, which I shall derive formally a little later on. The resulting formulae:

$$STPR = (1 + m)(1 + g)^e - 1$$

where m is mortality-based time discount rate, g is growth rate of real income over time, e is the elasticity of marginal utility of income. For the United States the figure turns out to be:

$$STPR = (1 + 0.02)(1.023)^{1.83}$$

$$= 6.2\%$$

Suppose that the growth rate of consumption is zero and thus future generations are not going to be better off than the present one. With no growth in real incomes, $g = 0$ the $STPR$ would be:

$$STPR = 2\%$$

Figure 4.2 illustrates the modified factors with and without income growth. Clearly, the new method differentiates between income levels. For example, the weight used for utility of richer generations, say, 1,000 years from now, is 0.22; the figure would be 0.52 if they were predicted to be at the same income level as we are. Note that the ordinary discounting method, by using either rate, would give a weight of 0.000 to both utility levels 1,000 years ahead.

In contrast, Price prefers to discount future utilities by using the ordinary criterion based solely on the diminishing marginal utility of income concept.

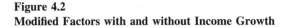

Figure 4.2
Modified Factors with and without Income Growth

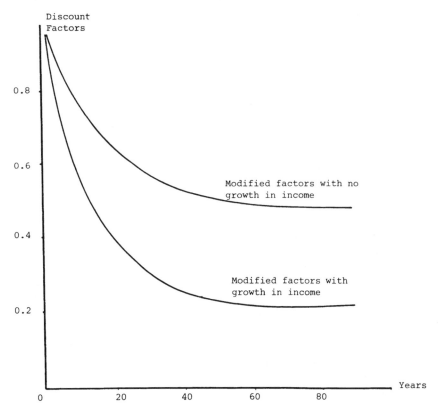

With this the *STPR* would be 4.2 percent and the weight to a 1,000-year benefit would be 0.000! However, what is really flawed in his analysis is this: the concept of diminishing marginal utility of consumption implies that a person, or persons, must experience a continuous increase in consumption capacity over time. The ordinary factor 1,000 years ahead, $1/(1.042)^{1000}$, implies that this experience for persons in 2992 starts from 1992, which is patently nonsensical.

According to Thomson (1988), it is not quite clear why the "at birth" expectation of life is relevant in the new model. I believe that choosing the date of birth as a reference point is appropriate. Imagine a large government project with a long life. Present individuals will be affected as soon as a decision is taken to go ahead with it. Future individuals will be affected at the point of their births as they will either receive a benefit from it or incur a cost. To give an extreme example, consider those babies born with leukemia as a result of radioactive contamination created by a publicly owned nuclear power generating unit nearby. Also, it is incorrect to argue that the modified discounting method assigns uniquely favorable distribution of weights to those who are alive at present. As far as discounting is concerned, the new method treats every single individual, present or future, in the same manner. True, there are differences between cumulative discount factors belonging to present and future generations; these arise due to age differences and consequently the length of time that individuals are associated with the projects, not because of unequal treatment.

Rigby (1989) correctly points out that although the modified discounting method does take into account the intergenerational distributional aspects of public sector projects, it does not deal rigorously with the intragenerational distribution. As I pointed out above, if some communal projects redistribute annual throw-offs unevenly, there may not be a need to alter modified factors that are computed here. Such effects can be taken into account in a variety of ways such as by giving weights to target groups.

Hutchinson's (1989) analysis, which implies that the use of the modified discounting method would increase the size and scope of the public sector, would only be correct under the assumption of an unlimited budget. But when the government is tied by budgetary constraint instead of a larger expenditure there will be a quite different project mix in the public sector portfolio. This will include some previously rejected long-term projects at the expense of "quick and dirty" ones.

Bateman sees modified discounting as an extension of ordinary discounting in view of the fact that both methods adopt a positive time preference to deflate the future net benefits of an investment project. It is certainly true that the ordinary discounting method is an integral part of the modified discounting method as it is used to deflate the net benefits which belong to mortal individuals. The fact of the matter is that the summation of these ordinary discounted individual net benefits over time yields results which are very different from the conventional factors.

SOCIAL TIME PREFERENCE RATE

The appropriate rate of discount in the modified discounting method is the social time preference rate, STPR, which is also called the consumption rate of interest, CRI, or the communal psychological discount rate, CPDR. As explained in Chapter 1, this rate is assumed to contain pure time discount rate, risk (in particular risk of death) and diminishing marginal utility of increasing income. The pure time preference is related to factors such as myopia, irrationality, backwardness and even pure selfishness (see Chapter 1, pp. 8–10), which is not compatible with the Rawlsian doctrine. Rawls implies that such tendencies may exist, but queries their primacy. Moreover, irrational myopic or excessively selfish tendencies will not help delegates at all to agree on the principles of a just society. In the original position, rationality and viewing all parts of life as equally important are essential. Discounting on the grounds of risk of death, or other risks, and diminishing marginal utility of income are permitted in the Rawlsian doctrine.

Below I shall obtain social time preference rates based upon annual risk of death and diminishing marginal utility of income for the United Kingdom and the United States. These figures do not contain pure time preference. Apart from Rawlsian objection the pure time preference rate is frowned upon by most economists. One reason for using cost-benefit techniques on communal projects is to bring rationality into investment decisions. Inclusion of various elements of irrationality into the decision-making process through the STPR does not coincide with this principle. Moreover, even if some wished to include the element of irrationality or pure myopia in an empirical study, they should, somehow, be able to find a way of quantifying a figure for it, or to argue that this part of human behavior in time discounting reflects upon a particular market transaction that is successfully measurable. As for risks other than mortality, one may handle them without tampering with the social time preference rate. Each communal project has a unique risk dimension in view of its nature, location, lifespan, starting point in time, target groups, and so on. Sensitivity analyses or other methods can be useful in assessing such risks.

Over the years I have calculated social time preference rates for a number of countries based upon two models: two-period analysis (Kula 1984a, 1987b, 1988a) and multiperiod utility function (Kula 1985, 1986b). Here I shall use the latter as it ties up well with the modified discounting method in which future utilities are discounted over individuals' lifetimes.

As explained in Chapters 1 and 2, the STPR, S, equals marginal rate of substitution of consumption at a location point along the communal indifference curve minus one. That is:

$$S = MRSC_{0,1} - 1 \qquad (4.5)$$

where $MRSC_{0,1}$ is marginal rate of substitution between two consecutive time points, 0 and 1. In order to obtain an operational formula let us assume a typical individual, Person Average, who represents society at a given point in time. Person Average has an indifference curve, shown as I^1 in Figure 4.3, which is a miniaturized version of the social indifference curve, I. Along this we locate him/her at point s, where the marginal rate of substitution is the same as point S on the social indifference curve, that is, OA/OB = Oa/Ob. Then Person Average's time preference equals the STPR.

Person Average has an intertemporal utility function over a finite horizon, his/her lifetime, and this function is additive, differentiable, and has constant elasticity. Its net present value, NPV, is given by:

$$NPV = \frac{AC_t}{1 - e} + \frac{AC_{t+1}^{1-e}}{(1 - e)(1 + m)} + \cdots + \frac{AC_{t+n}^{1-c}}{(1 - e)(1 + m)^n} \qquad (4.6)$$

where C_t is real consumption at time t, n is his/her life expectancy, A is a constant, e is elasticity of marginal utility of consumption, and m is mortality-based time discount rate. The marginal rate of substitution of consumption at any two consecutive time points, say, t and $t + 1$, will be:

$$MRSC_{t,t+1} = \frac{dNPV}{dC_t} \Big/ \frac{dNPV}{dC_{t+1}}$$

$$= (1 + m) \left(\frac{C_{t+1}}{C_t}\right)^e - 1$$

then by definition the STPR is:

$$S = (1 + m) \left[\frac{C_{t+1}}{C_t}\right]^e - 1 \qquad (4.7)$$

The growth rate of real consumption, g, between these two time points is:

$$g = \frac{C_{t+1} - C_t}{C_t} \qquad (4.8)$$

which yields:

$$(1 + g) = \frac{C_{t+1}}{C_t} \qquad (4.9)$$

Substituting this in (4.7) we get:

$$S = (1 + m)(1 + g)^e - 1 \qquad (4.10)$$

Mortality-Based Time Discount Rate. This can be calculated for Person Average, or for the nation as a whole, on the basis of individuals' survival probabilities and sex and age distribution of population (Eckstein 1961; Henderson 1965). In this, first the existing population is classified into quinquennial sex and age groups. Second, on the basis of recorded mortality rates and life expectancies, a long-term discount rate for each group is calculated. Finally, a weighted average of these long-term rates is taken on the basis of sex-age distribution of population to obtain an overall figure. To do this three types of statistical data are needed: the expected mortality rates of individuals, life tables and sex-age distribution of population. Mortality rates and life expectancies for 1970–1972 are shown for the United Kingdom and the United States in Table 4.2. Females are subjected to lower death rates and consequently live longer than males in almost all societies. Figures shown in Table 4.2 are the average for both sexes.

With this information in hand we can estimate a long-term mortality-based time discount rate for individuals in every sex-age group by taking the geometric average of death rates over the expected lifetime. For example, a 25-year-old

Figure 4.3
Marginal Rate as Substitution of Consumption in a Two-Period Analysis

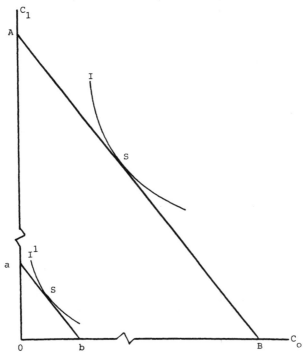

British person has 49 more years to live. During this time he/she faces death probabilities which are shown in Column 2. We can obtain a long-term time discount rate which is:

$$\beta = [(0.07)^5(0.09)^5(0.15)^5(0.26)^5 \ldots (3.17)^5(5.13)^5]^{1/49} \qquad (4.11)$$

where β is mortality-based time discount rate for a 25-year-old British person, which proves to be 0.6 percent. In old age the figure rises, of course, as the probability of survival diminishes. For example, at 60 years of age the long-term mortality rate, β_{60}, computed in the same fashion is found to be 3.8 percent.

The figure for the Person Average can be obtained by taking the weighted average of long-term rates for each age group. Weights depend on the distribution of population in each age group. This is done for the United Kingdom and for the United States for 1970–1972 and average figures of 2.23 percent and 1.79 percent are obtained respectively. Details of the derivation are shown in Table 4.3. In this calculation for quinquennial age groups, the median age is taken to represent the group, that is for the 20–24 age group the median age is 22, and so on.

It would be useful to look over a long period of time to observe the change

Table 4.2
Average Death Rates (%) and Life Expectancies (years) for 1970–1972 for the United Kingdom and the United States

Age Groups	Death Rates UK	Death Rates USA	Selective Ages	Life Expectancies UK	Life Expectancies USA
0- 4	0.39	0.46	0	72.0	70.0
5- 9	0.04	0.04	5	68.4	67.7
10-14	0.03	0.04	10	63.5	62.8
15-19	0.07	0.11	15	58.6	57.9
20-24	0.07	0.14	20	54.3	53.2
25-29	0.07	0.15	25	49.0	48.6
30-34	0.09	0.17	30	44.2	43.9
35-39	0.15	0.24	35	39.4	39.1
40-44	0.26	0.38	40	34.6	34.7
45-49	0.45	0.58	45	30.0	30.3
50-54	0.76	0.89	50	25.6	26.1
55-59	1.21	1.36	55	21.5	22.1
60-64	1.93	2.03	60	17.6	18.4
65-69	3.17	3.08	65	14.1	15.1
70-74	5.13	4.45	70	11.0	12.0
75-79	8.13	7.11	75	8.3	9.4
80-84	12.54	10.36	80	6.3	7.2
85-	22.40	16.38	85	4.5	5.3

Sources: For the United Kingdom: Central Statistical Office, *Annual Abstract of Statistics*, 1975 (London: HMSO). For the United States: *Statistical Abstract for the United States*, 1974 (Washington, DC: U.S. Government Printing Office).

in the volume of m for both countries. Figures calculated since the turn of the century are as follows:

Years	1900–1902	1910–1912	1920–1922	1930–1932	1950–1952	1960–1962	1970–1972
m, U.K.	2.2	2.1	2.2	2.2	2.3	2.3	2.2
m, U.S.	–	2.1	2.1	2.1	1.8	1.8	1.8

Average m, U.K. = 2.2 percent

Average m, U.S. = 2.0 percent

These results are quite unexpected for two reasons. First, the overall figures for both countries have proved to be quite high, contrary to the expectation of Henderson (1965) who guessed a figure of one percent. The reason for this is that, on the one hand, these countries have one of the lowest mortality rates in the world for almost all age groups, but on the other hand, they have a high concentration of population at older age groups. Since older people have much

Table 4.3
Long-Term Mortality-Based Time Discount Rate for Specific Age Groups and Age Distribution of Population, United Kingdom and United States, 1970–1972

Age	Long-Term Time Discount Rate		Distribution of Population	
	UK	USA	UK	USA
0- 4	0.26	0.34	7.9	8.4
5- 9	0.28	0.38	8.4	9.8
10-14	0.34	0.45	7.7	10.2
15-19	0.41	0.55	7.0	9.4
20-24	0.49	0.64	7.3	8.1
25-29	0.60	0.61	7.0	6.7
30-34	0.78	0.93	5.9	5.6
35-39	1.01	1.13	5.7	5.5
40-44	1.30	1.48	5.9	5.9
45-49	1.75	1.87	6.2	6.0
50-54	2.27	2.37	6.1	5.5
55-59	3.06	2.91	5.8	4.9
60-64	4.11	3.81	5.8	4.2
65-69	5.75	4.96	4.9	3.4
70-74	8.00	7.13	3.7	2.7
75-79	11.10	0.10	2.4	1.9
80-84	17.10	13.20	1.1	1.1
85-	23.20	16.40	0.9	0.7

higher long-term mortality-based time preference rates than younger ones, the higher the percentage of old people in the population the higher the national figure becomes. Second, the annual figures over the study period remained remarkably stable. Bearing in mind the improvements in the mortality figures over time, one would have expected a substantial reduction in the annual figures. This did not happen because, over the study period, age structure in the United Kingdom and the United States has been altered from a predominantly youthful composition to a much more mature one.

Growth Rate of Real Consumption. This is obtained by fitting the equation:

$$ln\ C = A + gt \tag{4.12}$$

to series in Table 4.4, where C is per capita real consumption, A is a constant, g is growth rate of per capita consumption, and t is number of years. The results are:

g, U.K.	2.0%	$R^2 = 0.98$
g, U.S.	2.3%	$R^2 = 0.98$

Table 4.4
Real Consumption, Per Capita, United Kingdom and United States

Year	Real Consumption UK, £ 1970 Prices	Per Capita USA, $ 1967 Prices
1954	414.8	1809.6
1955	430.3	1913.3
1956	431.5	1971.6
1957	439.5	1976.2
1958	448.9	1945.2
1959	465.7	2030.9
1960	480.1	2042.6
1961	487.3	2035.9
1962	493.3	2099.8
1963	512.2	2152.0
1964	525.8	2235.0
1965	529.4	2339.5
1966	536.8	2436.2
1967	545.2	2472.4
1968	556.4	2557.7
1969	557.8	2597.1
1970	571.0	2592.0
1971	584.5	2656.5
1972	616.6	2801.2
1973	641.5	2891.9
1974	636.3	2842.3
1975	632.3	2947.1
1976	630.1	2982.5

Source: Statistical Abstracts of the United States (1957–1976) (Washington, DC: U.S. Government
Printing Office).

Elasticity of Marginal Utility of Consumption

In order to calculate this parameter, a model is employed that is derived from
the earlier ideas of Fisher (1927) and Frisch (1932), and more recently was
developed by Fellner (1967), in which an additively separable utility function
is assumed in relation to two goods, namely, food and nonfood. In this model
the elasticity of marginal utility of consumption is measured by the ratio of
income elasticity to compensated price elasticity of the food demand function,
that is:

$$e = e_1/\hat{e}_2 \qquad (4.13)$$

where e_1 is income elasticity of food derived function and $\hat{e}_2$ is compensated
price elasticity which is obtained by eliminating the income effect from the
uncompensated price elasticity, e_2.

Table 4.5
Series for Regression Equations (4.14) and (4.15)

Year	Food Demand, D per capita adult UK 1970, £	Food Demand, D per capita adult USA 1967, $	Income, Y per capita adult UK 1970, £	Income, Y per capita adult USA 1967, $	Relative food price, P UK 1970=100	Relative food price, P USA 1967=100
1954	121	504	481	2144	101	104
1955	123	511	498	2271	110	102
1956	130	483	501	2343	110	101
1957	131	480	509	2351	108	101
1958	131	469	521	2316	107	103
1959	134	471	541	2420	108	101
1960	136	533	559	2436	105	99
1961	137	525	568	2428	102	99
1962	137	529	575	2501	97	99
1963	137	527	597	2561	101	99
1964	138	535	613	2656	101	99
1965	136	554	617	2774	99	100
1966	138	557	628	2880	99	102
1967	138	555	638	2917	99	100
1968	137	560	650	3007	98	99
1969	135	551	652	3041	99	99
1970	134	560	667	3049	100	98
1971	132	558	682	3095	102	97
1972	128	588	718	3295	104	98
1973	126	572	742	3352	112	108
1974	125	552	738	3282	115	113
1975	121	371	731	3283	116	112
1976	118	590	731	3435	121	100

Sources: Kula (1984a, 1985).

In order to find the required elasticity parameters in equation (4.13) the food demand functions are specified as:

$$ln\ D = ln\ \beta + y\ ln\ Y + p\ ln\ P + tT \qquad (4.14)$$

for the United Kingdom and

$$ln\ D = ln\ \beta + y\ ln\ Y + p\ ln\ P \qquad (4.15)$$

for the United States. D is the adult equivalent of per capita food demand, Y is the real income measured in the same adult equivalent unit and P is the relative price of food in relation to nonfood. The series for regression equations (4.10) and (4.15) are shown in Table 4.5. The results are:

Country	y	p
United Kingdom	0.39	-0.54
United States	0.51	-0.37

Then, in order to estimate the pure elasticity, $\hat{p}$, the following procedure, supported by Stone (1954) and Fellner (1967) is employed:

$$\hat{p} = y - (b)(p) \tag{4.16}$$

where b is the share of food in consumer budget (a percentage). (4.16) is also the standard Slutsky equation expressed in terms of elasticities. The budget share of food, b, is 20 percent in the United Kingdom and the United States. Substituting these together with other estimates in equation (4.16) gives:

United Kingdom $\hat{p} = -0.47$
United States $\hat{p} = -0.27$

Then by using equation (4.16) we get:

Country	Elasticity of Marginal Utility of Consumption, e
United Kingdom	-0.70
United States	-1.83

Substituting these estimates as equation (4.10) we get:

Country	STPR, %
United Kingdom	3.6
United States	6.2

NOTES

1. The stance taken by the rule utilitarians is somewhat different, as they tend to accept rules of equity along with their principles and thus advocates of egalitarian ethics quarrel, most, with the act utilitarians.

2. Quasi–public sector projects are ones in which externalities are created for future generations which are not equal to zero and not equivalent to net benefits to decision-making generations.

3. It is a well-known fact that our thoughts are influenced by our cultural and religious positions. This line of argument, which assumes a first and last generation and many in between, each consisting of different individuals (that is, living a life is a once-and-for-all affair), fits in well with our current Western way of thinking. This view is not universally accepted, especially within Eastern cultures in which the Rawlsian problem of a first generation with one and only one life receiving nothing for its sacrifice would not have following. However, it is not my intention here to push the argument into those territories.

Part II

Application of Ordinary and Modified Discounting Methods to Real-Life Projects

Chapter 5

Economics of Nuclear
Waste Disposal

INTRODUCTION

Developing a safe and permanent method of isolating highly dangerous nuclear
wastes is unprecedented in human history. Never before has it been necessary
to devise methods to isolate from the biosphere highly toxic nuclear wastes
which will remain active for millions of years and could affect the health and
safety of future generations. Add to this the fact that serious research efforts to
develop long-term nuclear waste disposal technology have begun only in the
1970s. In the excitement created by the development of nuclear energy in the
1950s and the 1960s, there was little concern about the "mundane" issue of
waste isolation. One is struck with both the vastness of the task and how little
has been done so far, as millions of cubic feet of highly toxic material are being
kept in temporary storage. Some environmental pressure groups contend that
just as governments brought top scientific minds together to start the nuclear
age, they must do the same again to help to devise a safe way out (Ulrich 1990).

Currently, there seem to be two conflicting views on the disposal policy. One
group contends that, in view of the rapidly increasing inventory of wastes in
temporary storage, there is no alternative but to figure out, quickly, some means
of isolating them geologically. In 1980 the U.S. government announced that
resolving waste management problems shall not be deferred to future generations. This, in some people's opinion, has created an atmosphere of imprudent
haste (Murdock et al. 1983). The other view is that a far safer policy would be
to keep wastes above ground at their present sites so that they would be easily
retrieved as the scientific knowledge on disposal makes progress. However, the
nature of the problem here is that it is virtually impossible to estimate when
enough will be known to proceed to the final stage.

In addition to the waste disposal problems there are other hazardous issues with nuclear power. A breeder reactor both produces and consumes plutonium and thus this highly toxic material on occasion gets transported long distances even across countries. In the past, many nuclear scientists argued that the probability of a significant accident during transportation or at power stations was negligible. This view has been changed following accidents at Three Mile Island in the United States, and Chernobyl in the Ukraine. Furthermore, the prospects of sabotage in power stations and the possible theft of plutonium for terrorism make it clear that present generations, too, are exposed to substantial risks.

However, it would be misleading to look at nuclear energy in isolation by focusing on its shortcomings without considering the problems created by alternative sources of energy. Take fossil fuel, for instance. Problems created by the use of coal and oil are widespread, causing concern in developed as well as developing countries. Apart from the scarcity issue (Meadows et al. 1972), some serious environmental complications such as continuing buildup of carbon dioxide in the earth's atmosphere and acid rain have now become issues for public debate. Indeed, the effects of global warming, although dimly understood at present, could be catastrophic to world systems as we know them. Agriculture may be greatly disrupted, marine life may be affected by the changing climate and ocean levels might rise, flooding many coastal regions and cities. It is well documented that acid rain is damaging forests, freshwater fish stocks, crops, historic monuments, human health and even plumbing systems in buildings.

Of course, there are more environmentally agreeable sources of energy vis-à-vis those of nuclear power or fossil fuel, such as solar, tidal, wind and hydro power, but not all nations of the world are well endowed with these resources. For example, solar energy does not seem to be a viable alternative in the sun-starved northern countries of Europe. Apart from a few countries such as Norway, Sweden and Scotland, hydroelectricity does not look attractive in the mostly flat but densely industrialized and populated northern Europe. Likewise, tidal power is not an option in landlocked countries or areas around closed seas such as the Mediterranean and the Black Sea.

A BRIEF HISTORY OF NUCLEAR POWER

The history of nuclear technology is young, going back only to the end of the last century. In 1895, Roentgen's discovery of the x-ray and, one year later, Becquerel's identification of natural radiation marked the beginning of the nuclear venture. In 1939, Hahn and Strassman achieved the splitting of the uranium atom in Berlin which started fission technology. Three years later another breakthrough came at the University of Chicago where Fermi proved that a fission chain reaction in uranium nuclei could be sustained and controlled, making it feasible to harness this energy. From this, nuclear technology developed along two paths: production of nuclear bombs and reactor development for commercial purposes.

During the height of the Second World War, attempts to build nuclear bombs intensified in the United States at Oak Ridge, Tennessee, and Hanford, Washington. In July 1945 the world's first atomic bomb was exploded in New Mexico as an experiment; on the 6th of August the same year, the first nuclear bomb was dropped on Hiroshima.

Creation of military devices was the original reason for the development of fission technology, but at the same time the United States government wanted to use this technology for peaceful purposes. After the war a five-year nuclear power research program was launched which resulted in the creation of the United States' first nuclear power plant at Shippingport, Pennsylvania, which began operation in 1957. Canada, the United Kingdom, France and West Germany followed quickly by developing their own nuclear projects. By the end of 1988 there were 423 nuclear reactors in operation, and an additional 105 units under construction or consideration around the world, providing about 20 percent of the world's electricity supply (Traiforos et al. 1990). In some countries nuclear power constitutes the bulk of the power generation; in France, for instance, the share of nuclear power is about 70 percent.

However, the accidents at the Three Mile Island and Chernobyl plants and the inability of governments to find a satisfactory solution to the waste disposal problem were beginning to put the brakes on the global expansion of nuclear power. For example, following the accident at Three Mile Island, many nuclear power plants were cancelled in the United States, including completed units. Sweden decided to phase out nuclear power by the year 2010, even though nuclear power currently provides almost half of the country's electricity.

NUCLEAR WASTES

Large quantities of nuclear wastes have already been created. They stem from three distinct activities: research, creation of military devices, and power generation for commercial purposes. Nuclear wastes are classified into four major groups reflecting their origin and potential hazard.

High-Level Wastes. They are the by-product of nuclear reactors which arise from the reprocessing of spent fuel. These by-products are locked up in the spent fuel rods, which are removed from nuclear power reactors when they have been used until they can no longer efficiently contribute to the chain reaction. Spent fuel can be reprocessed to separate the high-level wastes from the remaining fissile and fissionable material in the rods. When spent fuel rods are reprocessed, a much smaller volume of high-level wastes will need to be transported and stored. Furthermore, reprocessing provides an efficient utilization of uranium, which is a scarce natural resource. On the other hand, since bomb-grade plutonium is produced during reprocessing, this increases the security requirement of the operation. Because of this problem, in 1977 the U.S. government banned commercial reprocessing, much to the dislike of the nuclear power industry. High-level wastes from reprocessing are initially watery products, which are characterized by their intense energy radiation, as energetic alpha, beta and gamma radiation are emitted.

Mid-Level Wastes. These are characterized by slow decay rates, as some species of wastes remain active for millions of years.

Low-Level Wastes. They contain a small amount of radioactivity dispersed in a large amount of material which includes items such as rags, papers, filters and resins from commercial, medical and university nuclear facilities. Low-level wastes do not require extensive shielding as they do not generate too much heat, but some protective shielding may be needed for handling. They pose a relatively low potential hazard to the environment and thus are, sometimes, disposed of by shallow land burial in containers.

Uranium Mill Tailings. They are leftovers from uranium mining and milling, consisting of large volumes of soil and rock that contain natural radioactivity. Tailings are not a major radiological hazard.

Nuclear wastes usually contain a higher-than-natural concentration of radioactive atoms found in nature. Most atoms in nature, which are the building blocks for all matter, are stable, which means that they retain their form forever. But some atoms are unstable, called radioactive, and change into different forms. During the changing process atoms release energy in the form of electromagnetic waves or fast-moving particles, producing ions in materials they strike. Ionizing radiation can disturb the biological function of living tissues.

There are three types of radiation:

Alpha Radiation. This consists of positively charged particles. They are the least penetrating and can be stopped by the outer layer of skin or a sheet of paper.

Beta Radiation. This can pass through an inch of human tissue. It can be stopped by a thin sheet of aluminium.

Gamma Radiation. This is extremely penetrating and thus wastes containing this type of radiation are handled by remote control mechanisms. Deep pools of water and dense material such as concrete and steel can provide shielding.

Both high-level and transuranic wastes require isolation from the biosphere. In the United States, about 9 percent of the waste inventory, by volume, is high-level, 6 percent mid-level, and the rest is low-level. In 1988 there were over 100 nuclear power plants operated by electrical utilities in the United States which generated 20 percent of the nation's electricity. Nearly all spent fuel is currently stored in deep steel-lined concrete pools filled with water inside buildings at the reactor sites. About 18,000 metric tons of spent fuel was in storage in 1988 and this volume is estimated to increase to 40,000 metric tons by the year 2000.

In the United Kingdom it was decided that responsibility for developing the strategy to deal with radioactive wastes should lie with the government department concerned with the protection of the environment, rather than with that responsible for developing and promoting nuclear power. In this respect the

Secretary of State for the Environment is in charge of the radioactive waste management policy. In the United States, under provision of the Nuclear Waste Policy Act of 1982 and the Nuclear Waste Policy Amendments Act of 1987, the U.S. Department of Energy is responsible for establishing a system for the disposal of highly toxic nuclear wastes.

DISPOSAL METHODS

Quite a number of solutions have been proposed for the disposal of highly radioactive nuclear wastes, some of which appear to be dubious.

Space Disposal. This method was proposed for long-living and solidified radionuclides put into special flight containers for ejection into space. Once wastes are sent into space their potential for environmental impact and human health effects is judged to be zero. This proposal has been looked at in the United States by the National Aeronautics and Space Administration (NASA) since the early 1970s. The general idea is that first a space shuttle would carry waste packages to a low-earth orbit; from there a transfer vehicle would separate from the shuttle and repulse the wastes into the outer wilderness.

At first glance, space disposal looks attractive. However, there are two very serious problems with it. First, a large number of trips into space would be prohibitively expensive. Second, and more important, the likelihood of launch pad accidents and low-earth orbit failures would make this "option" a non-starter. Indeed, an accident could contaminate large areas of the earth, affecting the populations of many countries.

Ice Disposal. Disposal of highly radioactive nuclear wastes into Antarctica or Greenland ice sheets was studied by a group of scientists in the early 1970s (Zeller et al. 1973). This concept offers a number of attractive points such as remoteness from human settlements, long-term isolation of waste canisters in ice and a relatively simple technology, which is already available. However, the Antarctic Treaty now prevents waste disposal in the Antarctic region but excludes Greenland. Disposal in ice in Greenland would require authorization by Denmark and the island's local government.

Ice disposal involves three concepts: meltdown, anchored emplacement and surface storage. In the first one, waste canisters placed in holes would be allowed to sink right to the bedrock at a daily rate of three to six feet. In this way a canister would reach the bedrock in six to ten years. Anchored emplacement limits the descent to a certain level by a cable which would allow retrievability up to 400 years. Eventually, new ice and snow will cover the anchorage facilities on the surface. Surface storage would also allow retrievability for several hundred years.

Like space disposal, ice disposal has a number of serious shortcomings. First, transportation and operation costs could be very high in extremely remote and hostile regions like the Greenland ice. Second, it was argued that ice sheets are subject to periodic surges on a scale of thousands of years (Department of

Energy 1979). During these surges large chunks of ice get disgorged into the ocean, which could defeat the objective. Furthermore, it was argued that water pools exist between the ice and bedrock (Lipschutz 1981). In the meltdown concept, when ice canisters eventually sink into a water pool, with surge-like behavior they may get ejected into the ocean. The change in global climate could also melt sheets of ice. Disposal of too many hot canisters in a small area could raise the ambient temperature of the ice sheet and cause widespread melting (ERDA 1976). Thus, a great deal of research is necessary before the potential of ice disposal is determined.

Ocean Disposal. There are some attractive features of this proposal, which is under study by scientists in the United States, Japan and some other countries. The seabed is remote from human activities; there are large areas available; the technology is not too expensive; and seabed disposal provides less intractable political difficulties than that of land disposal.

Three areas have been proposed as suitable for emplacement: subsediment bedrock, ocean trenches and deep ocean sediments. There is somewhat less enthusiasm for bedrock disposal than other alternatives. In the second method it was argued that since some ocean trenches plunge deep into the earth, waste canisters dropped there would be drawn into the earth's crust to be safely isolated. However, it was estimated that the crust would move only about 250 feet in 1,000 years, leaving the waste on the ocean floor during the most critical period (Department of Energy 1979; ERDA 1976).

The most attractive area on the ocean floor is red clay sediments in the center of subtectonic plates about two to three miles below the surface. Kerr (1979) argues that particles have been settling to the ocean floor evenly and without interruption for millions of years. Areas where red clay sediments are found are seismically and tectonically stable and appear to be suitable for the disposal of radioactive wastes other than transuranic ones.

Wastes can be placed into sediments in a number of ways. One suggestion is to use ballistic penetrometers containing waste canisters dropped from a ship. Alternatively, canisters could be placed into sedimental bore holes from the surface by cable, which offers the potential for retrievability. On the other hand, a number of problems remain unresolved. For example, hot canisters could induce high water diffusion velocities in the clay. If the canisters reach the sediment surface, small currents could carry them long distances across the ocean floor, which could create danger.

The 1972 London Convention forbade the dumping of high-level wastes in international waters. The agreement does not prevent the dumping of low-level wastes in territorial waters, nor does it address the controlled disposal of other types of wastes in such water. However, some believe that ocean disposal is a more realistic alternative to land disposal (Lipschutz 1981).

Land Disposal. There are a number of concepts involved in land disposal, some of which are as follows:

Shale Disposal. Shales are sedimentary rocks containing matter that can produce oil. They have low permeability and good sorption properties. Wastes mixed with cement and clay could be injected into fractured shale deposits and allowed to solidify at depths of over 1,000 feet. Shale disposal is not suitable for high volumes of wastes.

Deep Injection Method. The idea is that watery wastes would be injected into porous or fractured strata at depths of 4,000–16,000 feet. Wastes in fluid form are expected to disperse and diffuse gradually. At this point in time not enough is known about the mobility of the wastes throughout the host strata.

Deep Hole Placement. In this, solidified wastes would be placed in holes up to 30,000 feet deep. Apart from incomplete knowledge about the earth's crust at that level, this method would be expensive and thus it is not suitable for large quantities of material.

Salt Disposal. Given the fact that salt is highly soluble in water, the existence of thick salt deposits underground implies that the area has not been in contact with circulating ground water for a very long period of time. The main problem with geological disposal is that of contact with ground water which may introduce wastes into the human environment. Also, salt fractures are self-healing, which ensures that entry holes would close soon after canister emplacement. More will be said later about this method, as the case study is based upon this concept.

Tuff Disposal. Tuff layers are volcanic rocks which are attractive for high-level waste disposal because of their sorptive qualities and strength. In 1983 the U.S. Department of Energy selected nine different locations for consideration as potential disposal sites. After studying these sites in 1985, then-President Ronald Reagan selected three sites for intensive scientific scrutiny, site characterization. The selected sites were Hanford (basalt rock), Washington; Deaf Smith County (bedded salt), Texas; and Yucca Mountain (tuff), Nevada. At the end of 1987 the U.S. Congress amended the Nuclear Waste Policy Act and directed the Department of Energy to study the Yucca Mountain site with a view to making it a permanent repository for high-level wastes.

Yucca Mountain is made up of layers of tuff created in a volcanic eruption eleven million years ago. At the time, large quantities of gases were released into the air and then fell to the earth in the form of ash. Still hot, this ash welded together and became compressed by its own weight and eventually became 6,000 feet thick.

Currently, Yucca Mountain is under study for a period of ten years by scientists who are focusing on: level and movement of the water in the area; the effects of volcanic activity and earthquake in the region; and environmental issues including socioeconomic matters. However, the U.S. government's decision has been criticized by many Nevadans on the grounds that the decision to select Yucca Mountain was unfair and improper.

Do Nothing Yet. This would mean keeping spent fuel and reprocessed wastes at sites where they are generated. In other words, this is a temporary measure to hold on to wastes until a lasting solution is identified. One appealing aspect of this policy is retrievability, as wastes would be kept in surface facilities. In 1991 the British government announced that transuranic wastes will be kept at Sellafield nuclear installation for the foreseeable future.

COST OF THE UNITED STATES' FIRST NUCLEAR WASTE REPOSITORY

The Waste Isolation Pilot Plant, WIPP, the United States' first federal nuclear repository, is in Los Medenos, in southeastern New Mexico, 25 miles east of the city of Carlsbad. The WIPP is a scheme run by the U.S. Department of Energy aimed at permanent storage of mid-level wastes generated by the nuclear weapons industry. The repository has been designed to dispose of approximately 185,000 cubic meters of wastes. The construction phase of this plant is now complete.

A 1979 Public Law (PL 96–164) exempted the WIPP from licensing by the Nuclear Regulatory Commission. The Department of Energy must, however, demonstrate compliance with the standards established by the Environmental Protection Agency to make sure that the long-term integrity of the waste in the repository is not in doubt.

The Department of Energy's interest in New Mexico's salt beds began in the early 1970s following the abandonment of the proposed repository site in Lyons, Kansas. The U.S. Geological Survey and the Oak Ridge National Laboratory recommended the Carlsbad area because of its well-known geological structure, due to extensive potash mining activities there. In effect, it was the collapse of the potash industry in the 1970s and the resulting unemployment which gave rise to the region's invitation to the Department of Energy to consider the salt beds as a potential repository.

The attractiveness of the Los Medenos site is that of dryness. The main body of the WIPP is about 2,000 feet underground in the lower part of a thick Permian age salt formation, about 225 million years old. Locations at this depth are likely to remain unaffected by surface erosion provided that there is no human intrusion, especially anything aimed at discovery of natural resources.

About one-third of wastes intended for the New Mexico site have been temporarily stored at the Department of Energy's weapon laboratories, awaiting transfer. The end of the cold war has increased the urgency of this project due to rapidly increasing inventory of wastes resulting from the dismantling of weapons. At the time of writing, the Department of Energy was planning experiments with a small quantity of waste for operational demonstrations. If everything works well, toward the end of this decade large quantities of wastes will be transported to the site.

The sealing of the WIPP is likely to take place around the year 2025, provided that operational experiments and placing containers into salt chambers turn out to be successful. Intended wastes, which are mixed with toxic chemicals, generate gases, plus the fact that there are reservoirs of brine and hydrogen sulphate gas under the site which could penetrate the repository through cracks. However, many experts believe that, on the whole, tests and other operations are likely to be successful even though a few problems are bound to crop up from time to time.

Table 5.1
Operating and Capital Cost of the WIPP, 1975–1991, in Terms of 1991 Prices

Year	Cost, $ Million, Construction	1991 Prices Operating	Total
1975	-	1.2	1.2
1976	-	12.8	12.8
1977	13.4	14.7	28.1
1978	45.1	22.5	67.6
1979	35.0	29.9	64.9
1980	39.9	55.5	95.4
1981	10.5	13.0	23.5
1982	26.7	37.3	64.0
1983	68.9	81.4	150.3
1984	30.6	46.4	77.0
1985	23.2	52.7	75.9
1986	89.9	59.7	149.6
1987	3.6	7.9	11.5
1988	69.7	45.7	115.4
1989	0.9	-	0.9
1990	23.4	-	23.4
1991	17.3	0.4	17.7
Total	498.1	481.1	979.2

Sources: U.S. Congress and Senate Committee on Appropriations, Energy and Water Development Bill, various volumes (Washington, DC: U.S. Government Printing Office); Project Managers Progress Report for the WIPP, U.S. Department of Energy, Albuquerque Operations, New Mexico.

COSTS SO FAR

The major cost items thus far are: construction, operating, improving the transport network and foregone benefits in exploitation of mineral resources such as potash and hydrocarbons in the repository area. Table 5.1 shows the construction and operating costs between 1975 and 1991 in terms of 1991 prices.

The safe transportation of nuclear wastes is essential for the protection of the public and the environment. The U.S. Department of Transport regulates all aspects of radioactive waste shipments, including packaging, labelling, handling, loading, unloading and routing. The Nuclear Regulatory Commission, on the other hand, tests standards for design and performance of waste containers. In order to be verified, a container must be able to withstand tests that measure its performance in severe accident conditions. Regulations regarding containers and transportation are constantly updated as new information is gained from research.

Increasing volumes of hazardous materials, including radioactive wastes, are

Table 5.2
Expenditure on Roads in Relation to WIPP, 1991 Prices (millions of dollars)

Years	1984	1985	1986	1987	1988	1989	1990	1991-2021
Million	8	21	20	17	6	16	15	300

shipped annually in the United States. In 1981 the state of New Mexico entered into an agreement with the Department of Energy for road upgrading and repair. During the 1984 financial year, eight projects for preliminary engineering were authorized and funds were created for use by the State of New Mexico Highway Department. Table 5.2 shows the expenditure levels since then in terms of 1991 prices.

Large-scale transportation is expected to begin around the turn of the century. The main collection points are expected to be: Argonne National Laboratory, Illinois; Oak Ridge National Laboratory, Tennessee; Mound, Ohio; Savannah River Site, South Carolina; Los Alamos National Laboratory, New Mexico; Rocky Flats Plant, Colorado; Idaho National Engineering Laboratory, Idaho; Hanford Site, Washington; Nevada Test Site, Nevada; and Lawrence Livermore National Laboratory, California. In addition to what has been spent on road improvement up to 1991, the Department of Energy earmarked a further $300 million for upgrading the transport infrastructure over the next 30 years (this figure is likely to change in future years as the disposal scheme gets underway). Some proposed legislation aims to double this sum.

Foreclosure of other development options such as exploitation of natural resources in the area is another cost item. As was mentioned before, the repository is situated in the United States' most extensive potash mining district. There are two types of potash deposits: langbenite and white sylvite, which is the raw material for muriate. In the absence of the WIPP these resources would likely be developed to benefit the local as well as the national economy. It was estimated by Cummings et al. (1981) that commercial exploitation of these resources would last about 23 years for langbenite and 13 years for muriate, generating an income (undiscounted) of about $2.5 billion for the region, in terms of 1991 prices.

Hydrocarbon deposits in the form of natural gas, oil and distillate exist five miles northeast of the WIPP. A reserve estimate reveals a foregone income of about $0.5 billion in terms of 1991 prices (Cummings et al. 1981).

In addition to mineable resources the WIPP will restrict grazing activities in the region. However, Cummings et al. (1981) estimate that loss of income in this way is rather small. Another possible repercussion from the presence of the WIPP is the potential for lost tourism in the region. There are three main tourist attractions in the area: Carlsbad Caverns, Guadalupe Mountains National Parks and the Living Desert State Park. However, there seems to be no conclusive evidence to suggest that the numbers of visitors to the area would decline significantly. Some even suggest that WIPP could become a tourist attraction as the first nuclear waste repository in the United States.

TIMESCALE FOR FUTURE COSTS

For the purpose of economic analysis identification of the WIPP's effective life is a rather complicated exercise. Some species of wastes in the repository will remain active for millions of years. For example, iodine-129, one of the longest-living species, has a half-life of 17 million years. Should the timescale for economic analysis be chosen on the basis of the longest-living species or should there be some other criteria? Economic theory recommends that all the expected incidents likely to affect society over time should be considered in cost-benefit analysis (Mishan 1972; Dasgupta and Pearce 1972). Then a strict application of the theory would link the life of this project to the longest-living waste species, a lifespan beyond the imagination of economists or any group of social scientists.

In this analysis three cut-off periods—10,000 years, 25,000 years and 1,000,000 years—are proposed with the following rationale. The U.S. Environmental Protection Agency (1985) recommends that a nuclear waste repository must be demonstrated capable of isolating radionuclides from the environment for at least 10,000 years. In this there must be reasonable assurances not only that future geological and hydrological changes at the site will not result in a leakage but also the construction and operation of the repository must meet the highest standards of safety. However, Malone (1990) argues that a number of factors could affect the repository's performance even during this period. Changes in precipitation, erosion and infiltration of water could affect the performance of the natural barriers and influence the movement of radionuclides. Deformation of the earth's crust, tectonic folding and volcanism could also compromise the integrity of the engineered barrier.

One important objection to the timescale suggested by the U.S. government is that 10,000 years do not consider the changing nature of the waste over a sufficiently long time period (Kirchner 1990). Based upon analysis, including isotopic composition of the waste, cycling in biosphere, probability of transport to human settlements and radio toxicity to humans, Kirchner shows that nuclear wastes involve risks over a period at least double the 10,000 years. In this regard an additional timescale, 25,000 years, which coincides with the half-life of one of the most toxic species, plutonium-239, is used.

Some studies by multidisciplinary teams of researchers comprising economists, sociologists, and medical and nuclear scientists provide data for the future health detriments of the WIPP for a much longer time period, 1,000,000 years, which is the basis for the third cut-off period. In Britain, NIREX, the nuclear industry's waste disposal company, takes a 1 million years' cut-off point in their calculations.

FUTURE HEALTH COST

The most sensitive aspect of the WIPP is that it may impose serious health risks on future generations. If nuclear wastes leak from the repository they could remain to poison future generations.

Findings in this section stem from the work of Logan et al. (1978), who consider two broad classes of health risks from exposure: total cancer including leukemia, stomach, lung, bone and breast, and genetic deformities. Their analyses are based upon the BEIR Report (1972), which is the most accepted source of information on health and the effects from radiation exposure in which the number of deaths per year by cancer, from a hypothetical increase in continuous exposure of 0.1 rem[1] to the United States population is estimated. The report also contains estimates for genetic effects, including chromosomal and recessive diseases, congenital abnormalities and regenerative problems.

According to the BEIR Report a continuous exposure of 0.1 rem per year by the current 254 million population would create an average excess death of about 5,100 for all cancers. Calculation of the excess deaths associated with genetic damage encounters greater uncertainty than that of cancer, as it depends on the mean age of reproduction as well as exposure rate. However, analysis by Logan et al. (1978) leads to a figure for annual excess death of about 5,050 for 254 million population.

The region within a radius of about 150 km from the repository in New Mexico and Texas is considered for the health effects with the assumption that most of any release of material would be dispersed within this area. In order to provide a realistic dispersal, which requires nonuniform spread, the area is divided into seven population zones. The entire area is assumed to have a long-term population of 1.88 million, engaged mainly in agricultural pursuits.

The methodology for calculating excess cancer deaths using the BEIR results can be illustrated by using the following formulation.

$$
N_K
\begin{bmatrix}
M_{1,1,k} & \cdots\cdots & M_{1,7,k} \\
\cdot & & \\
\cdot & & \\
\cdot & & \\
M_{25,1,k} & \cdots\cdots & M_{25,7,k}
\end{bmatrix}
\begin{bmatrix}
D_1 \\ \cdot \\ \cdot \\ \cdot \\ D_7
\end{bmatrix}
=
\begin{bmatrix}
TD_{1,k} \\ \cdot \\ \cdot \\ \cdot \\ TD_{25,k}
\end{bmatrix}
$$

where:

M_k = a matrix of doses M (i,j,k) for the kth zone in millirems per person in the tth time period, for the ith nuclide (there are 25 radionuclides) impacting the jth body organ (there are 7).

D = a vector of increased deaths per 0.1 rem of per million population.

N_k = population in the kth zone in time period t.

TD_k = a vector representing deaths associated with the dose from each nuclide in the kth zone in time t.

Genetic risk presents a special problem in that the equilibrium level of genetic damage may not be reached until 900 years after an increase in the continuous exposure level (BEIR Report 1972). Logan et al. (1978) assume that a serious genetic effect may be equated to a death for damage evaluation purposes. That is, genetic effects are handled in the same manner as cancer deaths.

Logan et al. (1978), Cummings et al. (1981) and Schulze et al. (1981) envisage some repository disruptions that could result in a release from the disposal site, either directly to surface or to surrounding groundwater. These are: a severe earthquake, volcanic action and meteorite impact. The first incident could lead to reactivation of old faults around the repository or even create new ones in the region, bringing wastes into contact with circulating groundwater, the major hazard in the geological disposal of nuclear wastes. In order to assign a probability to earthquake damage Logan et al. (1978) study tremors within $10,000km^2$ around the repository from 1964 to 1976 and identify 12 serious cases. Given the geological structure in the region, the probability of a repository fracture is estimated to be $1.4/10^7$ per year.

The risk of volcanic action which may affect the repository is estimated to be $8.1/10^{13}$ per year, a figure based upon observations that an average of one new volcano every 20 years has occurred during the last 225 years, and by using a random probability from the WIPP site relative to the total area of the earth. As for the third risk, meteorite impact, a figure of $1/10^{13}$ per year is obtained based upon the same logic as volcanism. Note that likelihoods of meteorite impact and volcanism are extremely small.

On the basis of these probabilities, the total health effects are calculated by using Logan et al. (1978) (shown in Figure 5.1), which represents average rates of deaths per year over segments of repository lifetime considered. The increasing rate of mortality in later years is due to breakthrough of neptunium in groundwater. The rate subsequently levels out as the neptunium contribution peaks around year 10^6. Different cut-off periods used in this analysis yield different death rates which are:

Cut-off Period, Years	Average Annual Excess Death Rates from Cancer and Genetic Illness
10,000	0.0002
25,000	0.0024
1,000,000	0.0048

The next step is to assign monetary values to the increased health risk for which compensation variation is used. This considers the amount of compensation required to induce individuals to accept a situation where the probability of death is increased. The main problem with this method is that as the proba-

Figure 5.1
Average Death Rates from All Cancers and Genetic Effects for the Study Region around WIPP

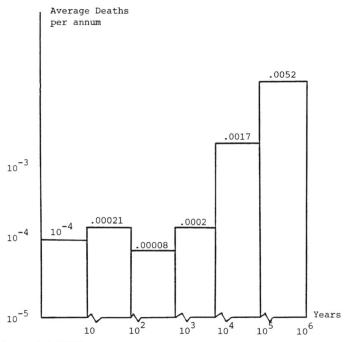

Source: Logan et al. (1978)

bility of death approaches unity, the compensation would approach infinity. However, this method is extremely useful in cases where the probability of death is increased only slightly, which is appropriate in this case (Cummings et al. 1981).

Thaler and Rosen (1976) study the U.S. labor market to identify cases in which individuals may accept a small increase in risk to life in return for higher earnings. In this a wage-risk analysis is conducted to ascertain how much individuals would require in additional income if they were to, voluntarily, accept jobs involving a marginal increase in risk of death. In order to estimate wage levels as a function of risk, Thaler and Rosen consider the existence of a job market for safety with the implication that job-associated risks and wage rates are positively correlated. Their research reveals that in the U.S. labor market, jobs with an extra risk of 0.001 paid between $176 and $260 extra per annum in 1967. Logan et al. (1978) note that these figures underestimate the value of risk to life as Thaler and Rosen's data base includes an exceptionally high-risk set of job classification which may attract fewer risk-averse individuals. In the event, they express a preference for the high figure, that is, each person would be willing to work for $260, in 1967 prices, per year less if the extra death probability were reduced from 0.001 to 0.0. By using OECD's labor statistics we can update the annual value to risk to life to $1,264 in terms of 1991 prices.

Since the community is prepared to pay, in 1991 prices, $1,264 to reduce the risk of death by 0.001, then the average annual payment for three different cut-off periods would be:

Cut-off Period, Years	Average Annual Payment for Risk Reduction on the Basis of Above-Mentioned Probabilities, $
10,000	2,528
25,000	3,034
1,000,000	6,067

Given these figures, the total undiscounted health cost over three cut-off periods becomes:

Cut-off Period	Total Health Cost, Million $
10,000	25.3
25,000	75.9
1,000,000	6,067.0

MONITORING COST

At the early stages of the "nuclear age" a good deal of scientists contended that once toxic wastes are safely isolated geologically there may not be a need for monitoring. Furthermore, timescales that are involved in nuclear waste disposal are so long that they dwarf the span of recorded history. No human society has remained in existence for periods anything like the timescales involved here. However, today most believe that it would be exceedingly irresponsible behavior to bury wastes into the ground and forget about the whole thing. As long as our societies remain intact we must monitor nuclear waste disposal sites with the utmost diligence (Weinberg 1972).

One proposed solution is the construction of large and durable mausolea, something like the Egyptian pyramids, to attract the attention of communities to the disposal site. However, experience with such structures indicates that they are unlikely to remain intact for significant periods of time (Lipschutz 1981).

Apart from natural hazards, there is the possibility of human intrusion in the form of search for natural resources; this is particularly relevant here as the WIPP is located in a mineral rich area. In the absence of monitoring, Channell et al. (1990) estimate an intrusion rate amounting to three boreholes per square kilometer per 1,000 years on the basis of historic records for the WIPP area. Drilling in the area could create serious problems undermining the safety of the repository. For example, a borehole into the repository could impact several interconnected salt chambers and bring wastes into contact with brine reservoirs under the repository. Some of these reservoirs contain several million cubic meters of brine and sufficient pressure to flow to the surface. Furthermore, intended wastes are expected to produce large quantities of gas from organic decomposition, anoxic corrosion of metals and radiolysis.

Channell et al. (1990) report on a number of cases of human indifference concerning sites where nuclear incidents took place. For example, the Gnome site, located 13 kilometers southwest of the WIPP, was the location of underground nuclear detonation in 1962. Since then the site has been cleaned up, although measurable radioactivity still exists at the surface. Following the experiment a monument was erected, but the access to the site was not restricted. Over the years the monument has degraded and there is little awareness by the residents of this event which occurred less than 30 years ago. A recent study by the Bureau of Land Management, which includes the WIPP area, found that there is widespread noncompliance by private industry with the government regulations to plug abandoned holes, or that it has been done improperly. In October 1990 it was rediscovered that a gas well located just outside the WIPP site had been slant drilled under the site in 1983. Gas had been produced from it between 1983 and 1988; the lease is still active. The Department of Energy had signed an agreement with the state of New Mexico in 1987 prohibiting slant drilling under the area. Neither the Department of Energy nor the Bureau of Land Management apparently remembered that the well existed during the period between 1987 and 1990; but when a newspaper reporter received information from an anonymous source, the event then became public knowledge. This incident suggests that drilling in a remote area in the future without the knowledge of the regulatory agencies is possible (Channell et al. 1990).

At the WIPP site only the operational experiments are imminent; sealing of the repository and monitoring are some distance away, beyond the year 2025. Many believe that as the time approaches toward the sealing operation there is likely to be a stringent regulation introduced for monitoring, which may even require more than one authority. Since the procedure to watch over the site is unknown at this point in time, it is difficult to identify the cost of this exercise. The State of New Mexico Environmental Evaluation Group, an independent technical appraisal body for the WIPP, guestimates that the annual cost of monitoring should be $1–2 million (1991 prices) provided that no extraordinary event such as a determined threat of sabotage takes place. In this section $1.5 million is used as an estimate for the annual monitoring cost. Then total costs for the three cut-off periods become:

Cut-off Period	Total Monitoring Cost, Million $
10,000	15,000
25,000	37,500
1,000,000	1,500,000

Table 5.3
Discounted and Undiscounted Future Monitoring and Health Costs for WIPP

Cut-off Periods Year 2025-	Undiscounted Costs $		Discounted Costs $ at 5% Discount Rate Ordinary Discounting		Modified Discounting	
	Health	Monitoring	Health	Monitoring	Health	Monitoring
10^4	2538×10^4	15×10^9	9300	57×10^5	6826×10^3	4037×10^6
25×10^3	7585×10^4	37.5×10^9	9400	57×10^5	171×10^5	10125×10^6
10^6	6067×10^6	15×10^{11}	9940	57×10^5	683×10^6	405×10^9

DISCOUNTED VALUE OF FUTURE COSTS

The discounted values for future costs, by using the ordinary criterion, can be obtained by using:

$$NDV = \int_{o}^{n} C_t e^{-st} dt$$

where:

NDV = net discounted value to base year 1991
n = cut-off period
C_t = estimated annual costs *from 2025 onward*
s = social rate of discount
t = time, years

Health and monitoring costs are assumed to fall upon society after the sealing of the repository in the year 2025. No allowance is made for risks during transportation or for possible accidents during placing containers into salt chambers. Furthermore, occurrence of ice ages during the life of the repository is not taken into consideration. In other words, the risk scenarios used in this analysis are based upon the most optimistic assumptions.

A recent estimate of a social time discount rate for the United States yields a figure of 5.3 percent (Kula 1984a). By using 5 percent as a very close approximation the ordinary discounting method yields the results seen in Table 5.3.

It is clear that ordinary discounting at a 5 percent interest rate practically wipes out all future costs of the WIPP repository. For example, on the basis of a one-million-year cut-off period, an aggregate health cost of $6,067,000,000 is reduced to $9,940.

Now let us use the modified discounting method with the same discount rate on the same cost stream. The last two columns of Table 5.3 show the results which can readily be compared with figures obtained by way of the ordinary criterion. In this respect discounted health cost, over one million years, becomes $683,000,000 as opposed to $9,940 in the ordinary method.[2]

From an economic angle one of the most interesting aspects of the WIPP is that it makes abundantly clear the devastating effect of ordinary discounting on future costs. By realizing the unacceptable consequences of ordinary discounting on distant costs created by nuclear projects, some writers such as Logan et al. (1978), Cummings et al. (1981) and Burness et al. (1983) recommended further study on the discounting philosophy, especially for cases concerning future generations.

There is a body of opinion, mostly outside the economics profession, that in the social decision-making process economic criteria should not play a decisive role. For example, an OECD committee (OECD 1980) contends that established and widely used economic principles are totally useless in dealing with nuclear waste storage projects. After studying radiation exposures the committee decided not to discount future health detriments attributable to long-lasting radionuclides while noting that the difference between zero and even a very modest discount rate can be enormous.

The WIPP was created to dispose of the United States' defense wastes. In a vastly political issue like defense there may be some grounds to disregard economic criteria, although some may question this by pointing out that there are economic consequences to any political decision. However, when wastes are generated for commercial purposes such as power generation it would be hard to dismiss economics as irrelevant in assessing the whole value of the project. A good proportion of the waste inventory in the United States stems from commercial activities. No matter how high future costs of nuclear projects may be (e.g., decommissioning power plants, monitoring wastes and health detriments), ordinary discounting makes a nuclear energy program look economically attractive. Modified discounting, on the other hand, makes nuclear projects economically less desirable.

The initial construction of the WIPP began in 1983 and the main structure was completed within the first five-year period. The Department of Energy had plans to start shipping waste to the repository in October 1988; as the deadline approached it became clear that the department had not completed all the necessary preparations to start the activity. In late 1992 the operation was still postponed. When completed the WIPP will consist of 8 panels and 7 rooms in each panel designed to be 91.5 meters long, 10 meters wide and 4 meters high. The bulk of the wastes would be emplaced in 55-gallon drums stacked 3 high in the rooms.

The long-term stability of the repository and the compliance with the Environmental Protection Agency standards will be documented by the Department of Energy. However, the Department must first experiment with wastes, which is likely to take at least five years to demonstrate safe disposal. Only after that will it be determined whether the site can become a permanent repository. Many believe that experiments will be successful on the whole and the WIPP will become the United States of America's first nuclear repository.

Finally, it is quite possible that figures used in this project are underestimates. There is a growing body of scientists who contend that health detriments calculated in BEIR reports, which are the basis for health cost study here, do not help us to understand the full impact of radiation on human health. Radiation levels less than 0.1 rem could cause a greater number of cancers and genetic deformities than those used in this study. Furthermore, it has been suggested by Dillingham (1985), Moore and Viscusi (1988) and Fisher et al. (1989) that Thaler and Rosen's figures to value human life are inadequate. For example, Dillingham implies at least two-fold whereas Moore and Viscusi's four-time increase in the figures is used by Thaler and Rosen.

With the use of ordinary discounting the economic analysis yields favorable results for nuclear power projects. This is because such analysis practically ignores the long-term when the real costs appear. A nuclear power plant is highly capital-intensive but after its construction it yields a steady stream of benefits until its closure in, say, 30 years' time. After that high costs occur in the form of decommissioning, transporting, storing and monitoring of nuclear wastes. Such costs do not bear heavily on the net present value or internal rate of return figures. Special interest groups armed with, say, high internal rate of return figures can present a ''strong'' case to decision-makers for the expansion of the nuclear industry. From a communal viewpoint the net present value or the internal rate of return conceal a lot of facts including the assumption that individuals live forever.

NOTES

1. A rem (roentgen equivalent man) is a measure of dose of radiation and its effects on human tissue. Sometimes doses of radiation received by people are measured in units called millirems. One millirem equals one-thousandth of a rem. The U.S. Department of Energy estimates that in the country the average person receives an effective dose of about 1 millirem per day, mostly from natural causes (DOE, *Managing the Nation's Nuclear Waste, Fact Sheet Series*, 1990, Washington DC).

2. Discount factors for the United States by way of the modified method are assumed to be similar to those in Appendix 2.

Chapter 6

Cost-Benefit Analysis of Afforestation in the United Kingdom

INTRODUCTION

Afforestation differs from many other investment projects in the sense that time intervals between establishment costs and benefits are unusually long for many species of trees. In most parts of the United Kingdom the average gestation period for softwood species such as Sitka spruce, Lodgepole and Scots pines is over 40 years. Hardwood trees such as oak, beech, ash, and so on require even longer periods (over 100 years) to reach commercially desirable maturity. Gestation periods for these species are even longer in continental Europe and in most parts of North America.

These long periods make it obvious that afforestation redistributes income between generations. When felling takes place now, the present generations reap the benefits of a plantation which was established by earlier generations a long time ago. When we plant trees now, the benefits that will arise from them will be captured, in the main, by future generations.

Separation of costs and benefits by long time intervals makes discounting a crucial parameter in the economic evaluation of forestry projects. Other important factors are: the future price of timber, the opportunity cost of land used to grow trees and, sometimes, valuation of environmental attributes of forestry. In the United Kingdom most afforestation projects are located on marginal land where rents are relatively low. In this chapter, after a brief historic review, a cost-benefit analysis will be carried out by using ordinary and modified discounting methods on a forestry project in the United Kingdom.

HISTORIC PERSPECTIVE

Toward the end of the Middle Ages, the British Isles were clothed with thick forests. The southern parts were largely covered with broad-leaved trees, whereas the northern parts contained a mixture of pine and birch. Today these islands are one of the least forested regions of Europe. There were a number of reasons for the destruction of forests in the British Isles. First, most of the trees located on fertile soils had to be cleared to make room for agricultural expansion to support the growing population. Second, clearance also took place for the purpose of providing fuel for the iron smelting industry, which was booming in the sixteenth and seventeenth centuries. This was so extensive that at the end of the seventeenth century, turf firing had to be introduced in many areas in place of wood. Around this period a traveller to Scotland wrote that "a tree in here is rare as a horse in Venice" (Thompson 1971). Third, the rise of Britain as a major industrial and naval power took its toll on forests. The industrialization process was based entirely on a single fuel, coal. Timber has always been a major input used as pit props in the coal mining industry. An expansion of this industry meant a decline of forests. Also, in the past, timber was widely used in the shipbuilding industry. However, the building of the first iron ship for the Royal Navy in 1860 signified an end to the shipbuilding industry's insatiable demand for oak. Fourth, destruction also took place for military purposes, especially in Ireland. During the colonial struggle settlers cleared the strategic locations of trees because they were providing cover for the local resistance groups. This was particularly extensive in Ulster.

Toward the end of the eighteenth century a revival of forestry took place in many parts of the British Isles. At the time the British aristocracy realized that woodlands were a desirable source of wealth and amenity which led to extensive plantation for commercial as well as for ornamental reasons. Forests in private estates were retained generation after generation for reasons of sentiment and prestige. Selling trees was usually an indication of the decline of the family. The decline of private forests began around the middle of the nineteenth century, a time when landlords, for various reasons, were in financial difficulties. Travelling mills moved into many estates to clear the land of trees. At the turn of this century the destruction was complete and one-time forest-rich islands became more or less treeless. Tree coverage of the total land surface was about 2 percent in places such as Ireland and Scotland.

The year 1903 was an important one for British forestry, as a forestry branch of the Department of Agriculture was established for the purpose of training young men as practical foresters. At first the department bought land in various parts of Ireland in order to establish forestry centers. Progress was slow to start with but it gathered pace in later years. Unfortunately, the First World War put a stop to the expansion of forestry projects. During the war Britain suffered a severe shortage of timber. The German submarine campaign reduced imports to practically nothing and domestic sources were nearly exhausted. After the war the Prime Minister, Lloyd George, admitted that Britain was nearer to losing the war from lack of timber than lack of food.

In 1917 a committee called the Acland Committee was appointed to examine the implication of inadequate supplies of homegrown timber. It recommended establishing a forestry authority to remedy the timber deficiency. On the basis of this recommendation, in 1918 the Forestry Commission was established and, in the 1920s, large-scale plantation of trees took place in many parts of the British Isles. In later years a strong anti-forestry lobby convinced the government that the state forestry was not a profitable investment and as a result many millions of young trees were destroyed. Then came the Second World War, which reminded the government of the reason why the Forestry Commission was established in the first place. After the war, further and quite extensive plantations were created in many parts of the Kingdom, and forests in general have enjoyed a period of growth under the protective policies of postwar governments.

The publication of a 1967 white paper "Nationalised Industries: A Review of Economic and Financial Objectives" (Cmnd 3437) somehow undermined the economic viability of afforestation projects in the United Kingdom. As explained in Chapter 2, this white paper suggested the use of an 8 percent test rate of discount by nationalized industries and two years later this was increased to 10 percent.

A number of forestry economists such as Price (1972, 1976) and Helliwell (1974, 1975) emphasized that the test rate of discount had ended the hopes of an economic rationale for afforestation in the United Kingdom. Indeed, research by Walker (1958), Land Use Study Group (1966), Thompson (1971) and Hampson (1972) concluded that by and large it was not possible to earn more than a 2–3 percent rate of return from afforestation projects without subsidies.

The publication of the 1978 white paper "Nationalised Industries" (Cmnd 7131) and recommendation of a 5 percent discount rate, the required rate of return, were not much comfort to the proforestry lobby. Figures revealed by the Forestry Commission in 1977 showed an expected rate of return of about 2–2.5 percent on 60 percent of the Commission's acquisitions in Britain (Forestry Commission 1977a).

The forestry lobby contends that in forestry rate of return calculations the increasing value of land over time is not normally taken into account. This understates profitability. Likewise, the future price of timber as opposed to current prices should be used in appraisal. Indeed, there is historic evidence that the price of timber has been rising in the long run (Potter and Christy 1962; Barnett and Morse 1963; Hiley 1967). Furthermore, recreational and environmental benefits from afforestation must be incorporated into social profitability calculations. Assumptions must be made about the expected visits to plantations by the general public as trees grow mature and become more attractive, about wildlife and water conservation, and so on. In this respect an interdepartmental government study carried out research on British forestry to ascertain social profitability. The group considered environmental landscape and recreational spillovers alongside timber output, plus a 20 percent premium for import saving. Inclusion of all these factors increased the profitability to 4 percent, still below the 5 percent required rate of return (HMSO 1972a).

In 1989 the British government increased the rate of discount from 5 percent to 8 percent in real terms for nationalized industries and public sector trading bodies. For the nontrading sector 6 percent was recommended as suitable. The rationale for the increase in the official social rate of discount was that in the decade to 1988 the rate of return in the private sector has risen to 11 percent and thus the public sector bodies should improve their performance in line with private companies (Chapter 2).

Although forestry is, essentially, a trading sector, the forestry authorities in the United Kingdom are allowed to use rates well below those recommended for their counterparts. The justification for these low rates are: unquantifiable benefits of maintaining rural life, improving the beauty of the landscape and wildlife conservation.

At present, forestry policy in the United Kingdom is influenced by a number of factors. First, there is a need, demonstrated by two world wars, to reverse the process of deforestation and create sufficient domestic timber resources. Second, given the fact that dairy, meat and cereal sectors are overexpanded in the United Kingdom, and in some other northern countries of the European Community, there is a compelling need to take land out of agriculture in favor of forestry. The European Union is the largest importer of timber in the world and the United Kingdom is the largest wood importing nation in Europe. Third, afforestation projects create employment opportunities for rural communities. In effect, the employment creation aspect of forestry in remote regions was strongly emphasized during the time when the Forestry Commission was established. Finally, the British government believes that the private sector should be encouraged to participate in the expansion of forestry. For this purpose it allocates public money in the form of planting grants and tax exemptions to private planters.

Today, the Forestry Commission is the largest landowner in Great Britain, as it manages over 1.5 million hectares of land. The main duties of the Commission are: buying land, planting trees, harvesting and selling timber, helping private forestry companies by giving technical advice and cash grants, establishing forestry recreation centers and doing research. In Northern Ireland the Department of Agriculture's Forest Service is in charge of forestry policy. This is a separate body from the Forestry Commission, but has similar powers and duties to it.

In spite of over 70 years' effort by the authorities, forestry in the United Kingdom is still an infant venture. The tree coverage in Scotland is about 12 percent; in England and Wales it is about 8 percent. In Northern Ireland, however, only 6 percent of the land is under trees. Compare these figures with those for some other European countries: France, Italy and Belgium, about 20 percent; Poland and Switzerland, over 25 percent; Portugal, Germany and Norway, over 30 percent; Austria, nearly 40 percent; Sweden 56, percent; and Finland, a colossal 72 percent.

GROUND RULES FOR THE ECONOMIC EVALUATION OF FORESTRY

Afforestation projects in the United Kingdom must meet some basic criteria before approval can be given. These are: to maximize the value and volume of domestically grown timber in a cost-effective manner; to create jobs in the rural areas; and to provide recreational, educational and conservation benefits and enhance the environment through visual amenity. Furthermore, before acquisition of a plot the forestry authorities must make sure that afforestation on it represents value for money and for this purpose a cost-benefit analysis is normally carried out.

Cost-benefit analysis of a forestry project involves a number of steps such as identification of costs, identification of benefits, discounting, weighing up uncertainties regarding future timber prices and the felling age, and studying the environmental and distributional effects.

Identifying Costs. The concept of opportunity cost is the main criterion in evaluation of costs. The prices attached to cost items should reflect society's valuation of these items and in some cases may differ from the prices actually paid. In this respect all costs should be included no matter who accrues them.

Market price of land should normally reflect its opportunity cost; it may also reflect some elements of the capitalized value of agricultural subsidies. Where applicable, an adjustment to exclude all subsidies from the market price of land should be made. Normally, the analyst takes a percentage reduction in the market price of land to eliminate the effects of subsidies. In Northern Ireland, most forestry acquisition is generally confined to marginal land. For many years the Forest Service has taken a 55 percent reduction in the market price of less-favored locations and a 45 percent reduction in other areas (Policy Planning and Research Unit 1987).

All costs should be, and are, expressed in real terms; in this way there is usually no need to forecast future changes in the general price level. Price changes only need to be taken into account if there is a change in relative prices.

Operational costs in forestry include labor, machinery and materials. Estimates for these items are normally based on average costs with the assumption that these are likely to coincide with marginal costs. Opportunity costs are assumed to be equal to actual costs in most cases. In processing direct labor cost, some additions are made to its market price. These are 35 percent for sickness leave and employers' contribution to national insurance; 53 percent for unproductive time in view of bad weather, to and from work and subsistence; 33 percent Civil Service superannuation; 91 percent supervisory and administrative mark-up. These bring the labor conversion factor to 2.12 (Policy Planning and Research Unit 1987).

Identification of Benefits. Broad benefits include revenue from thinnings and felling plus recreational, educational and conservation benefits, employment creation factor in the rural sector and terminal values such as land and roads.

Revenue from thinnings and felling depends on yield and the future price of timber. Estimation of the latter requires judgement on the price increase in real terms and the base price to which any such changes should be applied, which is not an easy task. Few investment projects require economic analysts to predict prices that will rule in 40 to 150 years' time.

During the lifetime of forestry projects many variables which determine wood prices may change quite dramatically. The United Kingdom meets well over two-thirds of its wood requirement by imports and thus domestic prices are dominated by world prices. In the world market the price of timber, just like the price of any other commodity, is determined by the forces of demand and supply. The cost of transport also plays an important role in determining prices because wood is a bulky commodity in relation to its value. This gives protection, to a certain extent, to local growers in the United Kingdom. Transport by sea is much cheaper than by road, and no part of the United Kingdom is far from the coast where imported wood lands.

Most exporting countries rely on natural forests as opposed to plantations, a case which gives them a substantial cost advantage over the British growers who rely exclusively on plantations. As long as large areas of virgin forests remain within easy reach of water transport, the price of timber in the United Kingdom will be determined mainly by the cost of extracting, sawing and transporting by the exporting countries.

Some researchers estimated that in the United Kingdom between 1853 and 1967 the annual price increase for imported timber was 1.5 percent in real terms (Hiley 1967). In a similar study, Potter and Christy (1962) identified a 1.9 percent annual price rise between 1870 and 1957 in the United States. However, it must be pointed out that those estimates carry the effect of the two world wars which caused a sharp increase in the price of wood. The consensus amongst experts is that timber prices will increase between 0 and 2 percent per annum. When forest economists carry out a cost-benefit study they normally use 0.5 percent and 2 percent annual price rise in their sensitivity analyses.

In areas adjacent to existing forests it is thought that an additional investment would be unlikely to yield significant recreational and educational benefits. Therefore, in economic evaluation of such projects these benefits are normally not considered, except when they are large. If a project is located away from existing sites, particularly near a large population center, an estimate of recreational and educational benefits is normally calculated on an ad hoc basis. The multiplier of investment expenditure on further income is not normally taken into account, as it is not unique to forestry. The terminal value of land and roads is assumed to be equal to their initial value.

Identification of Other Items. As mentioned earlier, the Forestry Commission in Great Britain has, in most cases, used a 3 percent target rate of return as the social rate of discount in economic appraisal of afforestation projects. In Northern Ireland, however, 5 percent, the Treasury discount rate, has normally been used. It is common practice to take the base date for discounting as the date of the initial investment or the date of the appraisal if that is different.

A cost-benefit study of forestry may also include a statement on distributional equity. The job creation aspect of forestry in the rural sector, where employment opportunities are normally limited, was strongly emphasized during the time when the Forestry Commission was created in Britain. However, in actual calculations no shadow values are applied to the cost of labor. If a project fails purely on financial grounds, there may be circumstances in which it could be justified on the grounds of relatively cost-effective job creation. Also, additional information may be necessary to reveal the extent to which the project provides employment for those already in part-time employment.

If there are potential losers from a scheme, the analysis normally includes a statement. They may be conservation, sporting, amenity or some other groups. It is desirable to carry out a sensitivity test to show the effects of possible variations on the assumptions made and their effects on the stream of costs and benefits. Assumptions to which the analysis is particularly sensitive are normally emphasised.[1]

A CASE STUDY IN NORTHERN IRELAND

The size of the afforestation project is 100 hectares, located on a moderately high region, with moderate slope, in the western part of Northern Ireland. The Department of Agriculture describes the region as severely disadvantaged due to the fact that its agricultural potential is poor. After the publication of a white paper entitled *Forestry in Northern Ireland* (1970), afforestation was targeted at land which had little agricultural value. Nowadays the situation is changing somewhat as some environmental interests would criticize planting that sort of land. Furthermore, as agriculture itself contracts, forestry is moving down the hill into much better land. One problem which is encountered by foresters is that good agricultural land in Ulster is fragmented into small ownerships, making it difficult to achieve economies of scale.

The project is based upon a 45-year single rotation which includes a thinning regime. Thinning means the cutting out of select trees from a plantation to gain a harvest and improve the growth and quality of the remainder. Also, thinning provides early returns, mainly in the form of pulpwood. Economically, thinning can only be justified if the increased benefits from it outweigh the cost.

The species planted is Sitka spruce, the most favored tree by foresters throughout the British Isles. It is an oceanic species native to British Columbia and southern Alaska, which was introduced to Britain in 1831. It grows very quickly in oceanic climates such as those of Ireland and the west coast of Britain. If allowed to, it can grow for a long time and in favorable conditions can attain a height of about 60 meters. The timber quality of Sitka spruce grown in the British Isles is, on average, below that of North America but it makes very good pulp. It is also used in house building mainly as interior construction material.

Table 6.1
Cost Details of Afforestation of 100 Hectares, 1990/1991 Prices

Operation	Year	Total Cost £
Draining	0	4,150
Ploughing	0	6,505
Planting	0	31,818
Fertilizing	0	12,038
Fencing	0	5,387
Maintenance:		
Fertiliser	8,16	19,421
Drains	15,25,35	2,634
Re-space	20	6,917
Opportunity cost	throughout	2,993

The yield class is estimated to be 10, meaning that the stand has a maximum mean annual increment of about 10 cubic meters of wood per hectare.

Table 6.1 shows the plantation costs in terms of 1990/1991 prices. Draining could be a very expensive operation in some locations, especially where the land gets waterlogged, which is not the case here. Ploughing, planting and fertilizing constitute the bulk of the establishment cost. Weeding is not carried out on this plot as the soil does not encourage weed growth. Because of the poor quality of soil, in addition to the initial cost, the area will be fertilized in the eighth and sixteenth years. Other operational assumptions are: no beating-up,[2] no brashing, no fence repairs, no pruning and no new roads, as the existing structure is assumed to be adequate (the land has been in the Forest Service's possession for many years). For the opportunity cost, first the annual rental value of £6,650 for the whole area is identified, then in view of the argument presented above, a 55 percent reduction is made to the market value thus reducing it to £2,993 per annum. Costs such as fire protection and management fees are not included, but labor cost is included in each item.

Table 6.2 shows an estimate of future output. Thinning on this type of location imposes a risk on the remaining trees because of winds. Some foresters contend that this risk is worth taking, whereas others disagree. Thinnings start in year 25 and continue at five-year intervals. The wood output is divided into three categories: pulpwood, boxwood and saw quality timber. The output details are worked out on the basis of information given in the Forestry Commission's Forest Management Tables (Forestry Commission 1971). The management table figures are reduced by 10 percent to allow for the space lost by fencing, drainage and passageways.

The 1990/1991 average prices of coniferous timber in lorry lengths at roadside in Northern Ireland were: pulpwood, £18.50; boxwood, £24.40; sawwood,

Table 6.2
Output Details, Sitka Spruce

| Yield Class 10 | Thinning (m³)in Years | | | | Felling |
	25	30	35	40	Year 45
Pulpwood	2610	3060	2970	2880	15750
Boxwood	90	90	180	270	7470
Saw-wood	-	-	-	-	1170
Total Output	2700	3150	3150	3150	24390
Money Benefits, £	23,418	27,306	27,837	28,368	265,779

£30.80. From these about £10 must be deducted for felling and extraction costs. The net prices then become:

Pulpwood = £8.50
Boxwood = £14.40
Sawwood = £20.80

By using these prices the money benefits, by assuming that there will be no change in the real price of timber (assumption 0), are obtained and are shown in the last column of Table 6.2.

Table 6.3 shows the annual net benefits of this project. Figure 6.1 shows the behavior of the net benefit curve. On the basis of the computed net benefit figures, net present value of this project is calculated by using:

$$NPV = \sum_{t=0}^{45} \frac{1}{(1 + 0.05)^t} NB_t$$

NPV (assumption 0) = −91415

SENSITIVITY ANALYSES

Future Price of Timber. Table 6.4 shows the price trends for three classes of wood in nominal terms in Northern Ireland. Since Northern Ireland meets over 80 percent of its wood requirement by imports, the price of domestically grown timber is dominated by the world prices. Table 6.5 shows the price trend for imported sawn softwood since 1951, in real terms. The growth rate of real price of timber is obtained by fitting the equation:

Table 6.3
Net Benefit Stream of Afforestation Project, 1990/1991 Prices

Yr	Cost	Benefit	Benefit	Yr	Cost	Benefit	Benefit
0	62,891	-	-62,891	24	2,993	-	-2,993
1	2,993	-	-2,993	25	5,627	23,481	17,854
2	2,993	-	-2,993	26	2,993	-	-2,993
3	2,993	-	-2,993	27	2,993	-	-2,993
4	2,993	-	-2,993	28	2,993	-	-2,993
5	2,993	-	-2,993	29	2,993	- -	-2,993
6	2,993	-	-2,993	30	2,993	27,806	24,313
7	2,993	-	-2,993	31	2,993	-	-2,993
8	22,414	-	-22,414	32	2,993	-	-2,993
9	2,993	-	-2,993	33	2,993	-	-2,993
10	2,993	-	-2,993	34	2,993	-	-2,993
11	2,993	-	-2,993	35	5,627	27,837	22,210
12	2,993	-	-2,993	36	2,993	-	-2,993
13	2,993	-	-2,993	37	2,993	-	-2,993
14	2,993	-	-2,993	38	2,993	-	-2,993
15	5,627	-	-5,627	39	2,993	-	-2,993
16	22,414	-	-22,414	40	2,993	28,368	25,375
17	2,993	-	-2,993	41	2,993	-	-2,993
18	2,993	-	-2,993	42	2,993	-	-2,993
19	2,993	-	-2,993	43	2,993	-	-2,993
20	9,910	-	-9,910	44	2,993	-	-2,993
21	2,993	-	-2,993	45	2,993	265,779	262,786
22	2,993	-	-2,993				
23	2,993	-	-2,993				

$$\ln P = a + gt$$

to series in Table 6.5 where P is real price of imported softwood expressed in terms of 1966 prices, a is a constant and t is the number of years between 1951 and 1991. The results are:

$$\ln P = 4.35 + 0.0195t$$

$$(98.44)\ (10.61)$$

$$R^2 = 0.74$$

The numbers in brackets are t statistics. Annual rate of price increase is 1.95 percent in real terms.

Further net present value calculations are carried out under three assumptions:

Assumption 1: the real price of timber will increase by 0.5 percent compound;

Assumption 2: the real price of timber will increase by 1 percent compound; and

Assumption 3: the real price of timber will increase by 2 percent compound.

Figure 6.1
Net Benefit Profile of Forestry

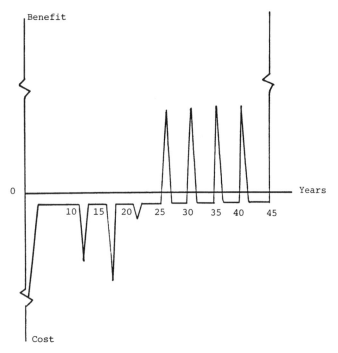

The results are:

$$NPV \text{ (assumption 1)} = -80338$$
$$NPV \text{ (assumption 2)} = -69024$$
$$NPV \text{ (assumption 3)} = -29884$$

With a 5 percent discount rate this project fails under all three assumptions regarding increase in the price of timber in future years.

Premium for Import Saving. As mentioned earlier in an interdepartmental study of forestry in 1972 (HMSO 1972), some economists argued that a 20 percent premium should be added to the benefits of forestry for import saving. At the time Her Majesty's Treasury did not accept the validity of this, even though they were curious about its effect on calculations. Nowadays this may be particularly relevant, as the United Kingdom seems to have a chronic balance of payment deficit which is likely to continue for some years to come. In view of this, timber benefits are inflated under four more assumptions:

Assumption 4:   no increase in real price of timber, plus 20 percent premium on wood output.

Assumption 5:   0.5 percent annual increase in timber price, plus 20 percent premium on wood output.

Table 6.4
Fluctuation in the Nominal Price of Wood in Northern Ireland

	Nominal Price Trends in Wood		
Year	Pulpwood cmtd around 12	Boxwood cmtd around 18	Sawwood cmnt around 24
1974/75	10.15	13.49	17.38
1975/76	7.90	10.58	12.97
1976/77	10.07	12.23	19.80
1977/78	11.66	16.11	21.46
1978/79	9.04	13.51	18.08
1979/80	8.44	10.94	18.30
1980/81	9.02	12.33	18.11
1981/82	7.76	10.48	14.04
1982/83	8.29	10.79	14.00
1983/84	10.07	11.76	14.32
1984/85	10.36	12.42	14.86
1986/87	17.82	22.47	25.41
1987/88	20.55	25.94	28.80
1988/89	18.30	26.10	27.33
1989/90	17.83	24.02	29.13
1990/91	18.50	24.40	30.80

Assumption 6: 1 percent annual increase in timber price, plus 20 percent premium on wood output.
Assumption 7: 2 percent annual increase on timber price, plus 20 percent premium on wood output.

The results are as follows:

$$NPV \text{ (assumption 4)} = -86935$$
$$NPV \text{ (assumption 5)} = -67820$$
$$NPV \text{ (assumption 6)} = -51700$$
$$NPV \text{ (assumption 7)} = -7619$$

The project fails even with the most optimistic assumptions regarding future timber prices and added premium for import saving.

RESULTS BY WAY OF MODIFIED DISCOUNTING

Net discounted values by way of modified discounting are shown below under eight sets of assumptions:

Table 6.5
Real Price of Saw-Quality Softwood in Northern Ireland (1966 = 100)

Year	Real Price of Softwood (P)	Year	Real Price of Softwood (P)
1951	101.4	1971	108.6
1952	93.1	1972	115.0
1953	86.3	1973	150.4
1954	87.0	1974	152.1
1955	87.0	1975	129.0
1956	91.2	1976	136.7
1957	84.6	1977	133.1
1958	77.7	1978	123.5
1959	81.9	1979	128.7
1960	88.7	1980	121.5
1961	86.2	1981	105.1
1962	93.7	1982	105.3
1963	99.8	1983	119.7
1964	104.9	1984	119.6
1965	105.7	1985	175.8
1966	100.0	1986	186.4
1967	103.4	1987	206.9
1968	113.8	1988	189.8
1969	113.8	1989	193.6
1970	114.6	1990	193.6
		1991	175.0

Source: Kula (1988b), and *Annual Report*, Northern Ireland, Forest Service, 1989/90.

NDV (assumption 0) $= -43617$
NDV (assumption 1) $= -18032$
NDV (assumption 2) $= +9999$
NDV (assumption 3) $= +100206$
NDV (assumption 4) $= -36363$
NDV (assumption 5) $= +9715$
NDV (assumption 6) $= +42302$
NDV (assumption 7) $= +150683$

As this case study demonstrates, a 5 percent discount rate fails many afforestation projects even with the most optimistic assumptions regarding future timber prices and import saving premiums. The modified discounting method, on the other hand, yields results which must be highly encouraging for foresters.

The forestry project used in this chapter has low profitability, as it is located in a high and exposed area. With the publication of the 1970 white paper *Forestry in Northern Ireland,* tree planting was targeted at land which had relatively little agricultural value; in practice that meant peaty and exposed locations. Good land in the Province, as in other parts of the British Isles, was allocated for the expansion of agriculture. In the 1970s and 1980s yield class 10 was quite common in Northern Ireland as well as in Scotland. This situation is now changing gradually as forestry is moving down the hill and onto much better land. Therefore, in future years yield class 14–16 for Sitka spruce is likely to become more representative for Northern Ireland than the one which is used here.

Although the climate and soil types in Northern Ireland are highly conducive to forestry, unfortunately the area is still one of Europe's least forested regions: the tree coverage is only about 6 percent of the land surface. Changing trends in land use are making forestry projects more attractive than they used to be. The continuous reduction in farm subsidies throughout the European Community is causing a decline in agriculture in many regions, including Northern Ireland. As more and more land is taken out of agriculture, farmers as well as governments are looking for alternative land-based projects. Another factor which will help afforestation projects is that of the greenhouse effect of atmospheric pollution. As the carbon dioxide concentration is increasing in the atmosphere foresters are advocating the expansion of forestry, as trees, with their absorption capacity, moderate the problem. It should be mentioned that it is quite difficult to quantify, in monetary terms, the environmentally beneficial aspects of forestry in cost-benefit studies.

Even with changing patterns of land use and environmental considerations favoring forestry, it would still be quite a struggle to justify afforestation projects by using a 5 percent discount rate in conventional appraisal techniques. Even in yield class 14–16 it would be difficult to pass the conventional economic tests, especially if costs in plantation were to go up and timber price rises moderate. As for many hardwood species in which gestation periods are as long as 100–120 years, conventional discounting methods even with a low interest rate become a kiss of death for forestry.

It should be made clear that this section is by no means suggesting that forestry projects in the United Kingdom must go ahead at all costs. Although British forestry has a much better chance to qualify as a viable venture by means of the new method, this does not mean that forestry should replace more beneficial projects in the public sector. Compared with forestry, if some other projects generate greater benefits to society, then they should be ranked above forestry.

NOTES

1. Economic appraisal methods of public sector investment projects are kept under constant review. For most recent changes, see HM Treasury (1984) and House of Commons (1992).

2. Beating-up is the replacement of plants that succumbed in the initial planting.

Chapter 7

Cost-Benefit Analysis of an Agricultural Project— Arterial and Field Drainage

INTRODUCTION

Drainage projects aim to remove excess water from land for a number of purposes such as flood control, safety in highway travel, to protect recreational and other facilities and to improve agricultural yields. A storm drainage project collects run-off from small drainage basins within urban or rural areas to prevent water from accumulating on the surface. A highway drainage scheme aims to remove storm or other water from roads used by motorists. Land drainage projects normally aim to increase incomes of farmers operating in areas where land is too wet for lucrative agriculture.

Arterial drainage means artificial widening and deepening of rivers and tributaries to increase their effectiveness in draining catchment areas. It improves the agricultural potential of land that is subject to flooding or waterlogging. Full benefits of an arterial drainage scheme cannot be realized unless farmers cooperate by having suitable field drainage carried out on their land and by putting the improved land to productive use.

Drainage projects should pass a number of feasibility tests. Engineering feasibility aims to ascertain whether the project is physically capable of performing its intended objectives. Economic feasibility is passed if discounted total benefits associated with the project exceed those which would accrue without the project by an amount in excess of the discounted costs. Economic argument depends on engineering feasibility because a project incapable of producing the desired output is not going to create sufficient discounted net benefits for its justification. Financial feasibility is passed if adequate funds can be raised to pay for the project's construction and maintenance. A drainage project may be economically feasible but financially infeasible because the benefits that it creates cannot be measured in monetary terms or are distributed amongst too many people for payment to be practical. Alternatively, a project may be financially feasible but economically infeasible because of substantial external costs such as loss of habitat and amenity.

Political feasibility is also essential, as required approval can only be obtained from politicians. Normally, political support is given after engineering and economic tests prove to be highly convincing, provided that the project does not create controversies to embarrass the government. It is quite common for political pressure to exist by potential beneficiaries even if the project's overall economic viability is in question. Almost every project harms someone, and if those who are to be harmed are sufficiently vocal and politically skillful they can prevent the project's construction. Nowadays, in environmentally conscious countries, drainage projects involving loss of plant and animal species may not be put into practice even if they turn out to be attractive as far as agricultural yields are concerned.

Last but not least, there is the social feasibility test which relates, in the main, to users of the project. For instance, will arterial drainage motivate farmers to take up the requested field drainage, to use modern equipment or to do whatever else is needed to realize a project's full benefits? There is little point in constructing an arterial drainage scheme if the farmers in the area are not going to respond and change their ways of operation.

Many water development schemes throughout the world are constructed and managed by governments because collective action is needed to overcome allocative deficiencies that exist in a market economy, to coordinate multiproject systems effectively, to provide extensive financial resources required and to ascertain the environmental implications of such projects in their entirety. Of course, there is a danger that some water projects may be considered by governments because a number of politicians look upon them as a means of furthering their political careers. In order to prevent this type of abuse, in most democratic countries public agencies are required to use objective assessment methods to make sure that projects are economically viable and will genuinely benefit the country.

Water projects played an important role in the development of economic assessment methods for public sector projects in general. For instance, the United States Bureau of Reclamation has been concerned with economic justification of its projects since the advent of its program in 1902. In 1936 the U.S. Flood Control Act established a principle that a project should be declared feasible if the benefits to whomever they may accrue are in excess of the estimated costs. After the Second World War two official reports, the U.S. Government Federal Inter-Agency River Basin Committee's Sub-Committee on Benefits and Costs (1950) and the Bureau of Budget's Budget Circular (1952), produced formalization procedures for costs and benefits of water development and other projects. A few years later a number of academics attempted to lay down cost-benefit criteria in relation to water development projects. In particular, O. Eckstein's *Water Resources Development* (1958), R. McKean's *Efficiency in Government Through System Analysis* (1958), J. Krutilla and O. Eckstein's *Multiple Purpose River Development* (1958), A. Maass's *Design of Water Resource Systems* (1962) and L.D. James and R.R. Lee's *Economics of Water Resources Planning* (1971) became major documents used by cost-benefit practitioners to evaluate the economic worth of water and other projects.

As progress on methodology was in motion some economists warned that cost-benefit analysis could become a bogus and corrupt discipline (see Clarenback 1955; Leopold and Maddock, Jr. 1954). They felt that the requirement that economic benefits exceed costs unduly restricted worthy water resources development. Furthermore, government agencies may inflate benefits and ignore costs in order to justify projects and thus perpetuate their own growth. The economic test may not be a proof of merit, but rather a number of concocted studies to gain more widespread acceptance of a decision already made on some other basis.

This chapter describes a cost-benefit analysis for the River Maigue Arterial Drainage Scheme (a live project) in the Republic of Ireland, mainly based upon procedures established by the above-mentioned documents. Both ordinary and modified discounting methods will be used in communal analysis of this investment project.

HISTORIC BACKGROUND

Arterial drainage is important in a country like Ireland because the heavy rainfall during the growing season, combined with the inadequate gradient of a number of rivers, causes large areas of agricultural land to be poor because they are excessively wet. The Office of Public Works estimates that about 3 percent of total land in the Republic of Ireland is dependent on arterial drainage works. The 1945 Arterial Drainage Act has given the Office of Public Works responsibility for carrying out arterial drainage projects. Since then the Office has constructed a number of major schemes, one of which is the River Maigue project.

The river flows northward through low-lying, good quality land in County Limerick to enter the Shannon Estuary about eight miles west of the city of Limerick. It drains an area of over a quarter of a million acres. Some 30,000 acres and 2,000 landholders in the river's catchment area benefit from the scheme (Figure 7.1). In an earlier scheme started in 1964, embankments were constructed on part of the tidal section of the river, draining about 17,000 acres.

In 1970 the River Maigue Arterial Drainage Project was made the subject of an in-depth cost-benefit study under the direction of a steering group drawn from the public sector, which took more than three years to complete. The study was done under the auspices of the Office of Public Works and within the context of the development of analytical studies in the Civil Service as an aid to policy formulation and review. The Maigue scheme was chosen for study because it was the next catchment on which a large drainage scheme was likely

Figure 7.1
River Maigue Catchment Area in Ireland

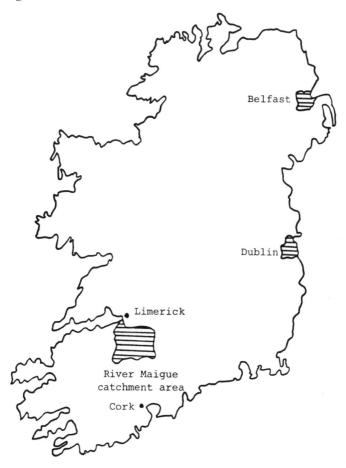

to be started by the Office. While the analysis was restricted to this project, it was recognized that the findings could be taken as indicating whether arterial drainage would be economically viable in Ireland.

Between 1945 and 1970 the Office of Public Works carried out analysis for 8 large and 25 small arterial drainage projects in Ireland. Some notable reports were:

- The Report on the Shannon Flood Problem by the U.S. Army Corps of Engineers, 1956.

- The Joint Study on the Shannon Flood Problem by the Office of Public Works and the Electricity Supply Board, 1961.

- The Report on Arterial Drainage in General by a group of civil servants, 1969.

These studies discovered that arterial drainage was uneconomic on the criterion of the increase in the market value of the drained land. It was then recommended that in cost-benefit analysis of arterial drainage projects an alternative criterion should be used in benefit measurement. In particular, the increase in net agricultural output and resulting income from the land improved plus increased employment opportunities should be focused on. The River Maigue study gives effect to these recommendations.

Article 45 of the Irish Constitution mentions the directive principles of the Republic's social policy and contains the following statement: "The state shall, in particular, direct its policy towards securing . . . that there may be established on the land in economic security as many familities as in the circumstances shall be practicable." The Irish government believes that arterial drainage schemes contribute to this policy by increasing the productivity of the land and hence the economic security of those who live off the land. In line with this, the 1945 Arterial Drainage Act suggests that such schemes should be initiated for the purpose of preventing or reducing flooding of lands or improving their economic worth.

On the basis of these statements the steering group recognized that the primary objective of arterial drainage was to increase the income of those whose lands were subject to flooding or drainage problems which could not be overcome without arterial drainage. In the analysis of the Maigue project landholders who benefit directly from the scheme are referred to as the project's target group. Although there are persons other than the target group that are affected by the project, this chapter will consider only the primary costs and benefits of the target group.

To start with, the steering group sought to answer four main questions in relation to the Maigue project and, by implication, in relation to the whole arterial drainage program.

1. Will the project achieve its objectives?
2. Will achievement of the objectives represent an economic return on the money invested?
3. Could the objectives of the scheme be achieved more economically by alternative means?
4. What principles of use for assessing future schemes may be derived from the analysis?

The analysis made it apparent that the scheme would achieve its objective of increasing the income of the target group provided the necessary follow-up work was undertaken by them.

ASSUMPTIONS AND CONVENTIONS

The original cost-benefit analysis was carried out by the Office of Public Works which forms the basis for calculations in this chapter. In order to bring the flow of benefits and costs over the future to a common time base, taken as 1973, a 3.5 percent discount rate was chosen, in real terms. The benefit-cost ratio method, which has historically been the most popular criterion to evaluate the worth of water projects, was used in the analysis. Benefits and costs were calculated on a gross basis when possible because when net costs are used, benefit-cost ratio may be distorted, a common problem associated with this method (Douglas and Lee 1971; Dasgupta and Pearce 1972).

The life of the project was estimated to be 58 years; 8 years of construction and 50 years of net life thereafter. The construction began in 1973 and the work was completed in 1981. The scheme is still in its early years of operation. There were some difficulties, mainly of a minor nature, between estimated costs and incurred costs. However, instead of carrying out a post-drainage study to test the underlying assumptions of the project, I will use the original figures as an illustration of the effect of the modified discounting method on its estimated economic viability.

The multiplier effect of this investment was excluded on the grounds that all public sector projects generate similar benefits. The Office felt that the multiplier effect was not relevant unless different multipliers could be justified for different public works.

PRIMARY COSTS

The primary costs of this project are:

- Survey and design.
- Execution of the major scheme.
- Maintenance of the major scheme.
- Field drainage.
- Maintenance of field drainage.
- Purchase of extra livestock by the farmers.
- Provision of building and milking facilities for the extra livestock, including fertilizer.

Like many other arterial drainage schemes this project is designed on a catchment basis and so the processes of all drainage and flood problems dependent on major drainage are examined. To the extent that it is feasible economically, the alleviation of these problems is provided in the scheme. Problems dependent on minor drainage are omitted. Such problems are assumed to be solved by landlords themselves with the aid of state grants for field drainage. The Commissions of Public Works are charged with the responsibility of maintaining all completed arterial drainage schemes including the Maigue project. Most channels tend, over time, to revert back to the predrainage conditions due to such factors as weed growth and deposition of silt. The channels, therefore, require maintenance work periodically in order to retain their effectiveness.

The field drainage is undertaken by the landholders, supervised and grant-aided by the Land Project Office. Grants up to two-thirds are payable. It was estimated that the field drainage would be spread over about 20 years. As for the maintenance, the landholder himself is encouraged to do the maintenance on the grounds that this work is in his own interests. If a landholder neglects to maintain the works which were grant-aided in the first place, he will not be considered favorably by the government for any further grants. The purchase of extra livestock arising as a result of the drainage scheme is assumed to continue to the end of the project's life. New buildings and extra milking facilities are assumed to be established in years 8 and 9, with upgrading in year 38.

Construction and maintenance constitute the bulk of the cost. Field drainage comes to just over 10 percent of the total cost. Table 7.1 shows the breakdown of primary costs year by year over the estimated lifetime of this project.

The scheme covers a total of about 450 miles of channel involving excavation of a total of about 5.6 million cubic yards of material. During the peak of construction years a total labor force of about 320 men and a fleet of some 25 excavators and a large volume of transport facilities were used. Great care was taken in the disposal and treatment of excavated material in response to criticism by conservationists regarding the adverse effects of the work on the environment. Improved disposal and treatment received strong support by the community because of its impact on land prices in the area.

The cost of maintenance was borne by the County Councils of those counties where lands benefiting from the scheme are situated. The costs were divided between the county councils involved on the basis of degree of agricultural benefit conferred on landholders in each district. Maintenance costs increase at a greater rate than the general rate of inflation because of the high labor content of maintenance combined with the fact that real increases in wages are not normally offset fully by increases in productivity.

The field drainage is undertaken by the landholders, supervised and grant-aided by the Land Project Office. Grants of up to 75 percent of the cost were paid. The work was carried out by contractors who were specialists in this type of operation. There were 2,081 landholders who stood to benefit from the arterial drainage scheme. About 10 percent of these did not need to undertake field drainage to benefit from the scheme. The remaining 90 percent, or 1,873 landholders, were advised to carry out field drainage operation. The Land Project Office estimated that about 10 percent of these did not respond and therefore did not derive any benefits from the project. As for the maintenance of field drainage, this, too, was done by landholders.

As mentioned before, estimated benefits are related to the general level of production in each year associated with the increase in livestock population. When a landholder took advantage of the drainage scheme it was assumed that he would acquire extra livestock to improve yield on the land. The number of livestock to be acquired in any year would be the amount by which the number of livestock, due to the scheme in that year, exceeded the corresponding number in the previous year. The livestock purchases were quantified in monetary terms on the basis of base year prices, 1973, taken as £200 and £190 per livestock unit for dairy and dry livestock, respectively, and on the assumption that these prices would increase by one percent over inflation. Figures for the duration of the analysis are shown in column 7, Table 7.1.

In order to accommodate extra livestock, farmers were assumed to invest in extra buildings for housing, feeding and milking facilities. The cost of accommodation and feeding for dry livestock was estimated at £65 per head. For dairy livestock the cost per head was assumed to be £115, including milking facilities. About 15 percent of these costs were met by state grants. Since the period considered in this analysis is 58 years, it was assumed that some of the buildings and other facilities would have to be replaced or upgraded in future years. To simplify the calculation it was assumed that all buildings and other facilities will be constructed in years 8 and 9 and upgraded around the year 2010, or year 38. The unit replacement costs were assumed not to change substantially in real terms.

PRIMARY BENEFITS

The primary benefits of this project are: gross margin resulting from the increased livestock numbers in dairy and dry stocks, and savings in public and private works.

The net productive area to benefit was calculated to be 29,023 acres, or about 12 percent of the river's catchment. Dairy is the predominant type of farming in this region. The increased agricultural output was measured in terms of livestock units which then converted to money benefits. The increase in livestock numbers due to the scheme was estimated at 1971 production levels and assumed 100 percent response from landholders. Then allowances were made for a number of factors such as nonresponding landholders, losses due to deposition of excavated material on river banks, timing of landholders' response, changes in farmers' attitudes, productivity and gross margin trends.

The study group concluded that because of the varying degrees of soil types and farming proficiency in the area, information on expected increase in productivity could best be obtained from individual farmers who will be affected by the project. Hence it was decided to interview potential beneficiaries. The sample for the project was provided by the Central Statistical Office. Each townland containing land benefiting from the project was identified and the number of farms in that townland was determined; a total of 3,029. From this benefit-population 76 were chosen for a survey questionnaire.

The questionnaire was designed to obtain information on levels of agricultural production before and after drainage. The holdings were surveyed by a team comprising an agricultural advisor and a senior officer from the Limerick office of the Land Project. Using soil maps of the region, the survey team estimated pre- and post-drainage potential of each holding, which was expressed in terms

Table 7.1
Primary Costs of River Maigue Drainage Scheme, Irish Pounds (000)

Yr	Survey and Design	Excavation and Structures	Maintenance of main Structure	Field Drainage	Maintenance of Field Drainage	Extra Livestock	Extra Building & Milking Facilities	Total
1	227	509	39	-	-	-	-	775
2	-	509	40	-	-	21	-	570
3	-	509	40	-	-	21	-	570
4	-	509	41	-	-	21	-	570
5	-	509	42	15	1	21	-	588
6	-	509	42	23	1	21	-	596
7	-	509	42	44	2	21	-	618
8	-	509	43	63	3	21	500	1,139
9	-	509	43	73	4	21	500	641
10	-	-	44	112	5	30	-	191
11	-	-	45	140	8	30	-	223
12	-	-	45	160	10	30	-	245
13	-	-	46	144	12	30	-	232
14	-	-	46	137	14	31	-	228
15	-	-	47	116	14	31	-	208
16	-	-	48	97	16	31	-	192
17	-	-	49	86	17	32	-	184

18	-	-	49	47	18	32	-	146
19	-	-	50	19	2	32	-	103
20	-	-	50	-	-	33	-	83
21	-	-	51	-	-	33	-	84
22	-	-	51	-	-	33	-	84
23	-	-	52	-	-	34	-	86
24	-	-	53	-	-	35	-	87
25	-	-	53	-	-	35	-	88
26	-	-	54	-	-	35	-	89
27	-	-	55	-	-	36	-	91
28	-	-	55	-	-	37	-	93
29	-	-	56	-	-	37	-	94
30	-	-	57	-	-	37	-	94
31	-	-	57	-	-	37	-	94
32	-	-	58	-	-	38	-	96
33	-	-	59	-	-	38	-	98
34	-	-	59	-	-	39	-	98
35	-	-	60	-	-	39	-	99
36	-	-	61	-	-	40	-	101
37	-	-	61	-	-	40	-	101
38	-	-	62	-	-	41	425	528
39	-	-	63	-	-	41	-	104
40	-	-	64	-	-	42	-	106

Table 7.1 (continued)

Yr	Survey and Design	Excavation and Structures	Maintenance of main Structure	Field Drainage	Maintenance of Field Drainage	Extra Livestock	Extra Building & Milking Facilities	Total
41	-	-	64	-	-	42	-	106
42	-	-	65	-	-	43	-	108
43	-	-	66	-	-	43	-	70
44	-	-	67	-	-	44	-	111
45	-	-	67	-	-	44	-	111
46	-	-	68	-	-	45	-	113
47	-	-	69	-	-	45	-	114
48	-	-	70	-	-	46	-	116
49	-	-	71	-	-	46	-	117
50	-	-	72	-	-	47	-	119
51	-	-	72	-	-	48	-	120
52	-	-	73	-	-	49	-	122
53	-	-	74	-	-	50	-	124
54	-	-	75	-	-	50	-	125
55	-	-	76	-	-	51	-	127
56	-	-	77	-	-	51	-	128
57	-	-	78	-	-	52	-	130
58	-	-	79	-	-	52	-	131

of livestock units. In order to estimate the population value of the increase in livestock numbers, a number of methods were considered. In the event the ''mean value'' method was thought to be appropriate. This method consisted of computing the main increase in livestock numbers per holding and applying the mean to the total number of benefiting holdings. Then the increase in livestock numbers due to the scheme turned out to be 4,156 livestock units for the 1,873 holdings on the basis of 1971 production levels. By considering the historic trends, the study group predicted a long-term increase of about one percent, per annum, in livestock numbers over the life of the project.

In the analysis the gross margin concept—defined as the output from any form of production minus the variable cost—was used in evaluating the increase in income of the landholders. Table 7.2 gives a summary of primary benefits over the lifetime of the project. Column 2 shows the incremental holding which becomes zero in the ninth year.

Column 4, cumulative gross margin, captures both dry and dairy stocks. Gross margin values of £125 per dairy live unit and £55 per dry live unit were applied in the analysis for the base year and it was projected that both gross margins would increase at one percent per annum. At the time of the survey, dairy cows constituted 61 percent and dry stock 39 percent of the livestock population on the holdings inspected. It was estimated that due to the different rates of increase in cow and dry stock numbers at the end of the first decade, cows would constitute 63 percent of the livestock population.

The penultimate column shows the savings in discontinued public and private maintenance. Limerick County Council is obliged by law to maintain 130 miles of channel in the Maigue catchment. These channels are in 14 drainage districts in each of which a minor drainage scheme was carried out under a previous Drainage Act. When a drainage district is entered in the course of executing an arterial drainage scheme, the Arterial Drainage Act of 1945 requires that responsibility for maintenance of previous arterial drainage works in the district be transferred to the Office of Public Works. There is, therefore, a saving to Limerick County Council of the maintenance expenditure. This amounted to £16,800 in year 1. In addition, the riparian landholders have saved maintenance amounting to £9,690 in the base year. The combined saving in maintenance, both public and private, at base year rates was £26,490. This figure was estimated to increase, in real terms, by 1.2 percent per annum.

DISCOUNTED VALUES

On the basis of information provided in tables 7.1 and 7.2 we are now in a position to calculate the benefit-cost ratio by using ordinary and modified discounting methods. The benefit-cost ratio by using the former would be:

Table 7.2
Primary Benefits of River Maigue Drainage Scheme, Irish Pounds (000)

Year	Additional Holding	Cumulative Holding	Cumulative Gross Margin	Savings on Public Works	Total Benefits
1	180	180	39	27	66
2	85	265	60	27	87
3	225	520	121	28	149
4	213	733	178	28	206
5	130	863	219	28	247
6	459	1322	351	28	379
7	326	1648	452	29	481
8	225	1873	537	29	566
9	-	1873	546	30	576
10	-	1873	559	30	589
11	-	1873	570	30	600
12	-	1873	580	30	610
13	-	1873	595	31	626
14	-	1873	607	31	638
15	-	1873	617	31	648
16	-	1873	629	32	661
17	-	1873	642	32	674
18	-	1873	668	33	701
19	-	1873	682	33	715
20	-	1873	693	33	726
21	-	1873	710	34	744
22	-	1873	721	34	755
23	-	1873	738	35	773
24	-	1873	749	35	784
25	-	1873	765	35	800
26	-	1873	778	36	814
27	-	1873	796	36	832
28	-	1873	813	37	850
29	-	1873	830	37	867
30	-	1873	849	38	887
31	-	1873	860	38	898
32	-	1873	875	38	913
33	-	1873	839	39	878
34	-	1873	913	39	952
35	-	1873	932	40	972
36	-	1873	951	40	991
37	-	1873	970	41	1011
38	-	1873	986	41	1027
39	-	1873	1003	42	1045
40	-	1873	1026	42	1068

Table 7.2 (continued)

Year	Additional Holding	Cumulative Holding	Cumulative Gross Margin	Savings On Public Works	Total Benefits
41	-	1873	1046	43	1089
42	-	1873	1068	43	1111
43	-	1873	1090	44	1134
44	-	1873	1112	44	1156
45	-	1873	1134	45	1179
46	-	1873	1155	45	1200
47	-	1873	1177	46	1223
48	-	1873	1200	46	1246
49	-	1873	1223	47	1270
50	-	1873	1247	48	1295
51	-	1873	1270	48	1318
52	-	1873	1294	49	1343
53	-	1873	1318	49	1367
54	-	1873	1342	50	1392
55	-	1873	1366	51	1417
56	-	1873	1391	51	1442
57	-	1873	1416	52	1468
58	-	1873	1441	52	1493

$$B/C \ Ratio \ (ord.Disc.) = \frac{\int_{0}^{N} B_t e^{-st} dt}{\int_{0}^{N} C_t e^{-st} dt}$$

where:

B_t = primary benefits at time t
C_t = primary costs at time t
N = project's life
s = social discount rate
t = time

By using a 3.5 percent discount rate the benefit-cost ratio turns out to be 2.25.
Discounted benefit-cost ratio, based upon the modified discounting method, on the other hand, would be:

$$B/C \text{ Ratio (mod.}disc.) = \frac{\displaystyle\int_0^N B_t \frac{1}{n}[e^{-st}(n - t) + \frac{1}{s}(1 - e^{-st})]dt}{\displaystyle\int_0^N C_t \frac{1}{n}[e^{-st}(n - t) + \frac{1}{s}(1 - e^{-st})]dt}$$

Where n is life expectancy/population cohorts, the figure is 2.9.

Unlike the afforestation project (Chapter 6), which fails decisively by using the ordinary discounting criterion, the situation here is different. The River Maigue drainage project, based upon primary costs and benefits, qualifies as a sound venture by using ordinary discounting, which yields a benefit-cost ratio of 2.25. The modified discounting method only enhances the economic viability of the project as the benefit-cost ratio improves by about 30 percent, from 2.25 to 2.9, at a 3.5 percent discount rate. If the social interest rate was higher then the improvement ratio would have been much higher.

The River Maigue drainage project has been in operation for a number of years. At the time when it was proposed, agriculture in Ireland, and indeed in many other parts of Europe, appeared to be expansive. Today, the situation is different, as agriculture is a contracting sector, especially in the European Union which has been sitting on food surpluses for many years. Due to subsidies, in particular meat, cereal and dairy sectors are overexpanded in the northern countries of the community and the Republic of Ireland has its fair share of these problems.

As subsidies are falling, farmers throughout the European Union are looking for alternative uses for their land. As mentioned in Chapter 6, natural conditions in Ireland and Britain are highly conducive for afforestation projects. At present the Community has a considerable trade deficit in forestry, which is likely to continue for many years to come. In this respect, forestry projects are being encouraged by the European Community as well as by national governments. For example, in the Programme for Government 1989–1993, the Government of the Republic of Ireland identified forestry as having the potential to make a major contribution to regional and economic development. Forestry was included as a priority measure because of the contribution it can make to the objectives of the reformed structural funds and the European Commission has approved the Irish government's decision to expand forestry in the face of declining agriculture.

There is no doubt that the River Maigue drainage scheme will be in operation throughout its estimated life of 58 years and possibly well beyond that. However, given the changing pattern of land use it is highly unlikely that new large-scale arterial drainage projects will be conducted in Ireland.

Chapter 8

Optimal Forest Rotation Problem

INTRODUCTION

A forest is a renewable capital asset that relies on replanting by forest managers as well as natural regeneration. Gestation periods in forestry are very long for some species of trees, as they take over 100 or 150 years to mature. When trees are harvested the area could be replanted or it could be transferred to other uses such as agriculture, horticulture, housing development, and so on. When an area is used for forestry on a long-term basis a cycle is observed that is planting, thinning, felling, replanting, thinning, and so on. The period between one felling and the next is called the rotation. Time intervals between planting, or replanting, and successive thinnings are phases of the rotation period. Thinning (cutting out select trees from a plantation to improve the growth and quality of the remainder) is a further investment in a stand of trees.

The identification of the optimum rotation is one of the oldest technical problems known to economists since the work of Von Thunen (1826) and Faustmann (1849). When is the right time to fell a forest? If undisturbed a plantation forest grows over time until the maximum volume of wood is attained; beyond this point trees begin to decay. Light-demanding trees grow in volume rapidly at first and reach a growth peak early. Shade-bearing trees grow slowly at first, building up to peak annual increment in later years. Figure 8.1 shows, for illustrative purposes, the growth cycle of a tree. After firm establishment the volume of wood grows at an increasing rate up to α, beyond which increase continues but at a slower rate until β when the maximum wood output is achieved. Table 8.1 shows the yield under a "no thinning" regime for a stand of Sitka spruce, yield class 12, 16 and 22, on a per-hectare basis. Figure 8.2 shows the relevant yield curves.

Figure 8.1
A Typical Tree Growth Schedule

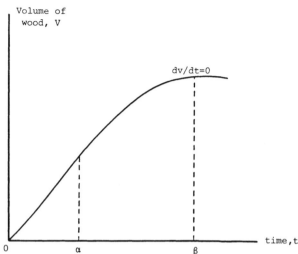

In silviculture the growth pattern of a tree can be altered by fertilizing, thinning, and pest control. Silviculture is intervention in ecosystems in order to modify the yield of trees for the intended purposes. Trees could be grown for a variety of reasons such as pulp, saw-logs, box-wood, Christmas decoration, bean sticks, amenity, pollution abatement, water conservation, flood control, avalanche prevention and species protection. When trees are grown for wood it has been recommended that the planning is best undertaken in reverse chronological order. First, the end product should be identified so that the desired species and rotation lengths can be attained. When species and rotation lengths are known, thinning and tending methods can be decided upon. Only then can it be resolved whether it is worthwhile to invest in forestry for wood (Price 1989b).

Many forest managers trained in forest biology and engineering have traditionally advocated that the goal of good policy is to have the maximum sustainable yield aimed at achieving maximum wood output. In Figure 8.1 this corresponds to the turning point of the volume/age curve. If all trees were cut down at this point in their lives the forest owner would achieve the objective, that is, maximum production of quality wood. As I shall explain below, economists, in the main, have challenged these criteria on the grounds that trees would be left in the ground for too long. Some even contend that at realistic profit rates, it may not pay to keep public or private forests in existence at all (Miller 1981; Samuelson 1976). The latter humorously points out that when he was preparing his celebrated lecture, "Economics of Forestry in an Evolving Society," he heard that a nearby consulting firm had applied, on behalf of a

Table 8.1
Growth Cycles for Sitka Spruce under a No-Thinning Regime, One Hectare, Three Different Yield Classes

Age, t	Volume, V, per Hectare		
Years	YC12	YC16	YC22
25	133	207	341
30	214	314	480
35	301	423	615
40	386	526	740
45	465	617	862
50	534	698	967
55	593	770	1065
60	462	834	1145
65	683	891	1220
70	718	940	1326
75	751	982	1326

Source: Forestry Commission (1971).

forestry company, dynamic programming analysis to the problem of optimal cutting age. Its computer spun out of control and generated an imaginary root for the equation designed to solve the problem, that is, there was no case for forestry.

Furthermore, Samuelson contends that over the last two hundred years when many economists tried to solve the problem of optimal forestation they misled their profession. Contributors such as Von Thunen (1826), Hotelling (1925), Fisher (1930), Boulding (1935) and Scott (1955) erred in their analyses and thus ended up with wrong solutions. The economic analyses in their works are either wrong or very wrong and in a limited number of cases not quite right. Errors made in this field have amply been duplicated in economics textbooks, leading users up the garden path. Now, at the Massachusetts Institute of Technology, postgraduate students are asked quizzes to identify and correct Irving Fisher's false solution to the optimum rotation problem, so Samuelson argues.

Later on, by using a criterion similar to Samuelson's most favored model, I shall employ modified discounting to identify the optimal forest rotation from the viewpoint of all individuals involved, present as well as future. The result will become very close to foresters' maximum sustainable yield.

RESTRICTIVE ASSUMPTIONS

Although a maximization model will be used below, unlike some economists I am not going to pretend that identification of a uniquely correct solution to optimal forest rotation exists in economics. Instead, my purpose is to demonstrate the extent to which a solution based upon modified discounting will diverge from previously known results. Having said that, my next step is to lay down the basic assumptions of this model purely for the purpose of illustration.

Assumption 1. Future timber yields from a publicly owned stand, which is

Figure 8.2
Yield Curves for Sitka Spruce

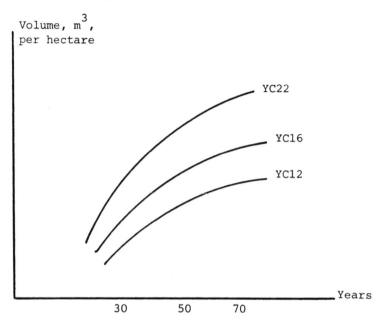

even-aged, are known with certainty. That is, when output details are worked out no substantial change is expected in climate, fertility of the land or in the management technology over time. Needless to say, all these could vary in the long run. Perhaps the fastest-changing item would be forest management technology, as it tends to improve over time.

Assumption 2. The objective of forest managers is to maximize the net benefits to society from the sale of timber. Other goals such as flood control, prevention of soil erosion, avalanche control, protection of species, recreation and pollution abatement are left out.

Assumption 3. Trees that are widely spaced and thus will not undergo thinning; that is, no-thinning regime is assumed. This is not an unrealistic assumption, as no-thinning regimes are used nowadays at many locations in Britain and Ireland.

Assumption 4. The trees will be sold standing, that is, harvesting and haulage costs will be incurred by the buyer. By this assumption we eliminate brushing, which means knocking off some of the lower branches of the crop when the trees become sufficiently tall. For some softwood species, such as Sitka spruce, brushing takes place about 15 years after planting when the trees reach about 20–30 feet in height. One reason for brushing is to provide easy access into the forest so that the growth of the crop can be monitored and the quality of the maturing merchandise can be seen closely. Only a few buyers would be prepared to make an offer for an unbrushed stand, as they would normally want to thoroughly inspect the forest for quality beforehand. However, inclusion of brushing would needlessly complicate the problem which is presented here.

Assumption 5. The future price of timber is constant and known. Obviously, this assumption is debatable. Nobody knows the future price of any commodity. By studying historic records, some researchers have observed a rising trend for lumber (Potter and Christy 1962; Barnett and Morse 1963; Hiley 1967). Although rising prices can be incorporated into optimal forest rotation models, not everybody would agree that the price of lumber will go up indefinitely.

Assumption 6. The price of wood is assumed not to be highly sensitive to the age or diameter of the tree, that is, a cubic meter of wood has a fixed value independent of the size and age.

Assumption 7. Planting and replanting costs are also known and they are constant for all future periods. Replanting is done immediately after the felling and the intervals between successive felling/replanting are uniform.

Assumption 8. The social discount rate is known and it is constant over all future periods.

Assumption 9. Forest land can be bought, sold and rented. If the land is in abundant supply its rental value would be zero, or near zero. In the case of land scarcity, which is more realistic, its opportunity cost will not be zero. As the reader will see below, a positive opportunity cost in land use will make a great deal of difference in identifying the optimum cutting age.

Assumption 10. Risks from fires, wind-blow and disease are assumed to be minimal and thus ignored. Of course, like other living creatures, trees are vulnerable to infestation, especially in nonnative soil. Forest fires are quite common in North America and southern Europe, whereas in Britain and Ireland wind-blow appears to be the major natural hazard.

Assumption 11. There is no taxation of any kind. It is well-known to forestry economists that site utilization and sales taxes make quite a difference to the optimum rotation decision.

Assumption 12. Intragenerational equity issues are not considered in the models. In the United Kingdom and the Republic of Ireland one of the objectives of forestry authorities is to provide jobs in, and increase the economic potential of, rural areas with declining agricultural employment, and to provide alternative sources of economic activity. That is, in deprived areas a forestry program may operate at a substantial financial loss in order to alleviate poverty in the region.

CONVENTIONAL SOLUTIONS

Single Rotation Solution. In this the forest manager tries to identify a time period to maximize profits over a single cycle. Let us assume a benefit function:

$$B_t = A(1 + t)^{1/2} \tag{8.1}$$

where:

> t = time expressed in terms of years
> B_t = revenue from the sale of timber at future years
> A = constant

At a given discount rate, r, the net present value, NPV, will be:

$$NPV = B_t e^{-rt} - C \qquad (8.2)$$

where C is initial establishment cost.

In order to find the optimum cutting age which would maximize the NPV, after differentiating (8.2) with respect to time and setting it equal to zero, we get:

$$\frac{dB_t}{dt} e^{-rt} = r B_t e^{-rt}$$

or

$$r = \frac{dB_t/dt}{B_t} \qquad (8.3)$$

This tells us that the net present value of this investment is maximized when the marginal benefit from the selling of timber is equal to the discount rate, which somehow measures the opportunity cost of capital locked up in forestry. The intuitive appeal of (8.3) is obvious; it is not profitable to maintain the stand when the marginal revenue becomes lower than the discount rate. It would then be more beneficial to cut the trees and invest the money in projects with greater returns.

In Figure 8.3 the single rotation solution is found geometrically. It is at the point where the revenue curve is tangent to the opportunity cost schedule, or if the two curves cut across it would be at the point of intersection. Since the vertical axis is in logarithmic scale, compounding discount rate appears as a straight line and this scale also compresses the revenue schedule.

Samuelson (1976) implies that it is the intuitive appeal of the single rotation solution that led many well-known economists up the garden path. The single rotation solution, as described above, is limited to a case in which the land is available in unlimited supply and thus the land rate is zero. Goundry (1960) contends that forest land in Canada is so plentiful as to be free; then maximizing over a single cycle would be appropriate.

Multiple Rotation Model. Samuelson (1976) demonstrates that when the land is not a free resource then the correct solution will be obtained either by assum-

Figure 8.3
Geometric Solution to the Optimum Rotation Problem

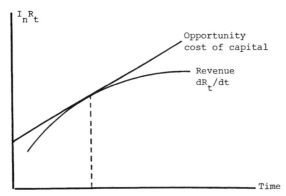

ing an infinite rotation with constant scale replication, but at the same time excluding all rents, or by taking the first cycle with the inclusion of the rental value. The former has now become textbook material. In this, once established trees are harvested, the same acreage is planted at a constant scale until kingdom come. If a private owner does not use this principle he/she will eventually end up in bankruptcy. If the owner is a public sector body with a view to self-financing its operation soon, it will turn to government for a subsidy.

The net benefit function to be maximized is:

$$NPV = -C + (B_t - C)e^{-rt} + (B_t - C)e^{-2rt} + (B_t - C)e^{-3rt} + .. \qquad (8.4)$$

The first term on the right-hand side is the initial planting cost which takes place at present, year zero, for which the discount factor is unity. The second term represents the discounted value of the first harvest and replanting which takes place at a future date. The third term is the second harvest and replanting, which takes place at a time twice as long as the first one, and thus it is discounted at e^{-2rt}, and so on.

Multiplying both sides of the equation by e^{-rt} and subtracting it from (8.4) yields:

$$NPV - NPVe^{-rt} = -C + Ce^{-rt} + (B_t - C)e^{-rt} - (B_t - C)e^{-2rt} + \ldots$$
$$+ \ldots (B_t - C)e^{-(n+1)rt}$$

All the terms on the right hand side cancel out except $-C$; Ce^{-rt}; $(B_t - C)e^{-rt}$ and $(B_t - C)e^{-(n+1)rt}$. Since n is a large number, then $(B_t - C)e^{-(n+1)rt}$ becomes practically zero. Then we have:

$$NPV(1 - e^{-rt}) = -C(1 - e^{-rt}) + (B_t - C)e^{-rt}$$

which is

$$NPV = -C + \frac{(B_t - C_t)e^{-rt}}{1 - e^{-rt}}$$

or

$$NPV = \frac{B_t - Ce^{-rt}}{e^{rt} - 1}$$

or

$$NPV = -C + (B_t - C)(e^{rt} - 1)^{-1} \tag{8.5}$$

For the optimum felling age we have to differentiate (8.5) with respect to time and set it equal to zero (the first order maximization condition), that is:

$$\frac{dNPV}{dt} = \frac{d}{dt}[-C + (B_t - C)(e^{rt} - 1)^{-1}] = 0$$

$$\frac{dB_t}{dt}(e^{rt} - 1)^{-1} - re^{rt}(B_t - C)(e^{rt} - 1)^{-2} = 0$$

which is

$$\frac{dB_t}{dt} = \frac{re^{rt}(B_t - C)}{e^{rt} - 1} \tag{8.6}$$

or

$$\frac{dB_t}{dt} = \frac{r(B_t - C)}{1 - e^{-rt}} \tag{8.7}$$

Samuelson contends that although Faustmann (1849) came close to this solution, he did not produce a clear formula. I call this Faustmann-Samuelson solution to the optimal forest rotation problem.

NEW SOLUTION

One point I would like to make at the outset is that, instead of perpetual rotation, I prefer quite a number of rotations in the following analysis. This is because, although familiar and fashionable they may be, concepts such as perpetual, *ad infinitum*, forever, from now until kingdom come, never-ending, and so on, cannot be relevant in a subject like economics. No investment decision can be forever; no firm or market can realistically be expected to remain in existence in perpetuity; no human institution or even a country can be expected to survive until kingdom come.

One reason why such concepts are used in economic analysis is that they yield mathematically convenient and neat results, as explained in Chapter 4. Samuelson (1976), in search of the correct solution to the optimum forest rotation problem, assumes the infinite chain of cycles of planting on the given acre of land from now until kingdom come. There are many similar examples in economic analysis, mainly for the purpose of model building. An idea which is untrue could help to build a convenient economic model but at the end of the day the model must be treated as untrue. Here I shall assume that the forestry project will be replicated at a constant scale for an unspecified period of time.

Using the modified discounting method in nondiscrete form, as explained in Chapter 4, the problem is stated as:

$$DNB = -C + (B_t - C)[e^{-st}(1 - \frac{t}{n} - \frac{1}{sn}) + \frac{1}{sn}] + \tag{8.8}$$

$$+ (B_t - C)[e^{-2st}(1 - \frac{2t}{n} - \frac{1}{sn}) + \frac{1}{sn}] + \cdots$$

$$\cdots + (B_t - C)[e^{-Nst}(1 - \frac{Nt}{n} - \frac{1}{sn}) + \frac{1}{sn}]$$

where:

DNB = discounted net benefits on the basis of modified discounting.
s = social time preference, constant over time.
n = number of cohorts in population, constant.
C = planting and replanting costs, constant.
B_t = benefit or revenue function.
N = number of rotations.
t = time in terms of years.

The first square bracket relates to the first harvesting and replanting activities. The second square bracket is for the second harvesting and replanting which is twice as long as the first time; that is, if the first harvest is realized in year 30, the second one would be in year 60, and so on.

The objective is to find the optimum cutting age which will maximize DNB. By using:

$$q = e^{-st}; P = \frac{1}{sn}$$

(8.8) becomes:

$$DNB = -C + (B_t - C)[(1 - P)q - \frac{t}{n}q + P] + \cdots \qquad (8.9)$$

$$\cdots + (B_t - C)[(1 - P)q^N - \frac{N}{n}q^N + P]$$

For maximization after summation we differentiate it with respect to time and set it equal to zero. Summation yields:

$$DNB = -C + (R_t - C)[(1 - P) \sum_1^N q^N - \frac{t}{n} \sum_{m=1}^N mq^m + NP] \qquad (8.10)$$

The first term in the square bracket is converging into:

$$q\frac{1 - q^N}{1 - q}$$

The second term will become:

$$\frac{q}{(1 - q)^2} - \frac{q^{N+1}}{(1 - q)^2} + N\frac{q^{N+1}}{1 - q}$$

Since N is a large number and $0 < q < 1$, (8.10) becomes:

$$DNB = -C + (B_t - C)[(1 - P)\frac{q}{1 - q} + \frac{t}{n}\frac{q}{(1 - q)^2} + NP] \qquad (8.11)$$

Substituting $q = e^{-st}$ back:

$$DNB = -C + (B_t - C)[(1 - P)\frac{e^{-st}}{1 - e^{-st}} + \frac{te^{-st}}{n(1 - e^{-st})^2} + NP] \qquad (8.12)$$

Differentiating (8.12) with respect to time and setting it equal to zero will yield:

$$\frac{dDNB}{dt} = \frac{dB_t}{dt}\left[\frac{(1 - P)e^{-st}}{1 - e^{-st}} + \frac{te^{-st}}{n(1 - e^{-st})^2} + NP\right] + \qquad (8.13)$$

$$+ (B_t - C)\left\{\left[\frac{-s(1 - P)e^{-st}}{(1 - e^{-st})^2}\right] + \frac{e^{-st}}{n}\left[\frac{(1 - st) - e^{-st}(1 + st)}{(1 - e^{-st})^3}\right]\right\} = 0$$

Then:

$$\frac{dB_t}{dt} = \frac{-(B_t - C)\left\{\left[\dfrac{-s(1 - P)e^{-st}}{(1 - e^{-st})^2}\right] + \dfrac{e^{-st}}{n}\left[\dfrac{(1 - st) - e^{-st}(1 + st)}{(1 - e^{-st})^3}\right]\right\}}{\dfrac{(1 - P)e^{-st}}{1 - e^{-st}} + \dfrac{te^{-st}}{n(1 - e^{-st})^2} + NP} \quad (8.14)$$

COMPARING THE RESULTS

We now have two discounted net benefit functions; one is obtained by way of modified discounting, based upon the assumption of a large number of chain cycles, equation (8.14), and the other by using ordinary discounting in perpetuity, equation (8.7). The optimum cutting age which will maximize these functions will not be the same. Since, for a given positive discount rate at a point in time in the future, the modified factor is greater than the ordinary factor, an investment decision based upon the former would yield longer rotations than the one when the latter is used. That is:

$$\left[e^{-st}(1 - \frac{t}{n} - \frac{1}{sn}) + \frac{1}{sn}\right] > e^{-st}$$

except when $t = 0$ and $t = 1$ the modified method would then recommend a longer cutting age than ordinary criteria. Another way of seeing this is that since the modified discounting method deflates future costs and benefits in a much more moderate fashion, then the ordinary method will result in longer rotation periods.

Assume the following values, purely for illustrative purposes.

$B_t = 60t - t^2$, revenue function.
$C = 140$, a constant cost function.
$s = 0.1$, the social discount rate (discount rate is r in 8).
$n = 73$, population cohorts and average life expectancy in the community.

Optimum rotation by using the Faustmann-Samuelson solution would be seven years. The modified method, on the other hand, would result in a figure between 29 and 30 years when the number is 25. Foresters' traditional solution, maximum sustainable yield, would give 30 years.

The practical implication of the modified discounting method to determine the optimum cutting age is substantial, as the bulk of the forest estate in many countries is owned publicly. Do public sector forest managers, in reality, use economic criteria in their felling decisions? In Britain and Ireland the economic viability of many afforestation projects is often worked out by using cost-benefit analysis over a single rotation, as explained in Chapter 6. Once an established stand is maturing, the felling decision is normally made in the light of maximum sustainable yield.

Almost all economic models assume constant timber prices over the project's lifetime, which is infinity in conventional analysis. Of course, the reality is different, and the price of wood fluctuates, sometimes quite sharply, from year to year. The demand for wood in the region where trees are to be sold may be very depressed at a time when cutting is contemplated. It is only common sense to postpone the felling decision a few years until the price is favorable. Alternatively, a customer may offer a very good price to buy a stand at a given time before its "predetermined" felling age. Therefore, a strict adherence of a cutting cycle cannot be beneficial in volatile market conditions.

Do private owners, in practice, make their decisions in the light of market inspired theories? To be able to answer this question we need a good deal of empirical research. Lönnstedt (1989) has studied the cutting decisions of private, small-forest owners in Sweden and discovered that many owners deliberately postpone the felling age as long as possible. The need for this study arose because of low cutting intensity prevalent among small-forest owners in Sweden, which is also observed in other Nordic countries, France, Germany and the United States. Lönnstedt concludes that most forest owners have a long time perspective and prefer to hold their estate in trust and hand it on to the next generation. That is, most owners look upon the estate as an inheritance from the grandparents and a loan from the children. Instead of cash benefits a mature forest passed on to the next generation tends to give owners more satisfaction that they are fulfilling their obligations to their offspring as well as their forefathers.

One worthwhile point is that the magnitude of discount rate will make a difference in identifying the optimum cutting age with or without modified discounting. Since the discount rate is a dominant parameter in equations (8.3), (8.7) and (8.14) any change in it will alter the final result. A high interest rate will shorten the optimum cutting age in all models. Conversely, the lower the discount rate the longer the felling cycle. Samuelson expresses his amazement at the low interest rate which abounds in forestry literature:

Faustmann, writing in the middle of the 19th century, uses a four percent rate. Thunnen, writing at the same time, uses a five percent interest rate. The 1960 Goundrey survey also uses a five percent rate. These will seem to an ordinary economist and businessman as remarkably low. . . . I can only guess that such low numbers have been used either as a form of wishful thinking so foresters or forest economists can avoid rotation ages so short they show up the foresters maximum sustainable yield; or because the writers have not had the heart to face up to the discounting. (Samuelson 1976)

Table 8.2
Real Redemption Yields on Index-Linked Bonds in 1988

Maturity Rate	Redemption Yield (%)
2001	4.0
2003	4.0
2006	4.0
2009	4.0
2011	4.0
2013	3.9
2016	3.9
2020	3.8
2024	3.8

Source: Financial Times, LBS inflation forecast.

However, empirical research reveals that for a social rate these figures are quite appropriate for the United States and Canada (Dorfman 1975; Kula 1984a, 1987b). Much lower figures are obtained for other countries: between 2.6 and 3.7 percent for the United Kingdom (Kula 1985, 1987a) and 2 percent for India (Sharma et al. 1991). As for the private sector, real average interest rates during the last couple of decades to 1990 remained remarkably low (Kula 1992). The average rate of interest for the whole period was only 1.3 percent in real terms. Table 8.2 shows the rate of return on long-term risk-free bonds; Table 8.3 shows the base rate of interest.

Samuelson believes that only a daft person will tie up his/her capital to long-term projects such as forestry, where rates of return are very low and risks are very high. I have amply demonstrated elsewhere that rates of return in forestry in the British Isles are well above those of market interest rates (Kula 1988b, 1992).

The use of modified discounting to find the optimum cutting age for publicly owned forests will bring about a solution which is much closer to foresters' maximum sustainable yield than the one which is prescribed by many well-known economists.

For publicly owned forest assets conventional economic models yield a cutting age which is well below the one obtained by using the modified discounting method. I tried to point out that the Faustmann-Samuelson model is not used by real-life decision-makers in the public sector where a "flexible maximum sustainable yield" appears to be popular. Likewise, in private sector forestry, when traditional values are involved, people do not live by mainly short-term rules of the market.

As far as public sector forest managers are concerned, revenue generation is one of many objectives in forestry. The chairman of the Forestry Commission in 1971, Lord Tylor of Gryfe, argued that the Forestry Commission should not

Table 8.3
Real Interest Rates in the United Kingdom

Years	Real Rate of Interest Before Tax
1969	4.3
1970	-0.5
1971	-5.3
1972	-2.8
1973	2.0
1974	-4.9
1975	-15.0
1976	-1.5
1977	-2.0
1978	1.5
1979	0.6
1980	-3.0
1981	2.5
1982	2.0
1983	4.4
1984	4.8
1985	5.4
1986	7.6
1987	4.8
1988	6.2
1989	6.4
1990	5.0
1991	5.0

Source: Bank of England, *Quarterly Bulletin and Economic Trends.*

be regarded as a large commercial state enterprise, but should be recognized for what it is—the forestry authority concerned not only about commercial factors but about the propagation and development of forestry as a whole in the country. Many foresters believe that the maximum sustainable yield is still the best way of achieving their overall objectives, economic, environmental and cultural. The modified discounting method brings the *communal economic* solution very close to the foresters' traditional criterion.

Chapter 9

Economic Appraisal of Transport Projects

INTRODUCTION

Just as water development projects played an important role in advancing cost-benefit appraisal techniques in the United States, the transport projects played a similar role in the United Kingdom. The water resource projects in the United Kingdom are small compared to the United States and also, they are under the control of diverse corporations. Transport projects in a densely populated but spatially distant region like the British Isles have always been important economically, socially and politically. It is therefore not surprising that they were the first ones to be subjected to in-depth cost-benefit analysis.

Toward the end of the 1950s, a substantial number of economists were recruited into the civil service who were familiar with the rudimentary appraisal techniques that were developing in the United States. They were quite keen to use, and even develop, early cost-benefit methods on the United Kingdom's expanding transport projects. At the time, Keynesian macro-economic policies were in fashion in Britain and, apart from the growth of nationalized industries, transport infrastructure was receiving increasing attention.

The London-Birmingham motorway project, M1, was the first major public sector investment which was subjected to a rigorous cost-benefit analysis. This retrospective study was conducted by Beesley et al. (1960) under the auspices of the Road Research Laboratory. The M1 project, in the main, was a methodological study, but the principles established there have been widely used on many other transport studies. After the M1, many other sizeable transport projects such as the Tay Bridge, Severn Bridge, London Victoria Underground Line, Cumbrian Coast Railway Line, and the siting of the Third London Airport received the scrutiny of cost-benefit analysts. Economic analysis for some of these case studies turned out to be highly expensive and time-consuming. For example, the study on the siting of the Third London Airport took two and a half years to complete and cost over £1 million, in terms of 1969 prices.

Apart from being vital for the nation's economic development, transport projects exhibit a number of interesting characteristics. First, most transport projects are creators of substantial environmental problems such as noise, pollution, loss of habitat and visual amenity. Incorporating environmental costs into cost-benefit studies is a substantial task in its own right; unfortunately, these attempts have largely been unsuccessful. Some transport projects were remarkably free of environmental issues such as visual intrusion and noise. The Victoria Line in London was a good example, due to its underground location, but this was an exception.

Second, financial analyses on transport projects produce ridiculous results (Pearce and Nash 1981). For instance, payments by road users by way of taxation, license duty and fuel tax fall well short of benefits accruing to the community. It is only when tolls are charged that the resulting revenue from the road use bears some resemblance to benefits such as time saved and comfort. However, introduction of nationwide toll charges is thought to be neither practicable nor socially desirable. Because of all these reasons many believe that cost-benefit analysis methods should be able to give a reasonably good idea to decision-makers about the worth of transport projects.

Most transportation projects incur high capital cost during their construction. Benefits, on the other hand, occur at later years after such projects are completed and put into use. Separation of distant benefits from the high capital cost makes discounting a crucial parameter in their economic evaluation. Transportation projects can be designed for a multitude of purposes such as to accommodate an increasing number of passengers and freight, to reduce journey time and to increase comfort or convenience.

When a transport project is designed to save journey time the primary benefits are normally measured by the willingness of the travellers to pay in order to save that amount of time. A popular approach is to assume the value of an individual's time as equal to the money he/she could earn during the time saved. If a person's average hourly earning was £5, a transport project which saves him/her 100 hours a year would be worth at least £500 per annum for that person. The rationale for this calculation derives from the individual's supply schedule of labor (Mishan 1988).

There are some reservations to be made. First, the hours of work for most people are fixed in negotiations between the employer and the trade union. This implies that the hourly wage rate is not a realistic method of measuring the value of time for individuals who work for fixed hours. Second, in cost-benefit analysis of transportation projects the social value of individuals' hourly income is relevant. If the price of labor input exceeds marginal social cost in the industry employing the worker then the marginal social valuation of an hour's work exceeds the hourly wage he/she is paid in terms of social opportunity cost. Third, in some transport studies, travelling time is assumed to be a burden on individuals, which cannot be true in every case. Travelling time can be spent in reading documents, preparing for meetings, marking exam scripts, and so on, provided that comfortable conditions exist. Travelling for holiday is not considered a burden by most people as it is a part of the whole experience. Of course, when travelling time is saved for the drivers of freight vehicles the situation is different, as man hours in this case are an input into the production process.

There is also the issue of marginal versus substantial savings in time. An investment project to save ten seconds' time on a daily journey may not be worth having even if millions of people make that journey, as nobody would care much about that amount of time. However as Mishan (1988) puts it, such considerations tend only to qualify the measurement of the value of time; they do not bring into question the idea of valuing time in terms of the social considerations. Having said this, I shall now turn to a cost-benefit analysis of the Victoria Line underground railway network in London.

THE VICTORIA LINE

The Victoria Line, which is currently active, links Victoria at its southern end to Walthamstow in northeast London, and was first proposed by the Inglis Committee (1946) and later expanded on by the London Plan Working Party. In 1962 its construction was authorized by the Treasury. It represented the first underground railway built in central London since before 1914. Figure 9.1 shows its position in central London.

A comprehensive cost-benefit analysis, which gave favorable results, was carried out by Foster and Beesley (1963, 1965) who aimed to measure the discounted surplus of social benefits over discounted social costs expected from the construction and operation of the Victoria Line. The team contended that a purely financial study based upon fare levels would most certainly make the project unattractive because revenue collected in this way would fall short of its operating cost, interest charge and depreciation. The main reasons for the divergence between the social and financial study were the pricing policy used on underground fares and relative prices on road and rail in London.

The importance of cost-benefit analysis in determining whether or not the project should have been built was debatable, but its favorable findings confirmed and even speeded up the decision (Barker and Button 1979). One of the shortcomings of the study was that it did not compare alternative transport schemes to the Victoria Line to ascertain that the line represented the best option. In other words, the study compared the Victoria Line with no alternative.

Assumptions and Conventions. The life of the project was assumed to be 56 years, 6 years' construction and 50 years' operation.[1] Analysts did not imply that all capital invested would need to be replaced by then. Indeed, tunnels and other earthworks will be usable for a very long time, but technological progress and spatial changes in population and industry could make the Victoria Line

Figure 9.1
Parts of London Underground; Victoria, Bakerloo and Central Lines

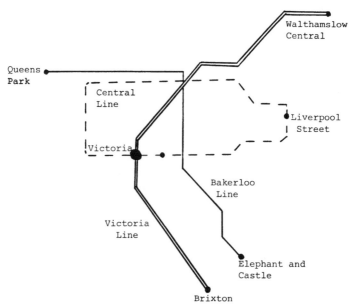

obsolete at some future date. To guard against obsolescence, the team felt that it was sensible to limit the operating life of the project to 50 years.

In their analysis Foster and Beesley used 4, 6 and 8 percent interest rates. Their inclination was that an investment project in the public sector should relate to the opportunity cost of capital but be measured in the form of the marginal social surplus rate of return. At the time, nationalized industries were beginning to increase their discount rates, partly due to the increase in the government borrowing rate, despite the fact that there was no officially agreed general rate of discount. As for the risk, rather than increasing the rates of discount, Foster and Beesley made allowances by way of a 50-year operational life, as explained above.

In this reappraisal of the Victoria Line I shall use 8 and 10 percent discount rates, as they were in line with the official discount rates introduced by the government at the time (Chapter 2). Other assumptions are: all costs and benefits are estimated in terms of 1962 prices, deflated to that year. Expected changes in land values are not included, as it would have meant a double counting because property values increase partly due to the improved transport infrastructure.

Costs. There are two items: construction cost and annual working expenses. The former includes such items as tunnelling, tracks and rolling-stock. Interest charges are not counted, as the focus of attention here is the net benefit of the project, not whether it can serve a particular fixed interest charge. Some capital items are assumed to have a scrap value of £5.3 million.

In addition, there was an £8 million expenditure to rebuild Kings Cross, Euston, Oxford Circus and Victoria stations. However, it was argued that these stations would have been rebuilt in any case and thus this expenditure is not incorporated into calculations.

Annual working expenses on track, structures, and rolling-stock were estimated to be £1.4 million per annum over a 50-year period.

Benefits. The measured benefits of the Victoria Line fall into three groups: the time savings to each class of people affected by the project; cost-savings to travellers and fleet operators as a result of reduced congestion and resulting diminished operating costs; and the value of increased comfort and convenience.

In the first category it was assumed that people choosing to travel directly on the Victoria Line or on other forms of transport speeded up by the line will save time, which has a value to them. In addition, those on other parts of the underground network benefit from the Victoria Line, where fewer passengers there means shorter station stops and so more trains can be run per hour. Furthermore, travellers on British Railways and on the roads benefit from reduced congestion.

The inclusion of comfort and convenience in the cost-benefit study was a novel and interesting approach. Less standing in coaches during the rush hours will improve travelling conditions greatly. Motorists on the roads value less-congested roads by more than what they save in time and vehicle operating costs. Driving along relatively less crowded roads may make the journey more pleasurable. The only element in comfort and convenience quantified in this analysis was the increased probability of getting a seat for passengers diverting to the Victoria Line and those remaining on existing lines.

COST-BENEFIT ANALYSIS

Construction and operating costs over the life of the project are shown in Table 9.1.

Benefits by source are put into three groups: (1) diverted traffic to the Victoria Line; (2) undiverted traffic; (3) generated traffic.

Diverted Traffic. It was assumed that all passengers would choose the quicker route between their existing route and Victoria Line. If both took the same time, half would use the Victoria Line and the other half would stick to their routines. Only passengers in central London were taken into consideration; those outside the central area were left out on the grounds that their numbers were too small to justify calculation.

The time saved was valued at different rates for work and leisure. For the former, the hourly wage rate was used which was 36.3 pence per hour in 1962. The leisure time was measured at a lower rate, 25 pence per hour. Average time economized by diverted journey on the underground was estimated to be 4.5

Table 9.1
Capital and Operating Cost of the Victoria Line

Years	Capital Cost Million £	Operating Cost Million £
1	3.6	-
2	6.4	-
3	9.6	-
4	9.2	-
5	13.7	-
6	5.6	-
7	-	1.41
8	-	1.41
:	:	:
:	:	:
55	-	1.41
56	-	1.41
Total	48.1	70.50

Source: Foster and Beesley (1963).

minutes, a total of 1.48 million hours per year. Five percent of this was assumed to be work time and 95 percent leisure time. That is:

5% of 1.48 m (work time) at 36.3 pence = £25,500
95% of 1.48 m (leisure time) at 25.0 pence = £352,500
Total = £378,000

There was assumed to be no increase in the value of work and leisure time, over time.

Another substantial benefit to the passengers diverted from the existing underground system to the Victoria Line was the increased comfort and convenience, which was measured by finding the value of the increased probability of getting a seat. The basic assumption was that comfort and convenience are positively related to the increased probability of getting a seat. It was envisaged that passengers would have a choice between saving time by opting for a fast but crowded train, and trying to look for a slow but comfortable carriage. If they chose the latter, the volume of comfort could be ascertained by the time sacrificed by opting for a longer journey in order to secure the increased likelihood of a seat. The figure for increased comfort and convenience was estimated to be £347,000 per annum, projected to fall to zero at the end of 50 years of operation.

A second category of diverted traffic was from British Rail, where passengers were assumed to save time on shorter trips after the Victoria Line was operating. In this a six-minute time saving was assumed by an average traveller which amounted to 0.8 million hours per year. The calculation was:

$$5\% \text{ of } 0.8 \text{ m (work time) at } 36.3 \text{ pence} = £15,000$$
$$95\% \text{ of } 0.8 \text{ m (leisure time) at } 25 \text{ pence} = £190,000$$
$$\text{Total} = £205,000$$

This traffic was projected to grow at 1.5 percent compound over time. No calculation was made for increased comfort and convenience in this case. The combined benefits of diverted traffic from the tube and British Rail are shown in Column 2, Table 9.2.

A third item of diverted traffic was from London city buses, which was calculated to be 5 minutes' saving per trip, amounting to 2.27 million hours per annum. Only 3 percent of the bus journey was assumed to be work time and the rest leisure time. The annual value of time saved in this way was calculated to be £575,000, with no growth over time.

The fourth case was diverted traffic from roads which involved two kinds of benefits: time savings and savings on vehicle operating costs. The proportion of travel by car in terms of work between central London and the outer regions was estimated to be 13 percent; by motorbike 6 percent. The average hourly income was assumed to be 59 pence for a car traveller and 36.3 pence for a motorcyclist. The annual value of time saved in this way was estimated to be £153,000.

As for the vehicle operating cost savings, the chief items were fuel, lubricants, tires, maintenance and depreciation. The study assumed that half of the saved journeys were performed by large cars (2250 cc or over) and the other half by small cars (1000 cc). The annual sum was estimated to be £377,000 at the outset with a trend of 5 percent compound for the first 15 years and 2 percent compound thereafter. These also apply to £153,000, time saved. The combined figures for time saved and operating costs for buses, cars and motorbikes are shown in Column 3, Table 9.2

The last item in diverted traffic was the estimates made on the number of pedestrians who would use the Victoria Line instead of walking. The starting annual value of benefit was estimated to be £20,000 to grow by 1.5 percent compound, Column 4, Table 9.2.

Undiverted Traffic. This contained two items: traffic remaining on underground and buses, and undiverted road traffic. Time savings to travellers in the underground network, in British Rail trains and on London Transport buses, were not taken into consideration. The main benefits were assumed to be to the operators. In the case of underground travellers, only increased comfort and convenience were taken into account. Total benefits for underground and buses were estimated to be £1,252,000 per annum, shown in the fifth column of Table

Table 9.2
Benefits from Diverted, Undiverted and Generated Traffic to the Victoria Line, £ (000)

| | Diverted Traffic | | | Undiverted Traffic | Savings In Time & Operating Costs | | |
Year	From British Rail & Tube	From Buses Cars & Motorbikes	Pedestrians	Underground & Buses	on Roads	Generated Traffic	Total
7	930	1105	20	1252	2662	822	6793
8	933	1132	20	1252	2664	834	6835
9	936	1159	21	1252	2664	847	6879
10	939	1188	21	1252	2664	860	6924
11	934	1219	21	1252	2664	872	6971
12	946	1251	22	1252	2664	885	7020
13	949	1285	22	1252	2664	299	7071
14	953	1320	22	1252	2664	912	7123
15	956	1358	23	1252	2664	926	7179
16	959	1397	23	1252	2664	940	7235
17	963	1438	23	1252	2664	954	7294
18	966	1481	24	1252	2664	968	7355
19	970	1526	24	1252	2664	983	7417
20	974	1574	24	1252	2664	998	7486
21	977	1624	25	1252	2664	1013	7555
22	981	1645	25	1252	2664	1028	7595
23	985	1667	25	1252	2664	1043	7636
24	989	1689	26	1252	2664	1059	7679
25	993	1711	26	1252	2664	1075	7721
26	997	1734	27	1252	2664	1091	7765
27	1001	1757	27	1252	2664	1107	7808

28	1005	1780	27	1252	2664	1124	7852
29	1109	1804	28	1252	2664	1141	7898
30	1014	1829	28	1252	2664	1158	7945
31	1018	1854	29	1252	2664	1175	7992
32	1023	1880	29	1252	2664	1199	8041
33	1027	1906	29	1252	2664	1211	8089
34	1032	1932	30	1252	2664	1229	8139
35	1036	1960	30	1252	2664	1247	8189
36	1041	1987	31	1252	2664	1265	8240
37	1046	2015	31	1252	2664	1284	8292
38	1051	2044	32	1252	2664	1303	8346
39	1055	2073	32	1252	2664	1323	8399
40	1066	2103	33	1252	2664	1343	8455
41	1065	2134	33	1252	2664	1363	8511
42	1070	2165	34	1252	2664	1383	8568
43	1076	2197	34	1252	2664	1404	8627
44	1081	2229	35	1252	2664	1425	8686
45	1086	2262	35	1252	2664	1446	8745
46	1092	2296	36	1252	2664	1468	8808
47	1097	2331	37	1252	2664	1490	8871
48	1102	2366	38	1252	2664	1512	8934
49	1108	2402	39	1252	2664	1535	9000
50	1114	2438	40	1252	2664	1558	9066
51	1120	2475	40	1252	2664	1582	9133
52	1126	2513	41	1252	2664	1605	9201
53	1132	2552	41	1252	2664	1629	9270
54	1138	2592	42	1252	2664	1654	9342
55	1144	2632	43	1252	2664	1679	9414
56	1151	2673	43	1252	2664	1704	9487

Table 9.3
Undiscounted and Discounted Costs and Benefits (£ million) Victoria Line

Item	Undiscounted Value	Discounted Value Ordinary Method		Discounted Value Modified Method	
		8 pc	10pc	8 pc	10 pc
Cost	118.6	46.6	41.2	54.5	48.5
Benefit*	408.3	56.6	40.7	100.9	80.9

*includes scrap value.

9.3. The breakdown of this sum was: £150,000 for cost saving, £457,000 increased comfort and convenience, and £645,000 cost saving by London buses.

The second item in the undiverted traffic category, namely, road traffic, turned out to be the most important group of social benefits, which were composed of two components: time saving and saving on operation cost. Both resulted from reduced congestion and consequently, increased speed. It was estimated that in central London alone the Victoria Line would save £1,200,000 vehicle hours per year. The average occupancy rate on buses was taken to be 18 and 1.5 for cars and taxis, which amounted to 1,940,000 hours for buses and 951,000 hours for cars. The saved time for bus travellers per hour was valued at 25.5 pence and 29.5 pence for car travellers was used. This totaled 770,000 per year.

In the area adjacent to central London the time saved was calculated to be 1,521,000 person hours per year, of which 57 percent was by cars, 42 percent by public transport and one percent by taxis. Time saving values for each group were 29 pence, 25.5 pence and 29.5 pence, respectively. Then time saving in the adjacent area became £420,550 per year.

In addition, there was relief to roads in the central region that would be associated with diversion of short distance travelling to the tube system. It was argued that this traffic would mostly take place during the off-peak hours and thus would involve little or no extra cost to the tube system. The annual value of this benefit was estimated to be £693,000.

Decreased congestion on roads also reduced the vehicle operating costs on the order of £781,000. The benefits of undiverted traffic are shown in Columns 5 and 6, Table 9.2.

Generated Traffic. The Victoria Line was assumed to generate new traffic which would be made as a result of quicker journeys. From the boroughs to central London, about 9 million new trips were assumed to be made per year. The average time saved was calculated to be 45 million minutes, valued at 25.6 pence per hour, which resulted in a £96,000 benefit per year. In addition, there were benefits by way of reduced fares payable by new passengers which roughly came to £63,000 per annum. Generated traffic was thought to increase London Transport's new revenues by £375,000 per annum; finally, for the central area, an additional £288,000 per annum by way of time saving, fare saving and some other benefits.

In total, the annual value of generated traffic turned out to be £822,000 assumed to grow by 1.5 percent per annum and shown in Column 7, Table 9.3.

OVERALL RESULTS

Discounted values by way of ordinary and modified methods using 8 and 10 percent discount rates are shown in Table 9.3. The benefit-cost ratio with an 8 percent discount rate becomes 1.21 by using the ordinary discounting method which implies economic viability. But the ratio turns out to be 0.98 when a 10 percent interest rate is used. That is, at a 10 percent discount rate, discounted benefits are not large enough to offset discounted costs and consequently the project, although only marginally, fails.

Like afforestation and land drainage projects, the use of modified discounting in economic appraisal of transport infrastructure projects would enhance their viability. Of course, the common characteristics of these projects is that they are all long-term undertakings in which the initial capital costs are well separated from later-year benefits, making discounting a crucial parameter in the equation.

It has been alleged that when the modified discounting is used to ascertain the commercial desirability of communal projects, especially transport investments, this would imply a large increase in road and rail networks, a case which could create environmental problems. This would not be so. If expansion of infrastructure projects generates costs such as noise, pollution and loss of visual amenity, they should be properly costed and included in cost-benefit calculations. If these costs are substantial, then they would reduce the desirability or, in some cases, could even eliminate the viability of transport projects altogether. Most environmental problems tend to occur in the long run due to the build-up of smoke, dust and noise resulting from increased use. These later-year costs, when deflated by modified factors, will have a substantial bearing upon the discounted overall sums. But when ordinary discounting is used, long-term environmental costs will be wiped out.

NOTE

1. In the original study, the construction period was assumed to be 5.5 years, but here this is rounded up to 6 years.

Appendix 1

The Ordinary Discount Factors

Percentage

Year	4.0	5.0	6.0	7.0	8.0	9.0	10.0	11.0	12.0	15.0
1	0.9615	0.9524	0.9434	0.9346	0.9259	0.9174	0.9091	0.9009	0.8929	0.8696
2	0.9246	0.9070	0.8900	0.8734	0.8573	0.8417	0.8264	0.8116	0.7972	0.7561
3	0.8890	0.8638	0.8396	0.8163	0.7938	0.7722	0.7513	0.7312	0.7118	0.6575
4	0.8548	0.8227	0.7921	0.7629	0.7350	0.7084	0.6830	0.6587	0.6355	0.5718
5	0.8219	0.7835	0.7473	0.7130	0.6806	0.6499	0.6209	0.5935	0.5674	0.4972
6	0.7903	0.7462	0.7050	0.6663	0.6302	0.5963	0.5645	0.5346	0.5066	0.4323
7	0.7599	0.7107	0.6651	0.6228	0.5835	0.5470	0.5132	0.4817	0.4523	0.3759
8	0.7307	0.6768	0.6274	0.5820	0.5403	0.5019	0.4665	0.4339	0.4039	0.3269
9	0.7026	0.6446	0.5919	0.5439	0.5002	0.4604	0.4241	0.3909	0.3606	0.2843
10	0.6756	0.6139	0.5584	0.5083	0.4632	0.4224	0.3855	0.3522	0.3220	0.2472
11	0.6496	0.5847	0.5268	0.4751	0.4289	0.3875	0.3505	0.3173	0.2875	0.2149
12	0.6246	0.5568	0.4970	0.4440	0.3971	0.3555	0.3186	0.2858	0.2567	0.1869
13	0.6006	0.5303	0.4688	0.4150	0.3677	0.3262	0.2897	0.2575	0.2292	0.1625
14	0.5775	0.5051	0.4423	0.3878	0.3405	0.2992	0.2633	0.2320	0.2046	0.1413
15	0.5553	0.4810	0.4173	0.3624	0.3152	0.2745	0.2394	0.2090	0.1827	0.1229
16	0.5339	0.4581	0.3936	0.3387	0.2919	0.2519	0.2176	0.1883	0.1631	0.1069

Percentage

Year	4.0	5.0	6.0	7.0	8.0	9.0	10.0	11.0	12.0	15.0
17	0.5134	0.4363	0.3714	0.3166	0.2703	0.2311	0.1978	0.1696	0.1456	0.0929
18	0.4936	0.4155	0.3503	0.2959	0.2502	0.2120	0.1799	0.1528	0.1300	0.0808
19	0.4746	0.3957	0.3305	0.2765	0.2317	0.1945	0.1635	0.1377	0.1161	0.0703
20	0.4564	0.3769	0.3118	0.2584	0.2145	0.1784	0.1486	0.1240	0.1037	0.0611
21	0.4388	0.3589	0.2942	0.2415	0.1987	0.1637	0.1351	0.1117	0.0926	0.0531
22	0.4219	0.3419	0.2775	0.2257	0.1839	0.1502	0.1228	0.1007	0.0826	0.0462
23	0.4057	0.3256	0.2618	0.2109	0.1703	0.1378	0.1117	0.0907	0.0738	0.0402
24	0.3901	0.3101	0.2470	0.1971	0.1577	0.1264	0.1015	0.0817	0.0659	0.0349
25	0.3751	0.2953	0.2330	0.1842	0.1460	0.1160	0.0923	0.0736	0.0588	0.0304
26	0.3607	0.2812	0.2198	0.1722	0.1352	0.1064	0.0839	0.0663	0.0525	0.0264
27	0.3468	0.2678	0.2074	0.1609	0.1252	0.0976	0.0763	0.0597	0.0469	0.0230
28	0.3335	0.2551	0.1956	0.1504	0.1159	0.0895	0.0693	0.0538	0.0419	0.0200
29	0.3207	0.2429	0.1846	0.1406	0.1073	0.0822	0.0630	0.0485	0.0374	0.0174
30	0.3083	0.2314	0.1741	0.1314	0.0994	0.0754	0.0573	0.0437	0.0334	0.0151
31	0.2965	0.2204	0.1643	0.1228	0.0920	0.0691	0.0521	0.0394	0.0298	0.0131
32	0.2851	0.2099	0.1550	0.1147	0.0852	0.0634	0.0474	0.0355	0.0266	0.0114
33	0.2741	0.1999	0.1462	0.1072	0.0789	0.0582	0.0431	0.0319	0.0238	0.0099
34	0.2636	0.1904	0.1379	0.1002	0.0730	0.0534	0.0391	0.0288	0.0212	0.0086
35	0.2534	0.1813	0.1301	0.0937	0.0676	0.0490	0.0356	0.0259	0.0189	0.0075
36	0.2437	0.1727	0.1227	0.0875	0.0626	0.0449	0.0323	0.0234	0.0169	0.0065
37	0.2343	0.1644	0.1158	0.0818	0.0580	0.0412	0.0294	0.0210	0.0151	0.0057
38	0.2253	0.1566	0.1092	0.0765	0.0537	0.0378	0.0267	0.0190	0.0135	0.0049

| | Percentage | | | | | | | | | |
Year	4.0	5.0	6.0	7.0	8.0	9.0	10.0	11.0	12.0	15.0
39	0.2166	0.1491	0.1031	0.0715	0.0497	0.0347	0.0243	0.0171	0.0120	0.0043
40	0.2083	0.1420	0.0972	0.0668	0.0460	0.0318	0.0221	0.0154	0.0107	0.0037
41	0.2003	0.1353	0.0917	0.0624	0.0426	0.0292	0.0201	0.0139	0.0096	0.0032
42	0.1926	0.1288	0.0865	0.0583	0.0395	0.0268	0.0183	0.0125	0.0086	0.0028
43	0.1852	0.1227	0.0816	0.0545	0.0365	0.0246	0.0166	0.0112	0.0076	0.0025
44	0.1780	0.1169	0.0770	0.0509	0.0338	0.0226	0.0151	0.0101	0.0068	0.0021
45	0.1712	0.1113	0.0727	0.0476	0.0313	0.0207	0.0137	0.0091	0.0061	0.0019
46	0.1646	0.1060	0.0685	0.0445	0.0290	0.0190	0.0125	0.0082	0.0054	0.0016
47	0.1583	0.1009	0.0647	0.0416	0.0269	0.0174	0.0113	0.0074	0.0049	0.0014
48	0.1522	0.0961	0.0610	0.0389	0.0249	0.0160	0.0103	0.0067	0.0043	0.0012
49	0.1463	0.0916	0.0575	0.0363	0.0230	0.0147	0.0094	0.0060	0.0039	0.0011
50	0.1407	0.0872	0.0543	0.0339	0.0213	0.0134	0.0085	0.0054	0.0035	0.0009

Appendix 2

Discount Factors for the United Kingdom on the Basis of MDM

Discount rate, percentage

Year (t)	1	2	3	4	5	6	7	8	9	10	11	12	13	14	15
1	0.99010	0.98039	0.97087	0.96154	0.95238	0.94340	0.93458	0.92593	0.91743	0.90909	0.90090	0.89286	0.88496	0.87719	0.86957
2	0.98043	0.96143	0.94298	0.92506	0.90765	0.89073	0.87428	0.85828	0.84272	0.82758	0.81285	0.79850	0.78454	0.77094	0.75770
3	0.97099	0.94310	0.91628	0.89048	0.86564	0.84173	0.81870	0.79631	0.77513	0.75451	0.73462	0.71543	0.69691	0.67904	0.66177
4	0.96178	0.92538	0.89072	0.85769	0.82620	0.79616	0.76749	0.74013	0.71399	0.68901	0.66514	0.64230	0.62046	0.59955	0.57953
5	0.95278	0.90826	0.86626	0.82661	0.78917	0.75378	0.72032	0.68866	0.65870	0.63032	0.60343	0.57794	0.55377	0.53082	0.50904
6	0.94401	0.89172	0.84286	0.79717	0.75441	0.71438	0.67687	0.64170	0.60871	0.57774	0.54865	0.52131	0.49560	0.47141	0.44864
7	0.93545	0.87574	0.82047	0.76927	0.72180	0.67776	0.63686	0.59886	0.56352	0.53064	0.50002	0.47149	0.44489	0.42006	0.39688
8	0.92710	0.86031	0.79906	0.74284	0.69120	0.64372	0.60003	0.55978	0.52269	0.48846	0.45687	0.42767	0.40067	0.37569	0.35255
9	0.91896	0.84541	0.77859	0.71782	0.66250	0.61210	0.56612	0.52415	0.48579	0.45070	0.41858	0.38914	0.36214	0.33735	0.31458
10	0.91102	0.83102	0.75902	0.69413	0.63559	0.58273	0.53493	0.49166	0.45246	0.41690	0.38461	0.35527	0.32857	0.30425	0.28207
11	0.90328	0.81714	0.74031	0.67171	0.61036	0.55545	0.50662	0.46205	0.42236	0.38665	0.35449	0.32550	0.29932	0.27566	0.25425
12	0.89575	0.80375	0.72244	0.65049	0.58672	0.53012	0.47983	0.43507	0.39518	0.35959	0.32779	0.29934	0.27385	0.25098	0.23044
13	0.88840	0.79083	0.70537	0.63041	0.56456	0.50662	0.45555	0.41049	0.37065	0.33539	0.30412	0.27636	0.25167	0.22968	0.21007
14	0.88125	0.77837	0.68907	0.61143	0.54380	0.48481	0.43324	0.38810	0.34852	0.31374	0.28314	0.25617	0.23236	0.21130	0.19264
15	0.87429	0.76636	0.67351	0.59348	0.52437	0.46457	0.41274	0.36772	0.32855	0.29439	0.26456	0.23846	0.21556	0.19545	0.17774
16	0.86752	0.75478	0.65865	0.57651	0.50617	0.44580	0.39390	0.34917	0.31054	0.27710	0.24811	0.22290	0.20095	0.18178	0.16501

Discount rate, percentage

Year (t)	1	2	3	4	5	6	7	8	9	10	11	12	13	14	15
17	0.86092	0.74363	0.64448	0.56047	0.48913	0.42841	0.37659	0.33228	0.29430	0.26166	0.23354	0.20926	0.18824	0.17000	0.15412
18	0.85451	0.73289	0.63096	0.54533	0.47320	0.41228	0.36071	0.31693	0.27966	0.24786	0.22064	0.19729	0.17719	0.15984	0.14483
19	0.84827	0.72254	0.61807	0.53102	0.45829	0.39734	0.34612	0.30296	0.26647	0.23554	0.20923	0.18679	0.16758	0.15109	0.13688
20	0.84221	0.71259	0.60579	0.51752	0.44435	0.38350	0.33274	0.29026	0.25459	0.22454	0.19914	0.17759	0.15924	0.14355	0.13010
21	0.83632	0.70301	0.59408	0.50477	0.43132	0.37069	0.32047	0.27872	0.24390	0.21473	0.19021	0.16952	0.15199	0.13707	0.12432
22	0.83060	0.69379	0.58292	0.49275	0.41914	0.35883	0.30921	0.26824	0.23427	0.20598	0.18233	0.16246	0.14569	0.13148	0.11938
23	0.82504	0.68493	0.57230	0.48141	0.40777	0.34785	0.29890	0.25872	0.22561	0.19818	0.17536	0.15627	0.14023	0.12668	0.11517
24	0.81965	0.67642	0.56220	0.47073	0.39715	0.33770	0.28945	0.25008	0.21781	0.19123	0.16920	0.15086	0.13549	0.12255	0.11158
25	0.81441	0.66823	0.55258	0.46065	0.38724	0.32832	0.28079	0.24224	0.21081	0.18503	0.16377	0.14612	0.13138	0.11900	0.10852
26	0.80934	0.66037	0.54343	0.45117	0.37799	0.31965	0.27286	0.23513	0.20451	0.17951	0.15897	0.14197	0.12782	0.11595	0.10592
27	0.80441	0.65283	0.53474	0.44224	0.36937	0.31164	0.26561	0.22868	0.19886	0.17460	0.15474	0.13835	0.12473	0.11333	0.10370
28	0.79964	0.64559	0.52647	0.43383	0.36133	0.30424	0.25898	0.22284	0.19378	0.17023	0.15101	0.13519	0.12206	0.11108	0.10181
29	0.79503	0.63865	0.51863	0.42592	0.35385	0.29741	0.25291	0.21755	0.18922	0.16635	0.14772	0.13242	0.11974	0.10914	0.10021
30	0.79055	0.63199	0.51118	0.41849	0.34687	0.29112	0.24737	0.21275	0.18513	0.16289	0.14482	0.13001	0.11774	0.10749	0.09884
31	0.78623	0.62562	0.50411	0.41150	0.34038	0.28531	0.24231	0.20842	0.18149	0.15982	0.14227	0.12790	0.11601	0.10607	0.09768
32	0.78204	0.61951	0.49741	0.40494	0.33435	0.27996	0.23768	0.20450	0.17818	0.15710	0.14003	0.12606	0.11451	0.10485	0.09670
33	0.77800	0.61367	0.49105	0.39879	0.32873	0.27504	0.23347	0.20095	0.17524	0.15468	0.13806	0.12446	0.11322	0.10381	0.09586
34	0.77409	0.60808	0.48504	0.39301	0.32352	0.27050	0.22962	0.19775	0.17261	0.15254	0.13632	0.12307	0.11210	0.10292	0.09515
35	0.77032	0.60274	0.47934	0.38759	0.31867	0.26633	0.22612	0.19486	0.17025	0.15063	0.13480	0.12185	0.11113	0.10216	0.09455
36	0.76668	0.59763	0.47395	0.38252	0.31418	0.26250	0.22293	0.19225	0.16815	0.14895	0.13346	0.12080	0.11030	0.10150	0.09404
37	0.76317	0.59276	0.46886	0.37777	0.31001	0.25898	0.22003	0.18990	0.16626	0.14746	0.13229	0.11988	0.10959	0.10095	0.09361
38	0.75980	0.58811	0.46405	0.37333	0.30615	0.25575	0.21739	0.18778	0.16459	0.14614	0.13126	0.11908	0.10897	0.10047	0.09324
39	0.75654	0.58368	0.45950	0.36917	0.30258	0.25278	0.21499	0.18587	0.16309	0.14498	0.13036	0.11839	0.10844	0.10007	0.09293
40	0.75341	0.57946	0.45522	0.36529	0.29927	0.25006	0.21281	0.18416	0.16175	0.14395	0.12957	0.11779	0.10799	0.09972	0.09267
41	0.75041	0.57545	0.45119	0.36167	0.29621	0.24758	0.21084	0.18262	0.16057	0.14304	0.12888	0.11727	0.10759	0.09943	0.09245
42	0.74752	0.57163	0.44739	0.35829	0.29339	0.24530	0.20905	0.18123	0.15951	0.14224	0.12828	0.11682	0.10726	0.09918	0.09227

Discount rate, percentage

Year (i)	1	2	3	4	5	6	7	8	9	10	11	12	13	14	15
43	0.74475	0.56801	0.44381	0.35515	0.29078	0.24322	0.20743	0.17999	0.15857	0.14153	0.12775	0.11643	0.10697	0.09897	0.09211
44	0.74210	0.56457	0.44045	0.35222	0.28838	0.24132	0.20596	0.17888	0.15773	0.14091	0.12730	0.11609	0.10672	0.09879	0.09198
45	0.73956	0.56131	0.43730	0.34950	0.28617	0.23959	0.20464	0.17788	0.15699	0.14037	0.12690	0.11580	0.10651	0.09863	0.09187
46	0.73714	0.55823	0.43435	0.34698	0.28414	0.23801	0.20344	0.17699	0.15634	0.13989	0.12655	0.11555	0.10633	0.09850	0.09177
47	0.73482	0.55531	0.43158	0.34463	0.28227	0.23658	0.20237	0.17620	0.15576	0.13947	0.12625	0.11533	0.10618	0.09839	0.09170
48	0.73261	0.55256	0.42900	0.34247	0.28056	0.23527	0.20140	0.17549	0.15525	0.13910	0.12599	0.11515	0.10605	0.09830	0.09163
49	0.73051	0.54996	0.42658	0.34046	0.27899	0.23409	0.20053	0.17486	0.15480	0.13878	0.12576	0.11499	0.10593	0.09822	0.09158
50	0.72851	0.54752	0.42433	0.33861	0.27756	0.23302	0.19975	0.17430	0.15440	0.13850	0.12557	0.11485	0.10584	0.09816	0.09153
51	0.72661	0.54522	0.42224	0.33691	0.27625	0.23205	0.19905	0.17380	0.15405	0.13826	0.12540	0.11473	0.10576	0.09810	0.09149
52	0.72481	0.54307	0.42029	0.33534	0.27506	0.23118	0.19842	0.17336	0.15374	0.13805	0.12525	0.11463	0.10569	0.09806	0.09146
53	0.72312	0.54106	0.41849	0.33390	0.27397	0.23039	0.19786	0.17297	0.15347	0.13786	0.12513	0.11455	0.10563	0.09802	0.09144
54	0.72152	0.53917	0.41683	0.33258	0.27299	0.22969	0.19737	0.17263	0.15324	0.13770	0.12502	0.11448	0.10558	0.09798	0.09141
55	0.72001	0.53742	0.41529	0.33138	0.27210	0.22905	0.19693	0.17233	0.15303	0.13757	0.12493	0.11442	0.10554	0.09796	0.09140
56	0.71860	0.53580	0.41388	0.33028	0.27130	0.22849	0.19654	0.17206	0.15285	0.13745	0.12485	0.11436	0.10551	0.09794	0.09138
57	0.71728	0.53429	0.41258	0.32928	0.27058	0.22798	0.19619	0.17183	0.15270	0.13735	0.12478	0.11432	0.10548	0.09792	0.09137
58	0.71605	0.53290	0.41140	0.32838	0.26993	0.22753	0.19589	0.17163	0.15257	0.13726	0.12472	0.11428	0.10546	0.09790	0.09136
59	0.71490	0.53162	0.41032	0.32757	0.26935	0.22714	0.19562	0.17145	0.15245	0.13718	0.12468	0.11425	0.10544	0.09789	0.09135
60	0.71385	0.53045	0.40934	0.32684	0.26884	0.22679	0.19539	0.17130	0.15235	0.13712	0.12464	0.11423	0.10542	0.09788	0.09134
61	0.71288	0.52939	0.40846	0.32619	0.26839	0.22648	0.19519	0.17117	0.15227	0.13707	0.12460	0.11421	0.10541	0.09787	0.09134
62	0.71199	0.52843	0.40767	0.32561	0.26799	0.22622	0.19502	0.17106	0.15220	0.13702	0.12457	0.11419	0.10540	0.09786	0.09133
63	0.71119	0.52756	0.40697	0.32510	0.26764	0.22599	0.19487	0.17096	0.15214	0.13699	0.12455	0.11417	0.10539	0.09786	0.09133
64	0.71046	0.52679	0.40635	0.32466	0.26734	0.22579	0.19474	0.17088	0.15209	0.13696	0.12453	0.11416	0.10538	0.09785	0.09133
65	0.70982	0.52611	0.40581	0.32427	0.26708	0.22562	0.19464	0.17082	0.15205	0.13693	0.12452	0.11415	0.10538	0.09785	0.09133
66	0.70925	0.52551	0.40534	0.32394	0.26686	0.22548	0.19455	0.17076	0.15202	0.13691	0.12450	0.11414	0.10537	0.09785	0.09132
67	0.70875	0.52501	0.40495	0.32366	0.26668	0.22536	0.19447	0.17072	0.15199	0.13689	0.12449	0.11414	0.10537	0.09784	0.09132
68	0.70834	0.52458	0.40462	0.32344	0.26653	0.22527	0.19442	0.17068	0.15197	0.13688	0.12449	0.11413	0.10537	0.09784	0.09132

Discount rate, percentage

Year (t)	1	2	3	4	5	6	7	8	9	10	11	12	13	14	15
69	0.70799	0.52423	0.40435	0.32325	0.26641	0.22520	0.19437	0.17066	0.15195	0.13687	0.12448	0.11413	0.10536	0.09784	0.09132
70	0.70772	0.52396	0.40414	0.32311	0.26632	0.22514	0.19434	0.17064	0.15194	0.13686	0.12448	0.11413	0.10536	0.09784	0.09132
71	0.70752	0.52375	0.40399	0.32301	0.26625	0.22510	0.19431	0.17062	0.15193	0.13686	0.12447	0.11413	0.10536	0.09784	0.09132
72	0.70738	0.52362	0.40389	0.32295	0.26621	0.22508	0.19430	0.17062	0.15193	0.13686	0.12447	0.11413	0.10536	0.09784	0.09132
73	0.70732	0.52356	0.40385	0.32291	0.26619	0.22507	0.19429	0.17061	0.15192	0.13686	0.12447	0.11413	0.10536	0.09784	0.09132

Bibliography

Alfred, A.M. (1968). The correct yardstick for state investment. *District Bank Review*, 166, 21–32.

Amalzak, M.B. (1945). *Frei Joao Sabrinho e as Doutrinas Economicas do Idade Media*. Lisbon: Grafica Lisbonense.

Anderson, J.L., and Dow, J.B. (1948). *Actuarial Statistics, Volume II, Construction of Mortality and Other Tables*. Cambridge: Cambridge University Press.

Annual Abstracts of Statistics. Official Publication Giving Statistics on Many Aspects in the United Kingdom. London: HMSO.

Arrow, K.J. (1963). *Social Choice and Individual Values*, 2d ed. London: Wiley.

Arrow, K.J. (1965). Criteria for social investment. *Water Resources Research*, 1, 1–8.

Arrow, K.J. (1966). Discounting and public investment criteria. In A.V. Kneese and S. C. Smith (eds.), *Water Research*. Baltimore, MD: Johns Hopkins University Press.

Ashley, W. (1920). *Introduction to English Economic History and Theory*, 4th ed. London: Longmans.

Association of University Teachers (AUT) Bulletin. (1992). January issue, no. 186. London.

Backhouse, R. (1992). Should we ignore methodology? *Royal Economic Society Newsletter*, no. 78 (July), 4–5.

Barker, P., and Button, K. (1979). *Case Studies in Cost Benefit Analysis*. London: Heinemann Educational Books.

Barnett H., and Morse, C. (1963). *Scarcity and Growth: The Economics of Natural Resource Availability*. Baltimore, MD: Johns Hopkins University Press.

Bateman, I. (1989). Modified discounting method: Some comments. *Project Appraisal*, 4, 104–6.

Baumol, W.J. (1952). *Welfare Economics and the Theory of State*. Cambridge, MA: Harvard University Press.

Baumol, W.J. (1968). On the social rate of discount. *American Economic Review*, 58, 788–802.

Baumol, W.J. (1969). On the social rate of discount—comment on comments. *American Economic Review*, 59, 930–33.

Baumol, W.J. (1991). Toward a newer economics, the future lies ahead! *The Economic Journal*, 101, 1–9.

Beesley, M.E., Coburn, T.M., and Reynolds, D.C. (1960). *The London-Birmingham Motorway-Traffic and Economics*. Technical paper No. 46, Road Research Laboratory, Department of Scientific and Industrial Research, H.M. Government, London.

BEIR Report (1972). *Biological Effects of Ionizing Radiation, the Effects on Population Exposure to Low Level of Ionizing Radiation*. Division of Medical Sciences, United States National Research Council, Washington, DC.

Bellinger, W.K. (1991). Multigenerational value; modifying the modified discounting method. *Project Appraisal*, 6, 101–8.

Bergson, H. (1910). *Time and Free Will*. New York: Henry Holt.

Böhm-Bawerk, E.U. (1884). *The Positive Theory of Capital*. New York: Stedard Co.

Böhm-Bawerk, E.U. (1889). *Capital and Interest*, 3 vols., translated by G. Hunche and H.F. Sennholz. Holland: Liberation Press.

Boulding, K.E. (1935). The theory of single investment. *Quarterly Journal of Economics*, 49, 475–94.

Broussalian, V.L. (1971). Discounting and evaluation of public investments. *Applied Economics*, 3, 1–10.

Brown, S.P. (1987). The fairness of discounting: A majority rule approach. *Public Choice*, 55, 216–26.

Budget Circular (1952). Budget Circular A-47, Bureau of the Budget. Washington, DC: U.S. Government.

Burness, H.S., Cummings, R.G., Gorman, W.D., and Lindsford, R.R. (1983). U.S. reclamation policy and Indian water rights. *Natural Resources Journal*, 20, 807–26.

Campbell, T. (1971). *Adam Smith's Science of Morals*. London: Allen and Unwin.

Casson, M. (1990). *Entrepreneurship*. Aldershot: Elgar.

Central Statistical Office (1955–1978). *Economic Trends*. London: U.K. Central Statistical Office, HMSO.

Channell, J.K., Chaturvedi, L., and Neill, R.H. (1990). Human intrusion scenarios in nuclear waste repository evaluations. *Environmental Evaluation Group Papers*. Albuquerque, New Mexico: Department of Energy.

Charles, F. (1970). *An Anatomy of Values*. Cambridge, MA: Harvard University Press.

Charles, F. (1978). *Right and Wrong*. Cambridge, MA: Harvard University Press.

Clarenback, F.A. (1955). Reliability of estimates of agricultural damages from floods, in U.S. Commission on Organization of the Executive Branch of the Government. *Task Force on Water Resources and Power*, vol. 3, Washington, DC: USGPO.

Clark, J.B. (1927). *The Distribution of Wealth*. New York: Macmillan.

Clark, J.M. (1939). *The Social Control of Business*, 2d ed. New York: McGraw-Hill.

Clough, S.B., and Cole, C.W. (1946). *Economic History of Europe*. Boston: D.C. Heath.

Cmnd 1337 (1961). *The Financial and Economic Obligations of Nationalised Industries*. London: HMSO.

Cmnd 3437 (1967). *Nationalised Industries: A Review of Economic and Financial Objectives*. London: HMSO.

Cmnd 7131 (1978). *Nationalised Industries*. London: HMSO.

Collard, D. (1979). Faustian projects and the social rate of discount. Working Paper 1073, University of Bath, Papers in Political Economy, Bath, England.

Cummings, R.G., Burness, H.S., and Norton, R.G. (1981). *The Proposed Waste Isolation Pilot Project (WIPP) and Impacts in the State of New Mexico, A Socio-Economic Analysis*. EMO–2–67–1139. Albuquerque: University of New Mexico, Department of Economics.

Dasgupta, A.K., and Pearce, D.W. (1972). *Cost-Benefit Analysis: Theory and Practice*. London: Macmillan Student Edition.

DeGraaff, J.V. (1957). *Theoretical Welfare Economics*. Cambridge: Cambridge University Press.

Department of Energy (1978). *Standards for the Management and Disposal of Spent Nuclear Fuel, High Level and Transuranic Radioactive Wastes*. Environmental Protection Agency, the USA Code of Federal Regulations 40 CFR Part 191, Washington, DC.

Department of Energy (1979). *Draft Environmental Impact Statement: Management of Commercially Generated Radioactive Waste*. DOE/E1S-0046-D, 2 vols., Washington, DC, April.

Department of Energy (1990). *Managing the Nation's Nuclear Waste, Fact Sheet Series*. Washington, DC.

Diamond, P. (1968). The opportunity cost of public investment: Comment. *Quarterly Journal of Economics*, 82, 682–88.

Dillingham, A.E. (1985). The influence of risk variable definition of value of life estimates. *Economic Inquiry*, April 1985.

Dimson, E. (1988). The discount rate for a power station. *Energy Economics* (July), 175–80.

Donagan, A. (1977). *The Theory of Morality*. Chicago: University of Chicago Press.

Dorfman, R. (1975). An estimate of the social rate of discount. *Discussion Paper 442*, Harvard Institute of Economic Research.

Douglas, J.C., and Lee, R.R. (1971). *Economics of Water Resource Planning*. Bombay, India: McGraw-Hill.

Dupuit, J. (1844). On the measurement of the utility of public works, translated from French in *International Economic Papers*, no. 2, London (1952).

Eckstein, O. (1958). *Water Resources Development, the Economics of Project Evaluation*. Cambridge, MA: Cambridge University Press.

Eckstein, O. (1961). A survey of theory of public expenditure. In J. Buchanan (ed.), *Public Finances: Needs, Sources and Utilisation*. Princeton, NJ: Princeton University Press.

Edgeworth, F. (1881). *Mathematical Psychics*. London: C.K. Paul and Co.

Energy Committee (1990). *The Cost of Nuclear Power*. Fourth Report, vol. 1, House of Commons, Session 1989–90. London: HMSO.

ERDA (1976). *Alternatives for Managing Wastes from Reactors and Post-Fission Operation in the LWR Fuel Cycle*, vol. 4, *Alternatives for Waste Isolation and Disposal*. Washington, DC: U.S. Energy Research and Development Administration.

Faustmann, M. (1849). Gerechnung des wertes welchen walkboden sowie nach nicht haubare Holzbestänce für die Waldwirtschaft besitzen. *Allgemeine Forst und Sogd-Zeitung*, 25, 441–45.

Feldstein, M.S. (1964a). The social time preference rate in cost-benefit analysis. *Economic Journal*, 74, 360–79.

Feldstein, M.S. (1964b). Net social benefits calculation and public investment decision. *Oxford Economic Papers*, 16, 14–31.

Feldstein, M.S. (1972). The inadequacy of weighted discount rates. In R. Layard (ed.), *Cost-Benefit Analysis*. London: Penguin Education.

Fellner, W. (1967). Operational utility: The theoretical background and measurement. In W. Fellner (ed.), *Ten Economic Essays in the Tradition of Irving Fisher*. New York: J. Wiley.

Fisher, A. et al. (1989). The value of reducing risk of death: A note on new evidence. *Journal of Policy Analysis and Management* (Winter 1983).

Fisher, I. (1892). *Mathematical Investigations into the Theory of Value and Prices*. Transactions of the Connecticut Academy of Arts and Sciences, vol. 9. New Haven: reprinted by Yale University Press (1925).

Fisher, I. (1907). *The Rate of Interest*. New York: Macmillan.

Fisher, I. (1927). A statistical method for measuring marginal utility and the justice of a progressive income tax. In W. Fellner (ed.), *Ten Economic Essays Contributed in Honour of J. Bates Clarke*. New York: Macmillan.

Fisher, I. (1930). *The Theory of Interest*. New York: Macmillan.

Forestry Commission (1971). Booklet 34, *Forest Management Tables (Metric)*. London: HMSO.

Forestry Commission (1977a). *Wood Production Outlook in Britain*. London: HMSO.

Forestry Commission (1977b). *Leaflet 64*. London: HMSO.

Forestry in Northern Ireland (1970). Government of Northern Ireland, November 1970. Belfast: HMSO.

Foster, C.D., and Beesley, M.E. (1963). Estimating the social benefit of constructing an underground railway in London. *Journal of the Royal Statistical Society*, Series A, 67–88.

Foster, C.D., and Beesley, M.E. (1965). Victoria Line, social benefits and finances. *Journal of the Royal Statistical Society*, Series A, 67–88.

Fried, C. (1977). *An Anatomy of Values*. Cambridge, MA: Harvard University Press.

Fried, C. (1978). *Right and Wrong*. Cambridge, MA: Harvard University Press.

Frisch, R. (1932). *New Methods of Measuring Marginal Utility*. Mahr Tubingen: Verlag Von J.C.B.

Frost, M.J. (1971). *How to Use Cost-Benefit Analysis in Project Appraisal*. London: Gower.

Fusfelt, R.D. (1966). *The Age of the Economist*. Glenview, IL: Scott and Foresman.

Galbraith, J.K. (1974). *Economics and the Public Purpose*. London: Andrea Deutsch.

Garrison, R.W. (1984). Time and money, universal of macroeconomic theorising. *Journal of Macroeconomics*,

Goldsmith, T. (1991). *The Way: An Ecological World View*. London: Rider Books.

Gossen, H.H. (1854). *Entwickelung der Gesetze des manschilchen Verkehrs*, 3d ed. (1927). Berlin: Prager.

Goundry, G.K. (1960). Forest management and the theory of capital. *Canadian Journal of Economics*, 26, 439–51.

Graham, H., and Walsh, V. (1980). *Classical and Neoclassical Theories of General Equilibrium: Historical Origins and Mathematical Structure*. New York: Oxford University Press.

Hahn, F.H. (1980). General equilibrium theory. *The Public Interest*, Special Issue, 123–38.

Hahn, F. (1992). *Reflections*. Royal Economic Society Newsletter, no. 77, April 1992.

Hampson, S.F. (1972). Highland forestry: An evaluation. *Journal of Agricultural Economics*, 23, 49–57.

Hansard (1989). *Investment Volume*, 150, no. 79, column 187, 5 April 1989. London: HMSO.

Harberger, A. (1968). The social opportunity cost of capital: A new approach. Paper presented at the Annual Meeting of the Water Resources Research Committee, December, U.S.

Harberger, A. (1969). Professor Arrow on the social discount rate. In G.G. Sommers and W.D. Wood (eds.), *Cost-Benefit Analysis of Management Policies*. Proceedings of a North American Conference, Industrial Relations Centre, Queens University, Kingston, Ontario.

Harberger, A. (1972). The opportunity cost of public investment financed by borrowing. In R. Layard (ed.), *Cost-Benefit Analysis*. London: Penguin Education, pp. 303–10.

Hayek, F.A. (1935a). The nature and history of the problem. In F.A. Hayek (ed.), *Collectivist Economic Planning: Critical Studies in the Possibilities of Socialism*. London: Routledge and Kegan Paul.

Hayek, F.A. (1935b). *Prices and Production*. New York: Augustos M. Kelly.

Helliwell, D.R. (1974). Discount rates in land use planning. *Forestry*, 47, 147–52.

Helliwell, D.R. (1975). Discount rates and environmental conservation. *Environmental Conservation*, 2, 199–201.

Henderson, P.D. (1965). Notes on public investment criteria in the United Kingdom. *Bulletin of the Oxford University Institute of Statistics*, February 27, 55–89.

Her Majesty's Treasury (1991). *Economic Appraisal in Central Government: A Technical Guide for Government Departments*. London: HMSO.

Hern, N. (1864). *Plutology: or The Theory of the Efforts to Satisfy Human Wants*. London: Macmillan.

Hey, J.D. (1981). *Economics in Disequilibrium*. New York: New York University Press.

Hicks, J.R. (1946). *Value and Capital—An Inquiry into Some Fundamental Principles of Economic Theory*, 2d ed. Oxford: Clarendon Press.

Hicks, J.R. (1965). *Capital Growth*. Oxford: Oxford University Press.

Hiley, W.E. (1967). *Woodland Management*. London: Faber and Faber.

Hirschleifer, J. (1958). On the theory of optimal investment decisions. *Journal of Political Economy*, 66.

Hirschleifer, J., DeHaven, J.D., and Milliman, J.M. (1960). *Water Supply, Economics, Technology and Policy*. Chicago: University of Chicago Press.

HM Treasury (1984). *Investment Appraisal in the Public Sector: A Technical Guide for Government Departments*. London: HMSO.

HMSO (1972a). *Forestry in Great Britain: An Interdepartmental Cost-Benefit Study*. London: HMSO.

HMSO (1972b). *Forestry Policy*. London: HMSO.

Hotelling, H. (1925). A general mathematical theory of depreciation. *Journal of the American Statistical Association*, 20, 340–53.

Hotelling, H. (1931). The economics of exhaustible resources. *Journal of Political Economy*, 39, 137–75.

House of Commons (1990). *The Cost of Nuclear Power*, Fourth Report, Volume 1, Session 1989–1990, London: HMSO.

House of Commons (1992). Northern Ireland Audit Office, Department of Agriculture: Forest Service, 5 November, HC-206. London: HMSO.

Hutchinson, R.W. (1989). Modified discounting method: Some comments. *Project Appraisal*, 4, 108–10.

James, L.D., and Lee, R.R. (1971). *Economics of Water Resources Planning*. Bombay, India: McGraw-Hill.

James, E. (1969). On the social rate of discount, comment. *American Economic Review*, 59.

Jennings, R. (1855). *Natural Elements of Political Economy*. London: Macmillan.

Jevons, W.S. (1871). *The Theory of Political Economy*, rpt. 1970. New York: Penguin.

John, A., and Pecchenino, R. (1994). An overlapping generations model of growth and environment. *Economic Journal*, 104, 1393–1410.

Joint Economic Committee (1968). *Economic Analysis of Public Investment Decisions: Interest Rate, Policy and Discounting Analysis*, The United States Congress. Washington, DC: U.S. Government Printing Office.

Kahn, H. (1976). *The Next 200 Years*. New York: W. Morrow.

Karatas, C. (1989). Third Bosphorus Bridge versus Bosphorus Road Tube Tunnel and combined alternative: An economic appraisal. *Project Appraisal*, 4, 67–79.

Kendall, M.G. (1971). *Cost-Benefit Analysis*. London: The English University Press.

Kerr, R.A. (1979). Geological disposal of nuclear wastes: Salt's lead is challenged. *Science*, 204 (May 11): 603.

Keynes, J.M. (1936). *The General Theory of Employment, Interest, and Money*. New York: Harcourt.

Kirchner, G. (1990). A new hazard index for the determination of risk potentials of disposed radioactive wastes. *Journal of Environmental Activity*, 11, 71–95.

Knight, F.H. (1946). *Readings in the Theory of Income Distribution*. Philadelphia: American Economic Association, Blakiston.

Kraus, S.J. (1930). *Scholastik Puritanismus und Kapitalismus*. Leipzig: Duncker und Humblot.

Krutilla, J., and Eckstein, O. (1958). *Multiple Purpose River Development*. Baltimore, MD: Johns Hopkins University Press.

Kuhn, T.E. (1962). *Public Enterprise and Transport Problems*. Los Angeles: University of California Press.

Kula, E. (1981). Future generations and discounting rules in public sector investment appraisal. *Environment and Planning A*, 13, 899–910.

Kula, E. (1984a). Derivation of social time preference rates for the United States and Canada. *Quarterly Journal of Economics*, 99, 873–83.

Kula, E. (1984b). Discount factors for public sector investment projects by using the sum of discounted consumption flows method. *Environment and Planning A*, 16, 683–94.

Kula, E. (1984c). Justice and efficiency with the sum of discounted consumption flows method. *Environment and Planning A*, 16, 835–38.

Kula, E. (1985). Derivation of social time preference rates for the United Kingdom. *Environment and Planning A*, 17, 199–212.

Kula, E. (1986a). The analysis of social interest rate in Trinidad and Tobago. *Journal of Development Studies*, 22, 731–39.

Kula, E. (1986b). The developing framework for the economic analysis of forestry projects in the United Kingdom. *Journal of Agricultural Economics*, 37, 365–77.

Kula, E. (1986c). Public sector forestry and intergenerational justice, a cost-benefit analysis of Ulster forestry with modified discounting. In M. Merlo, G. Stellin, P. Harou, and M. Whitby (eds.), *Multipurpose Agriculture and Forestry*. Kiel, Germany: Vauk.

Kula, E. (1987a). The developing framework for the economic evaluation of forestry in the United Kingdom, a reply. *Journal of Agricultural Economics*, 38, 501–4.

Kula, E. (1987b). The social interest rate for public sector project appraisal in the U.K., U.S. and Canada. *Project Appraisal*, 2, 69–75.

Kula, E. (1988a). The modified discount factors for project appraisal in the public sector. *Project Appraisal*, 3, 85.

Kula, E. (1988b). *The Economics of Forestry—Modern Theory and Practice*. London: Croom Helm; Portland, OR: Timber Press.

Kula, E. (1992). A rate of return for private forest property. *The Property Journal* (Northern Ireland), 3, 7–16.

Kula, E. (1994). *Economics of Natural Resources, the Environment and Policies*, 2d ed. London: Chapman and Hall.

Land Use Study Group (1966). *Forestry, Agriculture and Multiple Use of Rural Land*. London: HMSO.

Landauer, C. (1947). *The Theory of National Economic Planning*. Los Angeles: University of California Press.

Layard, R. (1972). *Cost-Benefit Analysis, Selected Readings*. London: Penguin.

Layard, R., and Glaister, S. (1994). *Cost-Benefit Analysis*, 2d ed. Cambridge: Cambridge University Press.

Leopold, L.B., and Maddock, T., Jr. (1954). *The Flood Control Controversy*. New York: The Ronald Press.

Lind, R.C. (1964). Further comment. *Quarterly Journal of Economics*, 78, 336–45.

Lindstone, H.A. (1973). On discounting the future. *Technological Forecasting and Social Change*, S, 335–38.

Lipschutz, R.D. (1981). *Radioactive Waste, Politics, Technology and Risk, A Report of the Union of Concerned Scientists*. Cambridge, MA: Bellinger.

Lipsey, R. (1960). *Positive Economics*. London: Weidenfeld and Nicholson.

Little, I.M.D., and Mirrlees, J.A. (1968). *Manual of Industrial Project Analysis for Developing Countries*. Paris: OECD.

Little, I.M.D., and Mirrlees, J.A. (1974). *Project Appraisal and Planning for Developing Countries*. London: Heinemann.

Logan, S.E., Schulze, W.D., Ben-David, S., and Brookshore, D.S. (1978). *Development and Application of a Risk Assessment Method for Radioactive Waste Management, Volume III, Economic Analysis*. Washington, DC: U.S. Environmental Protection Agency, Office of Radiation Programs, AW-453, EPA 520/6–78–005.

Lönnstedt, L. (1989). Goals and cutting decisions of private small forest owners. *Scandinavian Journal of Forest Resources*, 4, 259–65.

Lutz, F.A. (1940). The structure of interest rates. *Quarterly Journal of Economics*, 54, 36–63.

Maass, A. (1962). *Design of Water Resource Systems*. New York: Macmillan.

Magnus, A. (1894). *Commentarii in IV Sententiarum*. Petri Lombardi, Dist. 16, art. 46 in Opera, Omnia. XXIX, Paris.

Mainwaring, L. (1990). Marginalism and the margin. In J. Creedy (ed.), *Foundation of Economic Thought*. Oxford: Blackwell.

Malone, C.R. (1990). Implications of environmental program planning for siting a nuclear repository at Yucca Mountain, Nevada. *Environmental Management*, 14, 25–32.

Marglin, S. (1962). Economic factors affecting system design. In A. Maass (ed.), *Design of Water Resource Systems*. Baltimore, MD: Johns Hopkins University Press.

Marglin, S. (1963a). The opportunity cost of public investment. *Quarterly Journal of Economics*, 77, 274–89.

Marglin, S. (1963b). The social rate of discount and the optimal rate of saving. *Quarterly Journal of Economics*, 77, 274–89.

Marglin, S. (1967). *Public Investment Criteria*. London: Allen and Unwin.

Marglin, S., Sen, A., and Dasgupta, P. (1972). *Guidelines for Project Evaluation*. Vienna: United Nations.

McKean, R.N. (1958). *Efficiency in Government Through System Analysis*. Los Angeles: University of California Press.

Meadows, D.H., Meadows, D.L., and Randers, R. (1991). *Beyond the Limits*. New York: Chelsea Green.

Meadows, D.H., Meadows, D.L., Randers, J., and Behrans, W.W., II. (1972). *The Limits to Growth*. London: Pan Books.

Menger, C. (1871). *Principles of Economics*, edited by J. Dingwall and translated by J. Haselitz. New York: New York University Press.

Mesarovic, M.D., and Pestel, E.C. (1974). *Man at the Turning Point*. New York: Dutton.

Mill, J.S. (1826). *Elements of Political Economy*. London: Routledge.

Mill, J.S. (1862). *Principles of Political Economy*. New York: Appleton.

Miller, R. (1981). *State of Forestry for the Axe*. London: Institute of Economic Affairs.

Ministry of Overseas Development (1977). *A Guide to Economic Appraisal of Projects in Developing Countries*. London: HMSO.

Mirrlees, J.A., and Stern, N.H. (1973). *Models of Economic Growth*. London: Macmillan.

Mises, L. (1966). *Human Action: A Treatise on Economics*. 3d ed. New York: Henry Regnery.

Mishan, E.J. (1967). *The Cost of Economic Growth*. London: Staples.

Mishan, E.J. (1971). *Cost-Benefit Analysis*. London: Allen and Unwin.

Mishan, E.J. (1972). *Elements of Cost-Benefit Analysis*. London: Allen and Unwin.

Mishan, E.J. (1975). *Cost-Benefit Analysis*, 2d ed. London: Allen and Unwin.

Mishan, E.J. (1988). *Cost-Benefit Analysis*, 4th ed. London: Unwin and Hyman.

Monk, R. (1990). *Wittgenstein; the Duty of Genius*. London: Cape.

Moore, M., and Viscusi, K. (1988). Doubling the estimated value of life: Results using new occupational data. *Journal of Policy Analysis and Management*. (Spring).

Mourmouras, A. (1991). Competitive equilibrium and sustainable growth in a life-cycle model with natural resources. *Scandinavian Journal of Economics*, 91, 585–91.

Murdock, S.H., Leistritz, F.L., and Ham, R.R. (1983). *Nuclear Waste: Socio-economic Dimensions of Long Term Storage*. Boulder, CO: Westview Press.

Myrdal, G. (1939). *Monetary Equilibrium*. London: William Hodge.

Nash, C.A. (1973). Future generations and the social rate of discount. *Environment and Planning A*, S, 611–17.

Ng, Y.K. (1973). Optimum saving, a practicable solution. *Indian Journal of Economics*, 53, 258–94.

Ng, Y.K. (1979). *Welfare Economics*. London: Macmillan.

Nicholas, A. (1969). On the social rate of discount: Comment. *American Economic Review*, 59, 909–911.

Nisbet, E.G. (1991). *Leaving Eden: To Protect and Manage the Earth*. Cambridge: Cambridge University Press.

Nove, A. (1992). Alec Nove. In *A Biographical Dictionary of Dissenting Economists*. London: Elgar.

O'Driscoll, G., Jr., Rizza, M.J., and Garrison, R.W. (1985). *The Economics of Time and Ignorance*. Oxford: Blackwell.

OECD Committee (1980). Nuclear Energy Agency, *Radiological Significance and Management of Tritium, Carbon-14, Krypton-85 and Iodine-129 Arising from the Nuclear Fuel Cycle*. NEA, Expert Group, Paris: OECD.

Ormerod, P. (1994). *The Death of Economics*. London: Faber and Faber.

Parker, J.W. (1844). *Essays on Some Unsettled Questions of Political Economy*. London: Macmillan.

Pearce, D.W. (1971). *Cost-Benefit Analysis*, 1st ed. London: Macmillan.

Pearce, D.W. (1983). *Cost-Benefit Analysis*, 2d ed. London: Macmillan.

Pearce, D.W., and Nash, C.A. (1981). *The Social Appraisal of Projects*. London: Macmillan.

Pigou, A. (1929). *The Economics of Welfare*. London: Macmillan.

Policy Planning and Research Unit (1987). Methodology for cost-benefit acquisition of land for forestry, Economic Division. Belfast: Northern Ireland.

Potter, N., and Christy, F.T. (1962). *Trends in Natural Resource Commodities: Statistics of Prices, Output, Consumption, Foreign Trade and Employment in the U.S., 1870–1977*. Baltimore, MD: Johns Hopkins University Press.

President's Material Commission (1952). *Resources for Freedom*. Washington, DC: U.S. Government Printing Office.

President's Water Resources Council (1962). *Policies, Standards, and Procedures in the Formulation, Evaluation, and Review of Plans for Use and Development of Water Related Land Resources*. 87th Cong. 2nd Sess. Senate Document, 97, p12. Washington, DC: U.S. Government Printing Office.

Price, C. (1972). To the future with indifference or concern? *Journal of Agricultural Economics*, 24, 383–98.

Price, C. (1976). Blind alleys and open prospects in forestry economics. *Forestry*, 49, 93–107.

Price, C. (1984). The sum of discounted consumption flows method: Equity with efficiency? *Environment and Planning A*, 16, 829–37.

Price, C. (1987). The developing framework for the economic evaluation of forestry in the United Kingdom—a comment. *Journal of Agricultural Economics*, 38, 497–500.

Price, C. (1989a). Equity, consistency, efficiency and new rules of discounting. *Project Appraisal*, 4, 58–65.

Price, C. (1989b). *Forestry Economics*. Oxford: Basil Blackwell.

Price, C. (1993). *Time, Discounting and Value*. Oxford: Blackwell.

Rae, J. (1905). *The Social Theory of Capital*. London: Macmillan.

Ramsey, D. (1969). On the social rate of discount: Comment. *American Economic Review*.

Ramsey, F.P. (1928). A mathematical theory of saving. *Economic Journal*, 38, 543–59.

Rawls, J. (1972). *A Theory of Justice*. Oxford: Clarendon Press.

Reder, W.M. (1982). Chicago economics: Permanence and change. *Journal of Economic Literature*, 20, 1–38.

Review of Economic Studies (1974). Symposium on the Economics of Exhaustible Resources, Volume 41.

Rigby, M. (1989). Modified discounting method: Some comments. *Project Appraisal*, 4, 107–8.

Roberts, A. (1994). *Eminent Churchillians*. London: Weidenfeld and Nicolson.

Rothbard, M.N. (1970). *Man, Economy, and State*, 2 vols. Los Angeles: Nash.

Roover, R. (1970). The Concept of the Just Price: Theory and Economic Policy. In I.H. Rima (ed.), *Readings in the History of Economic Theory*. New York: Holt, Rinehart and Winston.

Samuelson, P.A. (1958). An exact consumption model of interest with or without the social contrivance of money. *Journal of Political Economy*, 66, 467–82.

Samuelson, P.A. (1964). Principles of efficiency: Discussion. *American Economic Review*, 54, 93–96.

Samuelson, P.A. (1967). In W. Fellner (ed.), *Ten Economic Studies in the Tradition of Irving Fisher*. New York: J. Wiley.

Samuelson, P.A. (1976). Economics of forestry in an evolving society. *Economic Inquiry*, 14, 466–92.

Sassone, P.G., and Schaffer, W.A. (1978). *Cost-Benefit Analysis, A Handbook*. London: Academic Press.

Schulze, W.D. (1978). Economic analysis in development and application of risk assessment methods for radioactive waste management. In S.E. Logan et al. (eds.), *Economic Analysis: Description and Implementation of AMRAW B Model*. Washington, DC: U.S. Environmental Protection Agency, 520/6–78–005.

Schulze, W.D., Brookshire, D.S., and Sandler, T. (1981). The social rate of discount for nuclear waste storage; economics or ethics. *Natural Resources Journal*, 21, 811–32.

Scott, A. (1955). *Natural Resources: The Economics of Conservation*. Toronto: University of Toronto Press.

Scotus, J.D. (1894). Quaestiones in librum quartum sentenarum, dist. 15. Qu2, no. 23, Opera Omnia, XVIII, Paris.

Sen, A.K. (1961). On optimising the rate of saving. *Economic Journal*, 71, 479–96.

Sen, A.K. (1967). The social time preference rate in relation to the market rate of interest. *Quarterly Journal of Economics*, 81, 112–24.

Sen, A.K. (1972a). Control areas and accounting prices; an approach to economic evaluation. *Economic Journal*, 82, special issue.

Sen, A.K. (1972b). The social time preference rate in relation to the market rate of interest. In R. Layard (ed.), *Cost-Benefit Analysis*. London: Penguin.

Shackle, G.L.S. (1971). *Epistermica and Economics*. Cambridge: Cambridge University Press.

Shackle, G.L.S. (1972). Marginalism; the harvest. *History of Political Economy*, 4, 587–602.

Sharma, R.A., McGregor, M.S., and Blyth, J.F. (1991). The social discount rate and land-use projects in India. *Journal of Agricultural Economics*, 42, 86–93.

Shell, K. (1967). *Essays in the Theory of Optimal Economic Growth*. Cambridge, MA: MIT Press.

Shradder-Frechette, K.S. (1991). *Nuclear Power and Public Policy, The Social and Ethical Problems of Fission Technology.* Boston: Reidel.

Shradder-Frechette, K.S. (1993). Burying uncertainty: Risk and cause against geological disposal of nuclear waste. Berkeley: University of California Press.

Sidwick, H. (1907). *The Methods of Ethics*, 7th ed. London: Macmillan.

Simon, J.L. (1984). *The Resourceful Earth—A Response to Global 2000.* London: Blackwell.

Simon, J.L. (1989). *Population Matters; Resources, Environment and Irrigation.* New Brunswick, NJ: Transaction.

Smith, A. (1976). *The Theory of Moral Sentiments.* Oxford: Clarendon Press.

Smith, A. (1979). *An Inquiry into the Nature and Causes of the Wealth of the Nations.* London: Penguin.

Solow, R.M. (1974a). Intergenerational equity and exhaustible resources. In Symposium on the Economics of Exhaustible Resources. *Review of Economic Studies*, 41, 29–46.

Solow, R.M. (1974b). The economics of resources or the resources of economics. *American Economic Review Supplement*, 64, 1–14.

Squire, L., and Van der Tak, H.G. (1975). *Economic Analysis of Projects.* Baltimore, MD: Johns Hopkins University Press.

Statistical Abstract of the U.S. (1957–76). Washington, DC: U.S. Government Printing Office.

Stigler, G. (1972). The adoption of the marginal utility theory. *History of Political Economy*, 4, 573–86.

Stone, R. (1954). *Measurement of Consumer Expenditure and Behaviour in the United Kingdom 1920–1928.* Cambridge: Cambridge University Press.

Strotz, R.H. (1955). Myopia and inconsistency in dynamic utility maximisation. *The Review of Economic Studies*, 23, 165–80.

Thaler, R., and Rosen, S. (1976). The volume of saving life: Evidence from the labour market. In N.J. Terlecky (ed.), *Household Production and Consumption.* New York: National Bureau of Economic Research.

Thompson, A.C. (1971). The Forestry Commission: A reappraisal of its functions. *Three Banks Review* (September), 30–44.

Thomson, K. (1988). Future generations: The modified discounting method—a reply. *Project Appraisal*, 3, 171–72.

Timbergen, J. (1956). The optimum rate of saving. *Economic Journal*, 66, 603–9.

The Times. (1971). 5 May.

Traiforos, S., Adamontiades, A., and Moore, E. (1990). *The Status of Nuclear Power Technology.* Washington, DC: World Bank.

Tullock, G. (1964). The social rate of discount and optimal rate of investment: Comment. *Quarterly Journal of Economics*, 78, 331–36.

Tullock, G. (1967). The general irrelevancy of impossibility theorem. *Quarterly Journal of Economics*, 81, 256–70.

Ulrich, J. (1990). 1199 Speech, *Emchanted Times*, Fall 1990. Albuquerque: New Mexico Research and Education Enrichment Foundation.

UNIDO (1972). *Guidelines for Project Evaluation*, Washington, DC: UN.

U.S. Bureau of Mines (1970). *Mineral Facts and Problems.* Washington, DC: U.S. Government Printing Office.

U.S. Environmental Protection Agency (1985). Environmental Standards for the Management and Disposal of Spent Nuclear Fuel, High Level and Transuronic Radioactive Waste, 40 CFR 191, *Federal Register*, 50, 38066–38089.

U.S. Government. Federal Inter-Agency River Basin Committee, Sub-Commitee on Benefits and Costs (1950). *Proposed Practices for Economic Analysis of River Basin Projects*. Washington, DC: U.S. Government Printing Office.

Usher, D. (1964). The social rate of discount and optimal rate of investment: Comment. *Quarterly Journal of Economics*, 78, 641–44.

Von Thunen, J.H. (1826). *Isolated State*. English translation by P. Hall, 1966. London: Pergamon Press.

Walker, K.R. (1958). *Competition for Hill Land Between the Agriculture, Industry and Forestry Commission*. Unpublished Ph.D. thesis, Oxford University Press.

Webber, M. (1964). *General Economic History*, translated by F.H. Knight. London: Allen and Unwin.

Weinberg, A. (1972). Social institutions and nuclear energy. *Science*, 177, 7–34.

Whitehead, A.N., and Russell, B. (1910). *Principia Mathematica*. Cambridge: Cambridge University Press.

Wiseman, J. (1991). The black box. *Economic Journal*, 101, 149–55.

Wright, J.F. (1963). Notes on the marginal efficiency of capital. *Oxford Economic Papers*, 15.

Zeller, E.J., Sounders, D.F., and Angino, E.E. (1973). Putting radioactive waste on ice. *Bulletin of the Atomic Scientists* (January), p. 4.

Zerbe, R.O., and Dively, D.D. (1994). *Benefit and Cost Analysis and Practice*. London: HarperCollins.

Index

About the Author

ERHUN KULA, a member of the New York Academy of Sciences, is Senior Lecturer in Economics at the University of Ulster. Widely published in journals of economics and environmental science, he is the author of four other books. He also teaches in the University of London's External Diploma and Master Programs and has held visiting professorships at the University of New Mexico and the University of Bosphorus.

ISBN 1-56720-090-7

EAN

9 781567 200904

90000>

HARDCOVER BAR CODE